BARE FISTS

BARE FISTS

The History of Bare-Knuckle Prize-Fighting

BOB MEE

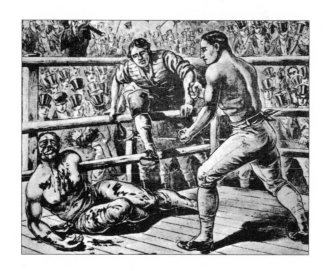

THE OVERLOOK PRESS
WOODSTOCK & NEW YORK

First published in the United States in 2001 by
The Overlook Press, Peter Mayer Publishers, Inc.
Woodstock & New York

WOODSTOCK:
One Overlook Drive
Woodstock, NY 12498
www.overlookpress.com
[for individual orders, bulk and special sales, contact our Woodstock office]

NEW YORK:
386 West Broadway
New York, NY 10012

Published by arrangement with HarperCollins UK

Library of Congress Cataloging-in-Publication Data

Mee, Bob.
Bare fists : the history of bare-knuckle prize-fighting / Bob Mee.
p. cm.
Includes bibliographical references (p.) and index.
1. Boxing—History—18th century. 2. Boxing—History—19th century. 3. Boxers
(Sports)—Biography. I. Title: History of bare-knuckle prize-fighting. II. Title.
GV1121 .M44 2001   796.83'09—dc21   2001021057

Manufactured in the United States of America
FIRST EDITION
1 3 5 7 9 8 6 4 2
ISBN 1-58567-141-X

To boxers everywhere. Thank you.

CONTENTS

'Almost everybody in our land, except humanitarians and a few persons whose youth has been depressed by exceptionally aesthetic surroundings, can understand and sympathise with an Admiral or a prize-fighter. I do not wish to bracket Benbow or Tom Cribb; but, depend upon it, they are practically bracketed for admiration in the minds of many frequented alehouses. If you told them about Germanicus and the eagles, or Regulus going back to Carthage, they would very likely fall asleep; but tell them about Harry Pearce and Jem Belcher, or about Nelson and the Nile, and they put down their pipes to listen.'

ROBERT LOUIS STEVENSON, *The English Admirals*, 1881

'For years the practice of pugilism has been one revolting to mankind, degrading to all the honourable and honest feelings of human nature ... A recent exhibition, with an illusion to which we will not pollute our page, has placed the Ring in a position to damage the character of any man who shall hereafter be known to endure a prize fight.'

The Illustrated London News, 27 September 1845

'It may not be generally known that Sir Isaac Newton, who died in 1726-7, above the age of eighty, used to strip up his shirt sleeve but a short time before his death, and showing his muscular brawny arm, would relate how dexterous he had been in his youth at the practice of boxing.'

RALPH NEVILL, *Sporting Days and Sporting Ways*, 1910

BARE FISTS

I

OUT OF TIME

We can never know the absolute truth about history. All we can do is recount or investigate what is known and interpret it to the best of our limited abilities. So be it.

As far as anyone can tell by peering into the fog of time, boxing first existed as a sport in Ancient Greece alongside wrestling and running. Homer, who is believed to have lived around 750 B.C., certainly knew enough about boxing to use it in *The Iliad*, when describing incidents in the Trojan Wars. The Greeks considered *The Iliad* a history book, not a work of fiction, and it's almost certainly a gathering of stories passed down by orators over several centuries, which indicates that boxing could indeed have been popular more than 3,000 years ago.

Hercules, Eryx, Amycus, Pollux and Antaeus, all of whom used the caestus, or gloved fist, are all mentioned in connection with boxing, but it is *The Iliad* that provides the first solid reference to a proper contest. Homer dramatised a showdown between Epeius, king of a tribe who lived on the Peloponnese peninsula in Greece, and Euryalus, an experienced fighter who was a son of King Mecisteus. They fought, sometime around the Fall of Troy, for a prize mule. Epeius boasted: 'The mule is mine ... I'm going to tear the fellow's flesh to ribbons and smash his bones. I recommend him to have all his mourners standing by to take him off when I've done with him.'

Homer, traditionally believed to have been blind, and some say not born until 300 years after Troy fell, creates a vivid picture of the fight, which indicates that, even if this particular account were pure fiction, such scenes were a common occurrence no matter when *The Iliad* was written. The fight followed the chariot race and preceded the wrestling bout and foot race in the festival that accompanied the funeral of Patroclus. The fighters put on shorts and gloves – 'well-cut ox-hide thongs on their hands' – and began.

'Fist met fist; there was a terrible grinding of jaws; and the sweat began to pour from all their limbs ...'

There's no need for a blow-by-blow account, but eventually Euryalus made a careless mistake and was knocked out.

'The legs were cut from under him and he was lifted by the blow like a fish leaping up from the weed-covered sands and falling back into the dark water ...'

Etc., etc. You get the picture. Epeius helped Euryalus to his feet and the unfortunate loser was dragged by his supporters, who had presumably lost gold and silver on the outcome and were therefore acting out of commendable charity, 'across the ring on trailing feet, spitting clots of blood, with his head lolling on one side. He was still senseless when they put him down in his corner'.

'Epeius w ko 1 Euryalus, Troy, 1184 B.C.' has never made the record books, but it established Homer as the father of all boxing writers and therefore provided the basis, or excuse, for the rather dubious literary tradition which has accompanied the progress of the sport.

At the site of Akrotiri, an Ancient Greek fresco of two boxers was also excavated. It shows two fairly stylish, stand-up gentlemen, with what appear to be dreadlock hairstyles, exchanging straight-armed punches. Boxing was also mentioned in an early Hindu poem, Mahabaratta.

Boxing played its part in Roman civilisation, too, as illustrated by Virgil's account of the meeting between Entellus, an old fighter making a comeback, and a young gentleman gladiator called Dares. The prize reflected the rise in inflation since the Fall of Troy – a bull with golden horns had replaced the mule. Boxing is traditionally a young man's game and comebacks usually end in disappointment, even humiliation, but Entellus obviously hadn't heard of that sort of thing. He knocked out Dares with a body punch and then sacrificed the poor beast with a single blow between its horns. 'The beast's brains are dashed out and splutter over the bystanders.'

And with that act of supreme bad taste, Entellus quit the fight arena for good. No doubt those accustomed to taking a ringside seat at his fights were delighted at the reduction in their cleaning bills.

There were other morbid accounts, but they have little bearing on our story. The function of including these two is to illustrate the existence of the boxing ritual all those years ago. We can skip other boring details like the use of cloth and leather gloves and the *caestus*, a glove with metal spikes on the surface or alternatively loaded with stone. And we can tread lightly over *muki*-boxing and *vajra-musti* in India, *shaolin* boxing in China, *muay-thai* in Thailand and *bama letwhay* in Burma. Each has its own history and should be recounted elsewhere.

Boxing did form part of a Gaelic festival at the site of an ancient Irish queen, Tailte, which ran for around 500 years, until the 12th century. But as far as anyone has been able to tell, it petered out. We can move swiftly down the centuries to the England of the Restoration, in 1681 to be precise, when the country was paying dearly for the last days of King Charles II and when the execution of opponents of the court, most recently the elderly, infirm and entirely innocent Lord Stafford, was commonplace. Old men could remember the beheading of Charles I and the subsequent rule of Oliver Cromwell's bloody Commonwealth. Young men could just about recall the Great Plague, the Fire of London, which was still popularly believed to have been started by Papists, and the frightening attacks on the Thames estuary and the Kent coast by the Dutch fleet. Christopher Wren was busy revolutionising the London skyline by building St Paul's Cathedral, although it wouldn't be finished for nearly 30 years.

Charles II's debaucheries led to, or were accompanied by, a relaxing of morals from the rigid days of Cromwell's Interregnum. And from somewhere among the pile of entertainments on offer – one celebrated activity was public farting – boxing began to emerge as a popular pastime. Samuel Pepys' diary for August 1660 refers to a Sunday morning set-to at Westminster Stairs between a Dutchman and a waterman, and in the January 1681 issue of the Protestant Mercury, it was recorded: 'Yesterday a match of boxing was performed before His Grace, the Duke of Albermarle, between the Duke's footman and a butcher. The latter won the prize, as he hath done many times before, being accounted, though a little man, the best at that exercise in England.'

(The first Duke of Albemarle was George Monk, a Royalist general in the Civil War who switched sides after being imprisoned in the Tower of London. He fought in Cromwell's army in Ireland and Scotland, but then upon Cromwell's death he helped arrange the return of Charles II. As a reward he was given the dukedom of Albemarle, the Order of the Garter and a £7,000 annual pension. He died in 1670. The Duke referred to here is presumably his son.)

James Figg

So much for the anonymous butcher. It's not such a long journey then to the belligerent, happy-go-lucky, shrewd and illiterate James Figg, born in the village of Thame in Oxfordshire, and the toast of Georgian society in the 1720s. Figg was spotted by the Earl of Peterborough, an old soldier and

James Figg

sporting patron, while displaying his ability in the arts of boxing, fencing and use of the quarter-staff on the village green. The Earl took him to London, which was a stinking, choking city then as now, but mercifully small by comparison.

Fume-clogged Tottenham Court Road was then a balmy, tree-lined country lane well to the north of the great city and among its meadows nestled the Adam and Eve, the first of boxing's major cathedrals: forefather of Madison Square Garden and Caesars Palace. The old building had been standing for more than a century even then and was talked of by the fat and rich for its syllabubs, cakes and strawberries and cream. (And, more discreetly no doubt, for its good English ale, wild women and slugging matches – which certainly occurred in London well before Figg appeared.) This was a chaotic, unpredictable time, before men had been trained to respond to the factory bell or alarm clock. They worked in single-minded rushes that might last two, three or even five days. Then they would spend the next half-week in the tavern with, presumably a quick check home, if home there was to speak of, fitted in as and when the demands of finance or fear of domestic reprisal grew too great. (Not dissimilar to the way my friends at *Boxing News* worked before the dreadful advent of computer technology!) Mondays were generally accepted as holidays.

Violence was a way of life. Public executions were held regularly at Tyburn, which is now Marble Arch, but which then was some half-mile beyond the last of the suburbs of the city. In the 1720s a kind of amphitheatre was erected for spectators near the gibbet.

Proof that boxing was relatively widespread comes from an unexpected source – the USA. In a 1938 book *Cities In The Wilderness*, Carl Bridenbaugh says a reference to prize-fighting was made as early as 1709 when attempts were made by British settlers and the rising, 'nouveau riche' of New York society to recreate the atmosphere of British entertainments. This included plays, horse races and prize fights.

By 1723 boxing was so popular that on the orders of George I a ring, a circular piece of ground encircled by railings, was erected in Hyde Park about 300 yards from Grosvenor Gate for the use of the public. It was broken up by a bunch of apparently humourless religious zealots in 1820.

Stories conflict. One newspaper account placed Figg in London working under one Timothy Buck of Clare Market in 1714. This is solid evidence but at some time after this, tradition says the Earl of Peterborough set up Figg in premises on the Oxford Road, Tottenham Court Road area, and the fighter was so successful at drawing clients, he soon had to move the expanding business a few hundred yards away into the Adam and Eve.

Travel along Oxford Street today from Tottenham Court Road and on the right hand side you will find an alleyway known as Adam and Eve Court, which we imagine marks the spot. It was there that Figg taught and fought anyone and everyone who shelled out the appropriate fee. This became known as Figg's Academy. It held about 1,000 people on the ground floor with up to 300 elite paying for the privilege of a seat in the gallery. In the centre of the hall was a 40-foot stage, where Figg and his underlings exhibited their skills. A famous sporting gentleman and chronicler of the day, Captain Godfrey, recorded that he had learned all he knew of 'self defence' from Figg.

'I have purchased my knowledge with many a broken head, and bruises in every part of me. I chose mostly to go to Fig (sic) and exercise with him, partly as I knew him to be the ablest master, and partly as he was of a rugged temper, and would spare no man, high or low, who took up a stick against him. I bore his treatment with determined patience, and followed him so long that Fig, at last, finding he could not have the beating of me at so cheap a rate as usual, did not show such fondness for my company.'

Figg was also mentioned in the *Tatler*, and other publications. For example, a writer named Bramstone referred to him in a poem called 'Man of Taste': '... In Fig, the prize-fighter, by day delight, And sup with Colley Cibber every night.'

(Cibber was the Poet Laureate of the day. More dramatist than poet, his appointment allegedly owed more to his quality as an agreeable eating and drinking companion than to his literary abilities, but he enjoyed his role immensely and didn't appear to give a damn about the angry reaction of the serious poets of the day.)

Figg also staged entertainments each September at Southwark Bowling Green Fair, where the master would close the ten-hour show with a demonstration of foil, back-sword, cudgel and fist. One of his prize-fighting staff around this time was the expert swordsman 'Mr Andrew Johnson', who also ran a booth at Smithfield, and whose nephew found longer lasting fame – Dr Samuel Johnson. A ring at Moorfields in London was run by an eccentric known as Old Vinegar, and a booth just a short distance away at the Death's Head and Cross Bones pub was owned by one 'Long Charles' Rimmington.

The fairer sex

Women's boxing became increasingly popular during the 1990s, with stars like Christy Martin, a coalminer's daughter and schoolteacher from America, and Regina Halmich, a German flyweight, commanding regular television exposure. Because it had lain dormant for the best part of a century, there has been a tendency to treat it as a fashionable, ephemeral icon to political correctness. In fact, history indicates this is not so.

The first reference was in the *London Journal* of June 1722, when, after a description of two women fighting 'with great valour for a long time, to the no small satisfaction of the spectators', the following advertisement appeared: 'I, Elizabeth Wilkinson, of Clerkenwell, having had some words with Hannah Hyfield, and requiring satisfaction, do invite her to meet me upon the stage, and box me for three guineas; each woman holding half-a-crown in her hand, and the first woman that drops the money to lose the battle.'

Shortly after came the reply: 'I, Hannah Hyfield, of Newgate Market, hearing of the resoluteness of Elizabeth Wilkinson, will not fail, God willing, to give her more blows than words – desiring home blows, and from her, no favour: she may expect a good thumping!'

No doubt there were hordes who would have loved to have witnessed Elizabeth and Hannah belting seven bells out of each other, but the women were threatened with jail if they persisted in a public prize fight. Could this be the first time boxing was driven underground? For an advertisement of the following year suggests that Wilkinson won. She refers to having beaten the Newgate Market basketwoman. Martha Jones, a Billingsgate fishwoman, challenged Wilkinson the following year, and Wilkinson declared herself the 'City Championess'. The bout took place 'at the Boarded House in Marybone Fields', and again Wilkinson won.

By 1728, Elizabeth Wilkinson had married a booth owner named Stokes and was calling herself 'European Championess'. She was challenged by an ass driver from Stoke Newington, Ann Field, at her husband's booth in Islington Road on 7 October 1728. Again, the formidable Elizabeth succeeded, but after that the presence of women in the ring is hardly referred to until the closing years of the century.

The early journalist, William Hickey, depicted what was probably an informal, impromptu fight between women early in the 19th century: 'The whole room was in an uproar, men and women promiscuously mounted upon chairs, tables and benches, in order to see a sort of general conflict carrying on upon the floor. Two she-devils, for they scarce had a human appearance, were engaged in a scratching and boxing match, their faces entirely covered with blood, bosoms bare, and the clothes nearly torn from their backs. For several minutes, not a creature interfered between them, or seemed to care a straw what mishap they might do each other, and the contest went on with unabated fury.'

This brawl had no bearing on the organised sport of pugilism, but remains evidence that boxing, or at least the settling of a dispute with the bare hands, was accepted as perfectly reasonable, both in itself and as a source of entertainment, in the early 19th as well as 18th centuries.

The Fancy

Meanwhile, Figg's supremacy was rarely challenged. One of the few occasions was on Wednesday, 6 June, 1727, when he took on Ned Sutton, a pipemaker from the isolated seaport of Gravesend, at the Adam and Eve. Some say Sutton first fought Figg in 1720. Some even say he beat him once. Their rivalry would seem to have been sustained and may have constituted the first great "series" of professional fights. Certainly, if the date of a poem by John Byrom – 1725 – is correct, then the 1727 battle was a rematch at least.

Byrom celebrates the heroism of the battle between Figg and Sutton, ending by proclaiming the victorious Figg 'lord of the field'. To be perfectly honest, nobody really knows what the details are. But they did fight in 1727. By this time the champion's business card, designed by a struggling young artist named William Hogarth, declared him to be the Master of the Noble Science of Defence. He was, we are told, less of a boxer than he was a swordsman and wielder of the cudgel and quarter-staff. Sutton, who when they first met had apparently never seen London before, was probably more of a boxer.

As was his wont, the dour King George I took himself and his court off to Hanover for the summer season, which meant Figg's business would be slow. He must have been delighted when Sutton agreed to meet him only three days after the departure of the King, who incidentally would never be seen again by the subjects he left behind. On 10 June, 1727, the German-speaking monarch suffered a terrible attack of diarrhoea, followed by a brain haemorrhage, and died in the early hours of the following day.

No matter. Among the crowds which pushed and jostled their way through the Academy gates that morning on 6 June were politicians, actors and writers: the Prime Minister, Sir Robert Walpole, sat down with several other Members of Parliament, Colley Cibber and the far greater writers Jonathan Swift and Alexander Pope. Swift, for whom prize fighting must have reflected his own love and disgust for life, was in London to oversee the publication of *Gulliver's Travels*. Pope, cynical and under-sized, and corsetted because of a weak back, had just celebrated his 33rd birthday. Anyone who was anyone, who was in London, walked, rode, was driven or carried out of the city along the north road.

Figg's pupils opened the show, and received the usual undercard treatment – barely anyone noticed them. Then the atmosphere changed, and the buzz of anticipation gave way to loud cheering as in came Sutton, taller but less muscular, and the shaven-headed Figg, who at 6ft and 13st had an enormous bull neck, broad shoulders and thick legs. In the first contest, the broadsword, nothing of note happened for half an hour. Then Sutton forced Figg back and the Master was gashed on his arm by his own sword. This apparently did not count. In the sixth round Sutton was scratched on the shoulder, which was enough to give Figg the first victory.

In the half-hour interval, great flagons of ale were passed among the masses, along with cakes and bread, until the fist-fighting began. For eight minutes they sparred, and then Sutton threw Figg at the umpire's feet. The crowd roared its approval, but Figg threw Sutton heavily on to his back and the challenger was given time to recover. A punch to the chest hurt Figg badly and he fell off the stage, but two or three members of the audience pushed him back. They took a 15-minute rest for some reason, during which time the new-fangled 'port-wine' was handed down from the gallery to the mob and the fighters. No doubt one or two drank it like beer. When the contest resumed, Figg gradually got on top and then knocked Sutton down with a punch to the chest. Figg jumped on him and pinned him down until he submitted. We are told he said: 'Enough indeed. You are a brave fellow and my master.'

In the third and final contest, Figg completed his day's work by breaking Sutton's knee with the cudgel.

Sutton may or may not have gone home afterwards. Certainly, he joined Figg's entourage at some time, and it's possible that was linked to the effects of a massive fire that destroyed a large part of Gravesend only a couple of months later. As we are uncertain on this point, it is possible that the Figg-Sutton contest was a staged affair, in that to drum up business the champion decided to fight the man he considered the best of his pupils. Others in the booth at the time are named: Timothy Buck, Thomas Stokes and Bill Flanders, who is sometimes written Flinders and who fought Chris Clarkson, 'The Old Soldier', at the booth in 1723.

Figg did not even bother to accept personally the other major challenge to his supremacy in 1733. When William Pulteney, the leader of the opposition to Walpole's Government and later the Earl of Bath, saw a giant gondolier, Tito Alberto di Carini, beat three men on one night in Venice, he brought him to England to fight Figg. But the great champion, now 38 years old, selected one of his pupils, the experienced Bob Whittaker of Whitby, to defend England's honour and, when the match was made at Slaughter's Coffee

House, put up a side bet of 50 guineas for Bob to win inside half an hour. Pulteney appears to have given him 2-1 ... and lost.

They fought at Figg's Academy in the presence of King George II (on a specially built throne) on 6 May 1733. Victorian ring historians were unkind to the King, who was described as 'a coarse, vulgar-looking German, with bloated cheeks and belly, a blotched nose and as beastly a voluptuous eye as his rascal of a Grandson, George IV, ever had.' This may or may not be an uncharitable representation, but he was certainly in his early 50s, a small man with blue eyes, whose relationship with his father had been at best tetchy and at worse volatile. George II's sons, the Prince of Wales, a hedonistic wastrel named Frederick, and the Duke of Cumberland, later to find infamy as the Butcher of Culloden, were also there. Tickets for the fight were priced upwards from one guinea – exceptionally high for the day – and still Figg was nailing up the "House Full" signs before the show began.

Di Carini did manage to knock Whittaker off the stage, but Whittaker clambered back and belted the Italian with a terrific blow to the belly, which knocked him down. A few minutes later the poor man quit. Another part of the great day was an exhibition between Figg and a star pupil, Jack Broughton, who made a big impression in front of the Royal gathering. A week later as Figg capitalised on the success of the Whittaker-Di Carini venture, Whittaker was beaten in the booth inside 10 minutes by another experienced fighter named Nathaniel Peartree, whose own career was to decline after he lost a finger. Figg had predicted Whittaker would lose.

Figg, still illiterate but famous enough to have been painted by Hogarth and Sir James Thornhill, who had worked on the Dome of St Paul's and on Hampton Court, did not have long to live. He died on 8 December 1734, at around 40 years of age, leaving a widow and several children. Even this is open to dispute. Some would have it that Figg lived on until 1740, a claim which would appear to be fairly eccentric, as his death was recorded in the *Gentleman's Magazine* of January 1735.

2

LIFE AFTER FIGG

On James Figg's retirement there were several who claimed to be the best fighter in England. Tom Pipes and George Gretting were among them and may even, for a short time, have been accepted as champions. Captain John Godfrey describes both in his 1747 work *A Treatise On The Science of Defence* which is acknowledged as the first boxing book.

'Pipes was the neatest boxer I remember. He put in blows about the face (which he fought at most) with surprising time and judgment. He maintained his battles for many years with extraordinary skill against men of far greater strength. Pipes was but weakly made; his appearance bespoke activity, but his hand, arm and body were small; though by that acquired spring of his arm, he hit prodigious blows; and at last, when beat out of his championships, it was more owing to his debauchery than the merit of those who beat him.

'Gretting was a strong antagonist to Pipes. They contended together for some time, and were almost alternate victors. Gretting had the nearest (sic) way of going to the stomach (which is what they call 'the mark') of any man I knew. He was a most artful boxer, much stronger than Pipes, and dealt the straightest blows. But what made Pipes a match for him was his rare bottom spirit, which would bear a great deal of beating, and this, in my mind, Gretting was not sufficiently furnished with; for after he was beaten twice by Pipes, [in 1733, he became] a mere sloven of a boxer, and everybody that fought him afterwards beat him. I must, notwithstanding, do that justice to Gretting's memory to own that his debauchery contributed to spoil a great boxer; yet, I think, he had not the bottom of the other.'

* * *

Lest we agree too wholeheartedly with the frowning of the good Captain, it should be pointed out that neither Pipes nor Gretting were the last boxers to be brought down by 'debauchery'.

The major figures of the post-Figg era were George Taylor, known as The Barber, and Jack Broughton, who had made such a favourable impression before George II. Broughton's reputation grew quickest, helped by his mastery of gentleman amateurs like Godfrey, and lasted longest, because of his ability to make the right type of social acquaintances.

Indeed, it is Broughton who is acknowledged as the Father of Prize-fighting. These were of course chaotic times and even though Broughton beat Taylor in 20 minutes, when Taylor was a young, inexperienced fighter, nobody seemed to mind when the Barber claimed the championship and ran Figg's old booth. Captain Godfrey, who was not a Taylor fan, described him as 'strong, able but deficient in bottom'. This would appear a harsh judgement. Taylor ran the old booth profitably, taking two-thirds of the gate, with one third divided between the main event boxers. The undercard survived from the proceeds of the hat which was passed among the customers. However, there is no basis in fact for historians to regard George Taylor as the next champion after Figg.

By the 1730s, prize-fighting was widely reported. One bout even reached the American press. The *Boston Gazette* recorded in 1733:

'On Monday last a Boxing Match was fought on the Bowling Green at Harrow on the Hill, between John Faulconer of Brentford, Carpenter, and Bob Russell, who keeps an Alehouse at Paddington.'

Another top man was Tom Smallwood, who lost to Dimmocks, a carman, in the Tottenham Court Road booth in 50 minutes in May 1741, but six months later beat Richard Harris in a severe fight for a prize of £50 in front of royalty. On the same day the celebrated Buckhorse also fought Harry the Clogmaker. In 1742 Smallwood beat an intriguing figure named Will Willis, the Fighting Quaker, for £100. He also lost a tough contest to a butcher named King in 1746, but was still fighting as late as 1757 when he beat the lightweight Ned Hunt in 50 minutes at Hounslow for a prize of 150 guineas. Hunt stood only 5ft 5in tall and weighed around 9st, yet had ability enough to handle most of the big fighters on the scene. He took a beating occasionally, as when the future champion Jack Slack hurt him unmercifully. His last fight was in 1758 when he lost after an hour's gruelling fighting to Richard Mills, who was known as the Onion Boy.

Buckhorse was another famous fighting man, whose ugliness was probably a result of some form of infantile encephalitis. Whatever the reason, his head was big and bulbous at the top and his face pinched and narrow. His real name was John Smith and he was born, according to *Eccentric Magazine*, 'in the house of a sinner' in the notorious Lewkner's Lane near Drury Lane, where rogues, thieves and ne'er-do-wells gathered to eke out their grimy, violent and precarious existences. Remember, these were days when the thieving of a pocket handkerchief could cost a young man his life.

Buckhorse

Buckhorse learned to steal, and then to fight, with equal mastery and through his appearances at Figg's Academy and then under Broughton, he became something of a cult celebrity. 'As ugly as Buckhorse' became a cliche of the time. Buckhorse was never a champion, but apparently his strange looks belied his talents. He was sought-after by ladies, who it was said regarded him as enthusiastic and energetic in the arts of love. Or something like that, anyway! Needless to say, he came to what is usually described as a bad end, but which hopefully was not completely devoid of happiness. He died in a ditch one wintry night, cuddling his last bottle of gin.

Boxing contests almost always passed unreported but they were common. The *Northampton Mercury* regularly printed the number of deaths in London for the preceding week. Between 13-20 July 1736, more than 420 were recorded, with the causes of death broken down as follows:

Old age	21
Consumption	57
Convulsions	144
Dropsy	20
Fever	60
Small-pox	83
Still-births	15
Teeth	20
Drowned	2
Killed accidentally	1
Overlaid	1
Hanged themselves	* (printing error omitted the figure)
Killed by boxing	2

In 1742, another newspaper carried a notice that 'Thomas Hodgkins, from Shropshire, and Jeremiah McCarthy, from Ireland, who fought on

Wednesday last a severe and bloody battle ... are to have a second combat for a great sum of money.'

Jack Broughton

Life was perilous, yet Broughton's might have been scripted for a Mills & Boon romance. He was born, possibly in 1704, in Baunton, a village a few miles north of Cirencester in a steep-sided valley on the Cheltenham road. At first his childhood was happy, but when his mother died, his father took to drink. Broughton Senior remarried, to a woman who shared his addiction to gin, and the home life Jack and his sister Rose had enjoyed under their natural mother was destroyed. When Jack was 12 and Rose 10, the atmosphere became so appalling that they packed their belongings into a bag and walked out.

It must be pointed out that according to social historians, this was not an uncommon thing for children of their age and place at the lower end of the social strata. Most kids probably spent whatever remained of their lives in wretched poverty, but the Broughtons were made from strong stuff and were luckier than most. They moved to Bristol and found work. Jack earned a decent living as a waterman and was a fine athlete even by his middle teens. When she was 18 he consented to Rose marrying a man who was described as a mechanic. She prospered.

Broughton left Bristol around 1725. Some say it was his work that took him to London, others report it was his performance at Figg's travelling booth at the traditional St James' Fair in Bristol. If the latter is true, he remonstrated loud and long with the winner of a mismatch on Figg's stage, the argument boiled over into a scuffle and the great champion, ever the entrepeneur, broke it up and matched them in a proper fight on stage. Broughton gave the professional slugger a hiding and Figg persuaded him to return with the fair to London to take up a job in the academy. In 1730 he used his old skills as a waterman to win the Doggett's Coat And Badge rowing event on the Thames.

Broughton, 5ft 11in and around 14st, was a model professional. He was regarded as intelligent and wise, a man who took as much joy from flowers as he did from the problems set him in a prize ring. He cut a

Jack Broughton

13

cultured, disciplined figure and must have stood out as an eccentric among his bent-nosed and buckle-eared companions. We are told that after a slow start, he learned his trade until he was more or less untouchable. He had fast reflexes, a sound defence and an acute boxing brain.

Broughton's life was that of a craftsman, working under the guidance of a master. Then on Figg's departure, Broughton fought in the Tottenham Road arena run by Taylor, who put other fighters up against him – including Jack James, and a sailor, James Field. Broughton beat everyone. He perfected the punch to the short rib, on to the liver, to the extent that the spot became known as 'Broughton's Mark'. He was strong, cunning, with a long reach and clever defence – he perfected the art of knocking away punches aimed at the body and in catching head punches with an open fist.

Broughton's career really took off the day he won an exhausting challenge with the small sword against a gentleman punter, whose confidence was such that he had assumed he would win as a matter of course. The startled loser was the Duke of Cumberland, otherwise known as Prince William, second son of King George II. History knows him better as The Butcher of Culloden, the man who set Bonnie Prince Charlie to flight and decimated the Jacobite army – and any woman and child who happened to be on the moor – in April 1746. When he lost to Broughton, the Duke was still a young man, but he knew a good investment when he saw one: he patronised Broughton and helped him .move from his old academy (in what became Hanway Street, almost on the junction of Tottenham Court Road and Oxford Street) to a new purpose-built place near the old Adam and Eve. The plans allowed for gentlemen's retiring rooms, in order for the bruised, puffed-out members of the upper classes to recover before returning home or into the social fray. Broughton also rented the place out for lectures. More darkly, during the 1741 elections, he also led a hired mob on the side of court candidates Lord Sundon and Sir Charles Wager against the more popular Admiral Vernon. Broughton was shrewd enough to know which side his bread was buttered.

George Stevenson

Broughton featured in two major battles, the first against George 'The Coachman' Stevenson, a Yorkshireman. There is a story, perhaps apocryphal, that Stevenson had worked in the stables of a Hull merchant, Richard Sykes, whose own misfortune was that he worked too much and left his young second wife at home in their large house in Sledmere, on the road from Bridlington to York. Mrs Sykes gave parties and balls, throwing herself into the social whirl of North Yorkshire. In 1739 she went to a party about 10 miles away and the head coachman, suffering an attack of gout or laziness, ordered

Stevenson, a strapping, athletic youngster, to drive her there. On the way home the coach was attacked by three masked highwaymen. Stevenson smashed one in the face with the butt of his pistol, knocked one out with a punch and shot the other one. As the Edwardian writer Fred Henning put it in his admirable *Fights For The Championship*: 'His mistress was grateful to him – some said too grateful.'

Stevenson was soon promoted to head-coachman and '...it was whispered there were more reasons for madam to be driven out into the country...than for the purpose of taking fresh air.'

The gossip eventually reached Sykes in London and Stevenson was dismissed. As he left Sledmere, legend has it that Mrs Sykes ran from the house and pressed a bag of gold into his hand. This story, however, does not fit with the currently published history and family tree of Sledmere. In 1739, Sledmere was inhabited by Mark Kirkby, whose sister Mary had married Richard Sykes. This Richard Sykes died in 1726, and his son Richard, whose wife was named Jane, did not inherit Sledmere until Kirkby's death in 1748. Nevertheless, as Mark Kirkby was childless, it's possible that Richard Sykes and his wife also lived there and employed Stevenson. If so, and the story is true, then it is a simple case that the lady in question's name was Jane and not Mary.

Whatever the exact details of his departure from Sledmere, Stevenson made his way to London, mostly on foot, and found rooms in Clerkenwell. He took his company on the wilder side of the grim London streets, met the royal whores, and eventually through them, the dissolute, extravagant Prince Frederick, who welcomed Stevenson into his circle with great relish. Obviously, the prize-fighter was not of interest to Frederick for his intellect or biting wit. At the same time Broughton was looking for an opponent and Stevenson, probably with one of Frederick's toadies having fun as letter-writer, issued a challenge:

'Mr Broughton, you think yourself a great fighter. Perhaps you are, but there's people living here in Clerkenwell says your fighting days are over, and you are good for nothing but to show off at them fights. I will meet you a month from today. If you don't come up, you are a coward. If you don't dust me you are a humbug. If I beat you, you are a dead man.'

Broughton, by then at least 36, agreed to fight Stevenson at a railed fair booth in Tottenham Court Road in February 1741 for a purse of £100. Broughton's training was affected by illness, but he went through with the fight as a matter of honour and because he believed himself sufficiently superior to any of his contemporaries, especially a young man whose pedigree was largely a matter of conjecture. Stevenson, revelling in his new role as royal companion, whored and drank almost to the eve of the fight.

Stevenson v Broughton: the death of the former led to the introduction of the first rules.

By fight time Cumberland, Broughton's patron, was there, alongside his brother Frederick, who was backing the Yorkshireman. No doubt their majesties had a good trip across London and were not subjected to the kind of inconveniences the roads, muddy from rain and thawed ice, had provided for the lesser multitudes. Only a few weeks earlier, it had been so cold the Thames had frozen solid. London had celebrated with a massive party on the thick ice, complete with an ox-roast, dancing and games.

The fighters entered the arena beneath the gaze of the royal brothers and their entourage. Other pugilists, some retired, were there too: men like Wells the Lamplighter, Boswell the Gipsy and Gray the Clogmaker, with their broken noses and mis-shapen hands. Broughton was taller but leaner. Stevenson was broad but half a stone lighter.

The 39-minute fight was brutal even for those days. The first two rounds lasted half an hour. Stevenson's cheeks streamed with blood after he had taken blow after blow to the head and when he rushed Broughton, he was smashed to the wooden boards. But the Yorkshireman refused to fold and fought back to bring blood pouring from the champion's nose. They both took terrific punishment and were reeling around, virtually exhausted, when Broughton pinned Stevenson to the ring stake, took a pace back and drove everything he had behind a punch that landed just beneath the heart. Stevenson went down and didn't get up. Broughton, as tired as he was, bent over him and said: 'Good God, what have I done? I've killed him.'

Stevenson eventually recovered his breath and senses in time to pay respect to Broughton, but retired to a room in the Adam and Eve and lost consciousness. He woke after several hours, but by then doctors knew he had two broken ribs. More serious than any of these were the injuries he had suffered to his internal organs. He lingered a month. Broughton visited every day and they became friends, the young man eventually dying in the older one's arms. At the funeral, so goes the story, there was a wreath from 'Mrs Sykes of Sledmere'.

Broughton was so upset by Stevenson's death that he devised a set of rules to make the business safer. Written by his friend Captain Godfrey, they were published on 26 August 1743. Destined to be used until the introduction of the London Rules in 1838, they exiled tactics like gouging and purring (kicking a fallen man) and generally tried to impose some kind of discipline on the competitors. Broughton also introduced the use of mufflers, or gloves, in order to increase the attraction to society gentlemen who wanted to gain a rudimentary grasp of the art without risking their looks.

This was the same year that the great man opened a new amphitheatre at the junction of Hanway Street and Oxford Street, christening it with a tournament between 'Evans, Sweep, Bellas, Glover, Rogers, Allen, Spikes and Gray' and a battle royal involving Buckhorse and several others. 'No person is to pay more than a shilling!' ran the notices in the *Daily Advertiser*.

Broughton's success was immediate – and his opening night was a deliberate spoiler designed to ruin the attendance at Taylor's booth where The Barber was fighting. Taylor was so furious that he accused Broughton of malicious practice and false boasts. He challenged him for £100, but Broughton ignored him. The same year Taylor was forced to shut down his booth. From then on he worked, presumably with a great deal of bitterness, alongside the other pugilists in Broughton's employ. Taylor had also accused Broughton of exploiting his pugilists by taking too great a cut of the gate.

BROUGHTON'S RULES

1. That a square of a yard be chalked in the middle of the stage; and every fresh set-to after a fall, or being parted from the rails, each second is to bring his man to the side of the square, and place him opposite the other; and till they are fairly set-to at the lines, it shall not be lawful for the one to strike the other.

2. That, in order to prevent any disputes as to the time a man lies after a fall, if the second does not bring his man to the side of the square, within the space of half a minute, he shall be deemed a beaten man.

3. That, in every main battle, no person whatsoever shall be upon the stage, except the principals and their seconds; the same rule to be observed in bye-battles, except that in the latter, Mr Broughton is allowed to be upon the stage to keep decorum, and to assist gentlemen in getting to their places; provided always, he does not interfere in the battle; and whoever presumes to infringe these rules, to be turned immediately out of the house. Everybody is to quit the stage as soon as the champions are stripped, before they set-to.

4. That no champion be deemed beaten, unless he fails coming up to the line in the limited time; or that his own second declares him beaten. No second is to be allowed to ask his man's adversary any questions or advise him to give out.

5. That, in bye-battles, the winning man to have two-thirds of the money given, which shall be publicly divided upon the stage, notwithstanding any private agreement to the contrary.

6. That to prevent disputes, in every main battle, the principals shall, on the coming on the stage, choose from among the gentlemen present two umpires, who shall absolutely decide all disputes that may arise about the battle; and if the two umpires cannot agree, the said umpires to choose a third, who is to determine it.

7. That no person is to hit his adversary when he is down, or seize him by the ham, the breeches, or any part below the waist; a man on his knees to be reckoned down.

By 1747 Broughton was more socialite than prize-fighter. He had travelled in luxury with Cumberland, who liked showing him off at home and abroad. On one trip to Prussia he had been introduced to Frederick the Great. He was well into middle age and was soft, and to be blunt, he shouldn't have been boxing competitively any more.

Jack Slack

Yet on Wednesday, 11 April 1750 he fought Jack Slack, a 29-year-old butcher from Thorpe, on the outskirts of Norwich. Slack, who best might be said to have lacked social graces, threw the champion's dinner-plate on the floor at Hounslow Races. Broughton whipped his legs and Slack, after threatening to knife the great warrior, was bundled away and calmed down. When he had cooled off, he issued Broughton with a challenge to a fight for the championship four weeks later.

Broughton's confidence was so high that he paid Slack 10 guineas just to turn up. He didn't worry too much about training – Slack, after all, was a brawler who had lost to George Taylor in 25 minutes three months before, on 31 January 1750. Taylor, however, backed Slack heavily. He knew that for all of his own technical superiority, the great strength of the Norfolk butcher could be a serious problem to anyone not fully fit. Taylor also knew that it had taken

Jack Slack

him 25 minutes to find a way to throw Slack, who had landed with a terrible crash and had been unconscious for a few seconds longer than Broughton's half-minute recovery time. Slack had ranted and raged, but rules had become rules. The butcher held Broughton, not Taylor, responsible for his defeat.

Like many an athlete before and since, Slack grew nervous and uncertain in the build-up to the big day, even to the point of wanting to pull out. But almost certainly his patrons leaned on him. Faced with the prospect of disgrace if he withdrew, not to mention causing his backers to lose their stake, Slack sorted himself out and prepared. Many a championship fight has been won on fear. This may have been the first. They met for a purse that eventually, when all receipts had been added up, amounted to around £600 in front of a crowd that paid half a crown for the cheapest vantage points. The arena was quickly filled. For a couple of minutes Broughton did as he liked, outboxing the shorter man. Then with gamblers offering 10-1 on Broughton, the man who had paid more attention to defence than anyone before him was caught by a sucker punch and blinded.

At first, when Cumberland called out to ask what was wrong, he said:

'I can't see my man, your Highness. I'm blind, but I'm not beat. Only let me see my man and he shall not gain the day yet.'

The rising panic almost bursts out from the words. After 14 minutes he admitted it was useless to fight on. The blank amazement of his plaintive: 'By God I'm done!' did nothing to impress Cumberland, who had wagered £10,000 to win £1,000 from the Earl of Chesterfield. The Duke stormed out, had the academy closed down and, for a time, fighting outlawed. Broughton's life was in ruins, but he turned the building into a furniture market and, such were his character and social contacts, he made money enough to dabble in stocks, was successful and lived in comfort to his old age.

As late as 1757 he was concerned with boxing, possibly as a promoter, in the tennis courts at James Street near The Haymarket. Broughton kept the job Cumberland had given him as Yeoman of the Guard and in old age even this generous, dignified man, with whom King George III would stop to chat, must have allowed himself a smile or two as he considered how Cumberland's fortunes nose-dived. Following the defeat of his armies abroad, Cumberland was in disgrace from 1757 until his death in 1765, when still only 44.

Broughton lived until six months before the storming of the Bastille and the symbolic beginning of a new Europe. By then the 'Father of Boxing' was 84 and had amassed a fortune of £7,000, which was left to his family. He died at the Ship public house, where he may also have been living at the time, in Walcot Place, Lambeth, on 6 January 1789, was buried in Lambeth churchyard and a stone tablet in his memory is in the place England reserves for its nearest and dearest, Westminster Abbey.

As for George Taylor, the great rival of Broughton's youth, his career ended when, as an out-of-shape, grey-haired, middle-aged man, he took a terrible, 75-minute thrashing from a raw youngster, Tom Faulkner of Deptford, a mile south of St Albans on 5 August 1758. That defeat must have rankled, for it was at Deptford that Taylor kept the Fountain Tavern. Twice in the past he had beaten Faulkner, but for some time before their third meeting he was blind in one eye and the battering took too much out of him. Both men were carried from the ring and within four months Taylor was dead.

At his best he was a brave, top class pugilist. In June 1741 he had suffered a broken jaw against a gipsy named 'Prince' Benjamin Boswell, son of the King of the Gipsies, but had won in three rounds. Godfrey is scathing about Boswell's lack of heart, but we cannot be certain of it because of his bias towards Broughton. He speaks of Boswell's 'worm-dread soul' and 'nurse-wanting courage'. In short, Taylor was probably very unlucky to have had Broughton for a contemporary. Boswell was a regular at the Tottenham Court booth and may have boxed Taylor on other occasions, and in 1743 lost to James Field, a sailor who would eventually be hanged at Tyburn.

Tom Faulkner, Taylor's final conqueror, was born in Hertfordshire in 1736 but moved with his parents to Deptford when he was a boy. He was more cricketer than boxer, but after beating Taylor, he fought Joe James near the White Lion at Putney in April 1759. James' father ran a small prize-fighting school at Newmarket and his elder brother Jack had worked without much recognition under Taylor and had boxed Broughton. Faulkner won in 10 minutes with a blow to the chest that raised the suspicions of the spectators, but no 'cross' was proven. Faulkner returned to the cricket arena but in his late middle age he had one last fling at prize-fighting: on 21 March 1791 at Studley in Warwickshire he beat William Thornhill in 50 minutes, ending the battle with a punch to the neck.

These were the years when sports were organised properly for the first time: in 1743 Broughton's laws were brought into boxing, in 1744 the Laws of Cricket were written; in 1752 the Jockey Club was formed. Before the end of the century the three great Classic races, The St Leger, The Oaks and The Derby were installed.

Wrestling without punching was a separate, but equally popular sport, with its own early master – Thomas Topham, who kept a pub in Hog Lane, Shoreditch, and who died after stabbing himself and his wife in a domestic quarrel in August 1749. Englishmen would watch anything they could bet on – including badger baiting, cock fighting, goose quailing and ratting, and would bet on anything, whether or not they could watch it! In 1743 a book was opened offering 4-1 against King George II dying in battle against the French, the first National Lottery ran from 1709 until 1824, and as late as 1820, a weaver named George Kettering won a 10-guinea bet that he could stand on one leg, with no other support, for four hours.

> 'The wager ... was decided before a large company, upstairs, at the house of Harmer, the pugilist, the sign of the Plough, in Gilt-spur Street ... when he stood in that attitude 3 and ¾ hours he became so weak he could not speak.'

However, he hung on for the last 15 minutes to earn his money. 'After his leg was fomented for some time, and some cordial given to him, he recovered so far as to be able to join in the festivities of the parties assembled.'

Life was a turbulent, violent mess, in which the line between survival and death was extremely thin. Sympathy for villains spread as far as handing a beer to a petty criminal who was put in the stocks for a night, but there were wooden grandstands at Tyburn, and huge crowds would gather to see a public lashing of a whore, witch, vagrant or Roman Catholic.

Jack Slack, who took over from Broughton as champion, was alleged to be James Figg's grandson. On the basis of what evidence, I know not. But whatever the truth of his heritage, he was by nature a swaggering, shiftless bully. Beating Broughton could have been the making of him. Instead, he thought nothing of involving himself in fixed fights, which, when he depended largely on an audience bent on gambling on the outcome, was a disastrous long-term tactic. Gentlemen might be swindled once, but rarely twice. Nevertheless, he did rule as champion for a decade and attracted the patronage of Cumberland, who had soon recovered from his fit of pique at Broughton's defeat and, in the time-honoured fashion, stepped over the fallen body to acknowledge and court his conqueror. Slack ran a booth in London, and when business was scarce, took his fighters on the road. He helped establish Bristol as a major fight centre.

Slack married a miller's daughter, had two sons, was a butcher by trade and a prize-fighter by inclination. When he set out for London in 1748, he had twice beaten the Suffolk champion, Daniel Smith. He arrived in the capital when Broughton was in Prussia with Cumberland, and contented himself by trouncing the lightweight Ned Hunt, who was one of the champion's favourite pupils. Hunt had once conceded six stones to a guardsman named Hawkesley and won in ten minutes. Against Slack, however, he took a fearful pounding. Hunt spent the rest of his active days as a teacher at Broughton's school and fought only occasionally, the last time in 1758.

Slack lost to Taylor, but then beat Broughton for the championship. And on 29 July 1751 the new champion of England beat a 6ft 4in Frenchman named Petit (presumably a joke) at Harleston on the Norfolk-Suffolk border. Petit's main ploy was to rush in and grab Slack by the thighs – illegal under Broughton's Rules – but then seemed to get the idea of it and grabbed Slack by the throat, propped him against the rails and thumped away with his free hand for 30 seconds. Slack was 'extremely black' – whether from bruising, lack of oxygen or temper, we know not – but somehow extricated himself and fought back. Both were thrown down. Once Slack went off the edge of the stage on to the ringsiders, who broke his fall and shoved him back. Slack hammered away on the inside and succeeded in virtually shutting one of Petit's eyes. Eventually, the weakened Frenchman was knocked off the stage – and fell the full eight feet on to the turf. To the disgust of the paying punters, Petit was so discouraged that he 'walked off without so much as civilly taking his leave of the spectators', according to one contemporary newspaper report.

On 13 March 1755 Slack knocked out Cornelius 'King Cole' Harris at Kingswood near Bristol. Harris is listed as a miner, but in fact was a dangerous, probably insane creature who was beyond the law. It's fairly certain that he killed a woman, with whom he had gone for a romantic interlude in the countryside, and her former boyfriend, who had disturbed them. The bodies were found, but nobody dared accuse him. Harris fought regularly on village greens after making challenges in public houses – and was also said to have left more than one man for dead in the coalmines where he worked. If a man upset him, he would challenge him to a fight to the finish in the bowels of the earth. This is why they called him 'King Cole'. He gambled 100 guineas on beating Slack and gave him a gruelling, desperate fight. But in the end Slack outlasted him and left him unconscious with a blow that landed between the eyes. When Harris awoke to find the champion had gone away to celebrate, he was so crazed by the defeat and the loss of his money that he ranted and raged like the madman he was, threatening all kinds of retribution. No doubt those who saw the fight were pleased to see him absorb a hammering for once. And no doubt they opted not to say so!

Slack alternated between his house in St George's Fields, where he gave lessons, and the road, when he toured with his employed band of 'pupils'. It was not until 20 October 1759, when he defeated a cowman named Jack Moreton near Reading in 35 minutes, that he can be considered to have defended his championship again. The price of the fight was only £50 a side, an indication of how much Slack's reign had devalued the championship. Nevertheless, he did accumulate a lot of money and ran a successful academy. His downfall came when he agreed to fight William 'The Nailer' Stevens on 17 June 1760 at the Tennis Court in James Street, Haymarket, which had been opened by Broughton three years earlier.

It was the first great pugilistic event in the capital since Slack had defeated Broughton those ten long years before. Once again, prize-fighting drew Royal patronage. Stevens, from Soho, Birmingham, was 24 years old – 15 years younger than the champion – slightly taller at 5ft 10ins but lighter at around 13 and a half stones. Stevens, the son of a female blacksmith, was patronised by the Duke of York, whom he had impressed by knocking out Jacob Taplin, a coal heaver and known pugilist, in February 1760 at Marybone Basin, fields beyond Oxford Street near where Marylebone is now.

Four months later he was pitched in with Slack ... and the championship changed hands. Early in the fight he knocked Slack down with a body punch, but was generally outwrestled and tried to keep the fight at long range, away from the champion's 'chopper-blow'. Nevertheless he had taken several of these when he caught Slack with a terrific punch to the forehead and quickly threw him over his leg. Slack's head cracked against the wooden boards and his seconds, Tom Smallwood and Ned Hunt, were unable to revive him in the half-minute allowed. Slack retired and was described by Pierce Egan, the first genuine boxing journalist and historian, as 'a brutish and untrustworthy character'. Egan did not know Slack, and so we must assume that this was Jack's reputation at the time Pierce was writing, half a century later.

Slack ran a butcher's shop in Chandos Street for a while and died in 1778, aged 57. His son Jem was also a prize-fighter, but didn't have the 'bottom' for it. In 1765 he did well for a round against Parfitt Meggs, then bolted when things began to go against him. Disgusted by another financial reverse, Cumberland broke all ties with boxing and, though out of favour with the court, became an outspoken critic of the sport. Four months after Slack's defeat George II died of a heart attack at the age of 76 and with him went the royal patronage.

England was changing dramatically. New towns were springing up and with them far better roads, and even the look of the country was being transformed by the controversial enclosure system. As to some in the 1990s, it may have seemed to the people of the 1760s that boxing was an activity which really belonged in the past, and had no place in these new, 'civilised' times. But it has a way of surviving, almost in spite of itself.

Like Slack, 'Nailer' Stevens was a shady individual. Within nine months, at the Haymarket Tennis Courts on 2 March 1761, he had taken a dive against George Meggs, who was trained by Slack. Stevens allowed the inferior Meggs to shove him around as he pleased, seemed stunned by the first blow he took, and then gave in tamely after 17 minutes. The general feeling was that Slack's role had been more than that of the trainer of the challenger – and it was soon confirmed. Slack had given Meggs a workout at the back of his butcher's shop, rated him worth a chance against Stevens, and made the match for £200 a side. But when Meggs began to baulk at the possibility of getting hurt, Slack made some further financial inducement which persuaded Stevens to throw the fight.

Soon after the fight, the Nailer admitted the dive. Stevens was disgraced, but carried on fighting with little or no backing. He boxed an Irishman named McGuire at Bloomsbury Fields, which is said to be the site where the British Museum now stands, on 4 July 1769. He beat McGuire and the same month lost in 130 minutes to a strong novice named Bill Turner in Hyde Park. Eventually, long bereft of his athletic powers, he lost in ten minutes to Harry Sellers in the summer of 1778 for the paltry purse of £25. Stevens died 'in a miserable condition' in London in 1781. He was 55.

Meggs, a Bristol collier, was an ordinary prize-fighter who struck lucky. He did not last long as champion. On 2 July, 1762, he was beaten decisively by George Millsom, a baker from Bath, at Calne in Wiltshire. In a return a month later at Lansdown, north of Bath, Millsom won easily. Then at Beckhampton in 1763 Millsom gave a severe 40-minute beating to Parfitt Meggs, a bruising countryman who was George's brother, for £100.

Millsom lost a gruelling fight with Tom Juchau which lasted an hour and ten minutes at Colney Bridge near St Albans on 27 August 1765. Juchau, nicknamed 'The Disher' and 'The Paviour' (pavement-maker) was 'a most excellent bit of flesh and a glutton of the first order', in the opinion of Pierce Egan. Juchau had first attracted attention the previous year when he beat Charley Coant, a butcher, in 47 minutes at Guildford, and may have been related to a prize-fighter named Phil Juchau, who died after a £10 contest against a builder named Jack Warren on a stone surface opposite the gates of the Bedlam hospital for lunatics at Moorfields, London, in April 1765.

Tom Juchau, the next so-called champion, was good enough to attract a little attention from the nobility and gambling gentry – and they turned out to see him defend against Bill Darts for the gigantic sum of 500 guineas a side at Guildford in May 1766. Around 600 people sat in a specially erected grandstand and thousands more milled around on the turf. But it was a fight riddled with fouls – and when Darts won with a low blow after 40 minutes, it seemed the prize ring was still an unsavoury and financially unstable business. The rich withdrew again to their racing.

Dr Samuel Johnson is recorded by James Boswell as saying: 'I am sorry prize-fighting is gone out. Every art should be preserved and the art of defence is surely important ... Prize-fighting made people accustomed not to be alarmed at seeing their own blood or feeling a little pain from a wound.'

Bill Darts, a dyer born in 1741, was able enough: brave and a big puncher with some skill and plenty of strength, but he ran a tavern in Holborn and lived recklessly, shortening his time at what passed for the top in these depressed years. Darts had previously beaten Parfitt Meggs in a terrific struggle near Shepton Mallet in Somerset in 1764, and after becoming champion he trounced a West Countryman named Dogget, known as the Bargeman, in an hour for £100 near Melksham in Wiltshire in July 1767. Three months later he beat Swansey, the Butcher, in Epping Forest.

He didn't mean much to the sporting world, however, and when he lost to a waterman, Tom Lyons, in 45 minutes at Kingston in June 1769, Lyons thought so little of his achievement that he was back working on barges two weeks later and, as far as we know, never bothered to fight seriously again. Darts beat Stephen Oliver, who was nicknamed Death because of his unnaturally pale skin, at Putney in March 1770, but then lost a fixed fight against an Irish farmer's son, Peter Corcoran, at Epsom Racecourse on 18 May, 1771. The 'fight' lasted less than a minute. Darts had agreed to take a dive in return for £100 from Corcoran's patron, a rogue named O'Kelly, who had been in debtors prison after running up gambling bills, had bought himself an army commission, called himself Captain and if he felt like it, Colonel. With £100 of O'Kelly's money in his pocket, Darts put up no fight at all and Corcoran finished it with unnecessary violence, smashing the champion's head against a ring post.

Darts was ostracised from the sporting world, customers no longer wanted to be seen in his Holborn tavern and he died a pauper in 1781, the year O'Kelly's horse Young Eclipse won The Derby at odds of 10-1. (He was to win again in 1784 on 3-1 favourite Sergeant.) O'Kelly made more than half a million pounds with his stud, but died in his house in Piccadilly at the age of 51 with his mistress Charlotte Hayes at his side. Some say he had never recovered from a private thrashing given him by a truculent, unsporting young gentleman named Richard England as a result of a personal row. O'Kelly sued him for damages, but although the case was proven, such was his own reputation that he was awarded only a shilling by the courts. When he died he left his fortune to his nephew, with a spoilsport restriction that he forfeit £500 for every bet he made on the turf.

Corcoran was another man doomed to leave a stained name. From

Ballyconneely in Galway, he is said to have fled Ireland after killing a man who shared his enthusiasm for a village girl. His father sent him to London to escape the law, and he worked as a coalman, then at sea and eventually settled as landlord of the Black Horse in Dyot Street, St Giles. At first he was popular, but after beating Darts he was a scandalous figure and was avoided. It probably made matters worse that he hadn't seemed much of a prize-fighter either. He had already lost to Bill Turner for £20, even though he had beaten two of his customers, Davis and Dalton, presumably to make a point. People trusted him so little after the Darts shambles that they called his win over Sam Peters near Waltham Abbey, Essex, in June 1744, a fake, even though he was badly bruised for days.

With money from this fight he took over the Blakeney Arms in St Martin's Lane, but eventually lost another allegedly fixed fight, this time to Harry Sellers of Bristol in front of the Crown Inn at Staines, Middlesex, on 10 October, 1776. Corcoran, heavily backed by his Irish followers, knocked Sellers across the stage with the first punch. Sellers fought extremely cautiously for nearly 20 minutes, apparently drawing Corcoran's strength, and then took over, hitting him as he pleased for ten minutes until Corcoran could not go on. The prize was 100 guineas. On face value, it didn't sound like much of a fix, but it was accepted as such. Egan was convinced he was a rogue, but William Oxberry, the author of the 1812 volume *Pancratia*, was more generous and, I think, probably in this case fairer.

> 'Peter, as a pugilist of his period, stands first rank as a fair fighter; being generally engaged with powerful pugilists, he was unfortunate in the events of his contests, and indeed had little reason to triumph when victorious, for as he never shifted or fell, unless accidentally, without a blow, he seldom escaped a severe drubbing.'

Corcoran was eventually reduced to begging on the streets. He died around 1784.

Boxing may have had a poor reputation, but its appeal was spreading rapidly among the poor and working classes. The *Daily Advertiser* of 13 May 1773 records a boxing match for £10 a side between two shoemakers, John Pearce and John White, at the Riding School, Three Hats, Islington, that was terminated by the intervention of the high constable and his attendant officers of the law.

Harry (Henry) Sellers was born on 10 August, 1753, and was 23 when he outboxed Corcoran. He had some ability but certainly seems to have been a character of dubious moral fibre. When proceedings got too rough, he had a habit of falling down, cunningly letting go a surprise punch as he fell. That should really be put down as an eccentricity rather than a revolutionary tactic. It didn't catch on!

Sellers was a classic bully. When someone stood up to him, he quit – as he did against an obscure Irishman named Jack or Duggan Fearns outside the Crown Inn, Slough, on 25 September, 1780. He fell over from the first half-decent blow and refused to go on. It was all over in 90 seconds. Fearns, who was a boatswain (a bosun – a ship's officer in charge of sails and rigging) was never heard of again, presumably because he went back to sea, but nobody was inclined to give Sellers the time of day. Between the Corcoran and Fearns

Harry Sellers

fights, he twice beat Joe Hood, the first time for 50 guineas a side at Ascot races, and 'Nailer' Stevens. The old champion was humiliated for the last time when he offended another Irishman, named William Harvey. In an asses' field near a pub named the Black Dog at a place named Holywell Mount, which has been sometimes transcribed as Holloway Mount, but may well have been the small area which is now Holywell Row and Holywell Lane in Shoreditch, Harvey, apparently a complete novice, somehow won in 20 minutes. Sellers was 31. Of the rest of his life, nothing is known. A story existed that he died of grief at being unable to fight Tom Johnson in the 1780s.

Prize-fighting was on the brink of extinction, only 40 years after the heyday of Broughton, because it had lost its sense of honour and dignity: it had become too crooked to be gambled on safely.

England was still largely the same mixture of rough, ragged and royal life as it was in George II's day. What we would judge now to be the most appalling cruelty to man and beast was then accepted as good sport. But no sport could thrive if men were not prepared to bet on it. It is also important to stress that although stake money was sometimes high, the boxer did not necessarily receive that amount. The stake money was handed to the backer of the winning boxer, who then divided it as he saw fit. The general rule of thumb was that the boxers should be given the gate money, if any, or a proportion of it, plus whatever the patron believed was fair. Obviously, if he had won, then a fighter might expect to receive more, as the patron had presumably increased his own income from the fight by gambling. If a fighter had lost, then he was likely to come away with little or nothing at all, as his patron would presumably make some attempt to recoup his losses before paying a man he might feel had let him down.

Pugilism might have drifted away then, had not a string of honourable men come to champion it. Because of them it managed to hold its own alongside ratting, bear-baiting and the rest – and also found a home as a reasonable alternative to duelling for the purpose of the settling of grudges. Accordingly, as the rich once had to learn to fence, now an education in the finer points of boxing was considered a social necessity. By the end of the century boxing was an accepted form of sport at Eton, although we are told the schoolboys were advised to maintain some kind of decorum by continuing to wear their top hats during competition.

At this point it is probably also apt to warn against too great a sensibility in the modern reader. We have different standards of sport and a wholly different set of values by which to judge the world from those that seemed appropriate and reasonable to the right-thinking, civilised man of the 18th and 19th centuries. We are now squeamish about hanging, for example, both in terms of the law and the ugly reality of the act. Yet in the era we discuss here, hanging was a weekly occurrence and considered worthy of public attendance. Animals were routinely tortured in all kinds of sports. The very basis of the British penal code was expressly concerned with crimes against property and contrastingly unconcerned by violence against the person. What we would consider assault very rarely brought prosecution in those days. Wives were a husband's property to do with as he pleased. You could be executed for more than 150 offences, most of which amounted to crimes against property or personal wealth. General fighting between ordinary people, so long as it stopped short of murder, was not a thing for the law to be unduly bothered about.

3
THE GOLDEN YEARS

Tom Johnson is one of boxing's less remembered heroes, yet the sport owes him an unpayable debt. In short, he saved it. His real name was Thomas Jackling and he was originally from Derby, but like so many others moved to London to find his fortune. He found a job as a porter in the docks and was well-liked and respected. A story of his generosity survives. A workmate was taken sick, which in those days meant he earned nothing and probably lost his job to the first available and willing hand. Johnson saved the man's livelihood, and quite possibly his family, by carrying both of their loads until he was well enough to return. Such chivalry is not easily forgotten among men and it's no wonder that when he turned to prize-fighting, the public took to him.

Johnson's first major win was when he trounced Jack Jarvis in 15 bloody minutes in June 1783. He went on to defeat a fighter known only as the Croydon Drover on Kennington Common in south London, and to destroy in half an hour the tragically declining Stephen 'Death' Oliver, who was cut so badly that he was unable to see. Oliver, who had worked in the great booth of Broughton, may then have been in his 60s.

By 1784 the Prince of Wales, the future George IV, was an enthusiastic supporter of the Prize Ring – and of Johnson. In 1786 Johnson beat Bill Love, who was a butcher, and fighters named Jack Towers and Fry. By this time he was widely acknowledged as head and shoulders above every other pugilist in the country and at last, after beating Bill Warr of Bristol in a nonsensical encounter at Oakingham in Berkshire on 18 January 1787, he was called champion. Warr realised he was outclassed and kept dropping to the canvas from light punches to buy time, but eventually Johnson landed with a legal blow as Warr was on his way down and finished it. Johnson was a throwback to the wise, tactically astute Broughton. He planned his fights in advance, was cautious, infinitely patient and determined, and rarely wasted a punch. He

Tom Johnson

did not retreat, did not run, simply switched the angle of his punches by sidestepping and cleverly parried or blocked the blows thrown at him. He was an adept counter-puncher.

The re-emergence of boxing was threatened briefly in 1788 when the Prince of Wales retreated from it in horror, following the death of a fighter named Earl. He gave Earl's widow a pension of £1 a year and, under fierce criticism from the Court, declared he would shun the prize ring in the future. Fortunately for boxing, he was merely being politic. Within a month he is said to have scalded Lord Barrymore for not fighting like a man in a private struggle with a Brighton perfumer named Donadieu. He retained his interest.

Johnson also beat the 6ft 4in, left-handed Irish champion Michael Ryan twice – on 19 December 1787 at Wradisbury, Buckinghamshire, in 24 minutes in front of 1,000 people; and on 11 February 1789 for 300 guineas a side at a spot known as Rabbit Dell in the grounds of the Earl of Essex at Cassiobury near Rickmansworth in Hertfordshire.

In his first fight with Ryan, Johnson was lucky. Floored heavily in the first round by a man said to be the heaviest puncher in the land, he was stumbling dazed and defenceless in the second when his cornerman, Richard 'The Gentleman' Humphries, grabbed hold of Ryan. There was uproar but Johnson was not disqualified, recovered his senses and went on to win in half an hour. Johnson learned from the experience and in their second fight, which drew The Fancy from far and near, he won decisively. The champion was floored after what was apparently a marvellous first round, but then took over and cut Ryan's eyes and broke his nose.

After 33 minutes, the sponge was thrown in by Ryan's second 'Rolfe, the baker'. Johnson made, including bets and tips, more than £500, including £20 a year for life from one of his successful backers, Mr Hollingsworth, who had once employed him as a corn-porter. After the fight Johnson was also crowned with a hat decorated with ribbons – and the pigeons of victory were set loose. One of the gentlemen present was the M.P. and future Secretary of War, William Wyndham, who was late back to Parliament following delays to the bout caused by the weather. He expressed his regrets but said: 'The occasion was one of those on which not to have gone would have been as much a matter of remark as the going.'

And on 22 October 1789 at Banbury in Oxfordshire, Johnson used his science and body attacks to weaken a 6ft 2in giant engine-worker from Birmingham, Isaac Perrins, then knocked him out after an hour and a quarter. On a 24-feet square turf stage raised five feet above the ground they laid before the public a horribly grim struggle. Their eyes swelled to slits, Perrins' nose poured blood, and eventually after 62 rounds and 75 minutes of severe fighting, Johnson won. He took more than £500 in gate money and was also given £1,000 by a gentleman gambler, Mr Bullock, who had won £20,000 on his victory. Perrins' friends, having been impressed by tales of his phenomenal strength, had gambled heavily ... and fattened the pockets of a sporting few like Bullock. Perrins worked for a Smethwick firm named Boulton & Watts and also preached the Gospel at a chapel in Handsworth, but later took over a pub in Manchester. He died of fever in 1800 shortly after he had rescued people trapped in a burning house.

Johnson should have lived on in comfort into old age, but his passion for gambling ruined him. He blew the £5,000 he had won in the ring, and then took on 'Big' Ben Brain, sometimes called Bryan, on the high road from London to Maidstone at Wrotham, Kent, in January 1791. Johnson was knocked senseless in 18 rounds on a 20-feet turfed stage. In the first round a blow to the nose sent Johnson pitching down face first and he never fully recovered. He also broke a finger on the rails and suffered damaged ribs and a bad cut on the lip that probably meant he was swallowing his blood most of the way.

After a pub in Lincoln's Inn Field – the Grapes in Duke Street – had failed, he moved to Dublin and kept another house in Cooper Alley, but was turned out by the magistrates. In his final months he tried to scratch a living by passing on his art to pupils, but there were few takers. Johnson died destitute in County Cork on 21 January 1797.

'Big' Ben Brain

Brain, a Bristol collier born in 1753, was a veteran of 37 with 17 years' ring experience when he beat Johnson. He had lived in Bristol until 1774, when he travelled to London to find work as a coal porter at the Adelphi Wharf. He had boxed in his home city, and fights are recorded against Clayton of Shropshire and 'Spaniard' Harris from Kingswood, both of which he won. A protege of the Duke of Hamilton, Scotland's senior peer, Brain was a straight puncher who 'when out of his business always appeared clean and respectable, mild and sociable', according to Egan. But nice guys rarely finish first, as we've been told a thousand times.

Brain had already gone through several grim battles, including a particularly tough one against John Boone, the Fighting Grenadier, in the Long Fields at Bloomsbury on 31 October 1786. His eyes were almost shut after half an hour, at which point the crowd spilled over into the ring. During the scramble, a doctor lanced the swellings and Brain went on to win ten minutes later. He was lined up to challenge Johnson in 1789 but was ill and forfeited £500. On New Year's Eve, 1788, Brain beat an Irishman named Corbally at Knavestock in Essex, in October 1789 he disposed of Jacombs, a Warwickshire pugilist, at Banbury in 36 minutes and in January 1790 he beat Tom Tring in 12 rounds and less than 20 minutes at Dartford. He also slugged out a three and a half hour draw with William Hooper, known as The Tinman, at Chapel Row, a few miles east of Newbury in Berkshire.

After beating Johnson, Brain retired, but he came back in 1794 and was training to fight William 'The Coachman' Wood, when he fell ill and died suddenly and agonisingly from a damaged liver at his rooms in Grays Inn Lane on 8 April, 1794 at the age of 41. He was buried in St Sepulchre's churchyard on Snow Hill, London. His tombstone carried lines written by a fellow boxer:

> 'Farewell, ye honours of my brow,
> Victorious wreaths, farewell!
> One blow from Death has laid me low,
> By whom such brave ones fell.
>
> 'Yet bravely I'll dispute the prize
> Nor yield, though out of breath,
> 'Tis not a fall, I yet shall rise
> And conquer even Death.'

Brain's opponents were good men. Jacombs, for example, fought Payne of Coventry at Stoke Golding in Leicestershire on 10 March 1790. They may have been lesser fighters according to the history books, but they hammered away at each other in 'a most severe conflict of two hours'. After 95 rounds, Payne won. Tom Tring was a gentle, polite and friendly man whose 6ft 2in, 15st frame was used by Sir Joshua Reynolds as the model for drawings of Hercules. Tring earned day-by-day money as a street porter, but like so many went on fighting for too long. In the end boxing killed him – he died as a direct result of a fight in 1815.

Pugilism was developing and spreading to an unprecedented level. Even minor prize-fights were sometimes recorded and boxing was put to extreme or eccentric uses. At Stockbridge in Hampshire on 1 March 1791, for example, a father beat his son for the purposes of paternal correction ... in 46 minutes! And at Chelmsford in August 1792, two women fought for three-quarters of an hour with their husbands as seconds. *Pancratia* recreates the scene:

> 'Being stripped, without caps, and their hair closely tied up, they set to, and for 45 minutes supported a most desperate conflict; when, although one of them was so dreadfully beat as to excite apprehension for her life, her husband possessed brutality enough still to prompt her to the fight; but, through the interference of the spectators, they were separated.'

If it seems niceties like concern for the welfare of boxers was virtually non-existent, we should remember that life itself was considered a reckless business anyway. Disablement of one kind or another was commonly seen on the streets of any of the major cities. Nevertheless, it is part of boxing's bloody nature that it appears to exhilarate both competitors and spectators alike. Athletes will often tell of being capable of ignoring extreme pain in the so-called 'heat' of battle. Even today, boxers who retire with a painful injury are often the subject of sidelong, even scornful glances from their peers. Fighters expect to see from their fellows bravery beyond the ordinary call – a sore or broken hand, even a dislocated shoulder, is sometimes considered no reason to retire from the fray, especially when a major prize is at stake.

There was a memorable occasion when a world title fight in the 1980s ended prematurely when one fighter, the Ugandan John Mugabi, effectively stopped fighting because of an eye injury. It transpired that he had a fractured orbital socket. His agony did not impress world middleweight champion Marvin Hagler, who was working for TV as an analyst. Hagler's attitude was simple: Mugabi had two eyes, and while he could see out of one of them, he should fight. Boxers do not 'play' by normal rules ... and it was even more the case in the 18th and 19th centuries. For example, on Monday 18 November 1793 a violent battle was recorded between an ass-driver named Hall and a brewer's servant, unnamed, in Harley Fields near Portland Place – presumably the site of what is now Harley Street. The fight ended after an hour and five minutes because the servant considered it time to give in ... he had just lost an eye!

Daniel Mendoza

Boxing was so popular that it was now capable of producing its first genuine superstar, a man who would at first brighten and then transform the sport, moving with it on its course towards its golden years at the start of the 19th century. Daniel Mendoza was a charismatic Jew of Spanish and English descent, born in Aldgate in the East End of London on 5 July 1764. His reputation was such at the end of the 20th century that he was placed 83rd in a strange book, the intent of which was to grade the 100 most influential Jewish people in history. Each contained a potted biography and drawing or photograph. Moses was No.1, Jesus of Nazareth No.2, King Solomon No.29 and Harry Houdini got in at 81. Daniel Mendoza did better than Bob Dylan, who only just crept in at 97!

Daniel Mendoza

To us Mendoza would have been nothing more than a middleweight – 5ft 7ins and 160 pounds. But he was a one-off, a fighting scientist who probably took boxing skills to their highest level since Jack Broughton was at his peak. He had lived on his wits since he was a child and at various times had been apprenticed to a glass-cutter, worked for a tea-dealer, sold oil and baked biscuits. For extra cash, and probably for the hell of it, he raced on foot against horses. He made repeated trips to debtors' prison, from which his friends always bailed him. He was a financial disaster area, but in the ring was a genius. After taking heavy punishment in his first prize fight, which he won in 40 minutes against Harry The Coalheaver, he taught himself a straight left and practised the art of side-stepping and boxing on the move.

He was by no means invincible and had to learn through experience like everyone else. Tom Tyne beat him in 1786 and Joe Ward in 1790. To the astonishment of the 'millers' around him, he used the whole ring in order to keep fights at long range, where he could dart in with fast punches and be away out of distance again before they could catch him. But more than that, he had the ability to attract crowds. Down the generations, this has proved a mysterious quality. Some of the greatest fighters who ever lived failed to move people, yet lesser men drew massive public support. Reputations are sometimes inflated by this tendency, yet this was certainly not so in Mendoza's case. He was as good as the publicity said.

He had a celebrated series of battles with Richard 'The Gentleman' Humphries, the man who had intervened in the Ryan-Johnson fight. Humphries, a dealer's son, had looked on the younger Mendoza as his protege, but Mendoza was disgusted by Humphries' tendency to embark on monumental benders in taverns and whorehouses, and they fell out. Humphries, who had good contacts in the Court and was himself a tough, scientific and cunning fighter, was considered Mendoza's superior for a while.

After a public argument at the Cock Tavern in Epping Forest in 1787 they retired to the rear of the premises to sort things out, but were prevented from doing so by the peace officer. Another time, Humphries tried to get Mendoza jailed for debt. Finally they set up a proper match for 150 guineas at Odiham, Hampshire, on 9 January 1788 which drew an incredible crowd, maybe as many as 60,000, even though it was a typically bleak, cold winter's day. After 28 minutes Mendoza was unable to continue after slipping and spraining an ankle. Humphries sent a message to his patron, Wilson Bradyll: 'Sir, I have done the Jew and am in good health.' But hours before that arrived, the people of the East End knew: the black pigeon, which signalled Mendoza's defeat, had flown home. It was acknowledged as the finest exhibition of fist-fighting in history, but the result rankled and festered in Mendoza's heart. He would not rest until he had proved it a freak.

Humphries' talents have been overlooked because he was eventually overshadowed by Mendoza, but he was a stout and surprisingly graceful fighter. He beat a Bath butcher named Martin near Newmarket in front of a gathering which included the Prince of Wales, the Dukes of York, Orleans and De Fitzsanes 'and the whole flower of the French nobility', whatever that meant. How many of them would survive the next ten years? Only 320 people watched, but it was said more than £30,000 was gambled. Humphries won after three-quarters of an hour.

Richard 'The Gentleman' Humphries

A crowd of 3,000 saw the second Humphries-Mendoza fight, for a prize of 850 guineas, in May 1789 at Stilton, Huntingdonshire, on the old Roman road, Ermine Street, which now forms the A1. An amphitheatre was built especially to stage it in a park belonging to a Mr Thornton. There was a tragic prelude to the occasion as the prize-fighter William Warr (also called Ward) got embroiled in an argument with a blacksmith named Swaine about Mendoza's ability at the Bell Inn in Enfield. Swaine stupidly challenged him to a fight and Warr hit him so hard in the stomach that he died. Warr was taken into custody and convicted of manslaughter at the Old Bailey. This was not a capital offence. A typical punishment was imprisonment with branding.

The fight was close for a while. After 22 rounds Humphries infuriated Mendoza's supporters when he seemed to go down without being hit, but the cries of 'Foul!' produced only a bad-tempered argument between the two sides. Mendoza's second Captain Brown called Humphries' chief attendant Tom Johnson a liar – and the furious Johnson, who was still recognised as champion at this time, was ready to make him pay for the insult there and then. It took several minutes to calm it all down and for the principal fight to continue. Mendoza was less reckless than he had been in the first fight and his punches seemed to hurt Humphries, even though Humphries taunted him contemptuously whenever they came up to the scratch mark for the start of a round. After 50 minutes Humphries had one eye shut tight, was barely able to see through the blood running down from a cut over the other eye and was gashed on his lip. He swallowed some blood and spat out plenty more. Eventually, after 50 minutes and 65 rounds, he fell down without being hit and Mendoza was awarded the fight.

The second half of the 18th century was turbulent and inflation-stricken. England was subject to riots and general unrest as the price of living soared. Whole cheeses were rolled down the streets from Nottingham Goose Fair in a strange incident in 1764 which became known as 'The Great Cheese Riot'! In the same city in 1788, there were more orthodox riots over the high price of meat. Large groups of labourers, who became known as 'Regulators', took to descending upon a village or small town (Maidstone in Kent was one, Abingdon in Oxfordshire another) and forcing down the price of food to a popular level. They once invited men 'with one voice, come one and all to Newbury in a body to make the bread cheaper'.

There were serious riots in Bristol in 1753 and again 40 years later. In Halifax people from the surrounding weaving villages came to the market place, surrounded the corn merchants and forced them to sell oats at 30 shillings and wheat at 21 shillings a load. For that heinous crime, the weavers' leader Thomas Spencer, and a companion, were executed. There were also religious demonstrations – in 1780 the Protestant Association organised a march to Westminster to hand in a petition opposing the toleration of Roman Catholicism. And back in the 1760s there had been blunt anti-monarchist activity. Apparently the mob had yelled: 'Damn the king, damn the Government, damn the Justices!' In 1776 Tom Paine, the 'free-thinker' who would later achieve notoriety and historical significance with his book *Rights of Man*, said of the English monarchy in a predecessor *Common Sense*:

'A French bastard landing with an armed banditti and establishing himself king of England against the consent of the natives is, in plain terms, a very paltry, rascally original ... The plain truth is that the antiquity of English monarchy will not bear looking into.'

Groups of working men demanded fairer wages and changes in conditions. For example, the Thames watermen presented themselves to the Lord Mayor of London and complained about their lot, but subsided when he promised to present a petition to Parliament if they could raise one. A terrible incident involving weavers from Spitalfields ended with the shooting of a 17-year-old youth in the house of one Elizabeth Pratt, shortly after the weavers had broken up the looms of a man named Nathaniel Farr, who lived nearby. Sawyers pulled down a saw-mill in protest that it cut out the need for the labours of many men, while in Liverpool the journeymen coopers 'in a cruel manner forced one of their masters on a pole' and paraded him through the streets. Even sailors in uniform presented a petition called 'Relief of Grievances' at St James Palace. The militia put down the 1780 Protestant Association riots, opening fire on the mob and killing hundreds, possibly thousands.

It's hard for us, two centuries later, to comprehend the extent of the unrest. Maybe the listing of the names of some of those who were hanged helps bring it home. Richard Roberts and William Lawrence, boys of 17, hanged in Bow Street for pulling down the house of Sir John Fielding; George Kennedy hanged in Bunhill Row for pulling down the house of a baker, Mr M'Cartney; William McDonald, a one-armed former soldier, hanged on Tower Hill for destroying a public house in St Catharine's Lane, and for assisting in the same crime Mary Roberts and Charlotte Gardener, who was described as a negress, hanged with him. George Bawton, a drunken cobbler, demanded six pence from a stranger, Richard Stone, in Holborn, saying: 'Pray remember the Protestant religion'. For that moment of extortion with menaces, Bawton was hanged. John Gray, Charles Kent and Letitia Holland were all hanged in Bloomsbury Square, for setting fire to the mansion of Lord Chief Justice Mansfield; James Jackson, Enoch Fleming, George Staples, Samuel Solomon, Jonathan Stacy, Mary Cook and Elizabeth Collins ... all of them perished on the scaffold.

On 18 June 1780, King George III said before Parliament:

'The outrages committed by bands of lawless and desperate men, in various parts of this metropolis, broke forth with such violence, into acts of felony and treason, had so far overborne all civil authority, and threatened directly the immediate subversion of all legal power, the destruction of all property and the confusion of every order of the state, that I found myself obliged, by every tie of duty and affection to my people, to suppress, in every part, those rebellious insurrections, and to provide for the public safety, by the most effectual and immediate application of the force entrusted to me by parliament.'

* * *

England never did quite have its revolution, possibly because of the experience of the Civil War of the 1640s and possibly because France reached that point first. In the summer of 1789 the world changed, once and for all. The ordinary people of France stood up and were counted, setting up their own National Assembly to force a constitution, and storming the horrific old Bastille prison, an act which had more value as a symbol of revolutionary possibilities and hopes than as a victory. (Most of the handful of freed inmates were quickly locked up again on the grounds that they were mad!) The French Revolution burned brightly from 1789 through its various bloodlettings, including the guillotining of Louis XVI in January 1793, followed by Danton and eventually the crazy Robespierre in July 1794. During the last six weeks of Robespierre's 'Reign of Terror' 1,376 people were guillotined. After that things calmed down a little and France drifted on until the arrival of Napoleon Bonaparte in 1799.

A revolution so close at hand obviously enveloped the whole of English thinking. Support for the French Revolution was from religious dissenters who hankered after another Cromwell, from young idealists like William Wordsworth and a few 'forward-thinking' artisans, who went to France just as English Communist sympathisers flocked fashionably to Spain during their Civil War in the 1930s. Although these revolutionaries represented little practical danger, the upheaval left the rich edgy, nervous of the ugly massed ranks of the poor, scared for the future and for the protection of everything time and power had provided for them.

I would contend it were no social accident that brought the previously frowned-upon activity of prize-fighting to its glorious years when its stature almost equalled the 'sport of kings', horse racing. Through pugilism, the rich met the poor and helped create a false image of 'one nation' with a common interest. Even if the common bond were no more than a shared enjoyment of legalised violence and gambling, the activity of attending a prize fight helped cement the national spirit that was needed to hold strong in the long years of war that lay ahead. In 1795 an Act of Parliament banned gatherings of more than 50 people – and yet boxing was positively encouraged by royal and aristocratic patronage. This was a two-fold benefit. It certainly helped maintain the social status quo. And it helped provide boxing with a traditional support throughout the social system which, in spite of the activities of generations of abolitionists, still holds good today.

The Mendoza-Humphries fights overlapped the French Revolution. The second one was shortly before 'Bastille' and the third was when things were in full swing. That was in the yard of the Rose and Crown on the outskirts of Doncaster on 29 September 1790, the day after Ambidexter had won the St. Leger at 5-1. The 18th century ticket spivs were out in force: there was room for 600 seated spectators and the half-guinea tickets were selling for £10 near fight time. Others watched from ships which had dropped anchor on the River Don, climbing high on to the rigging to get the best possible view of the 24 ft square ring on the stage that stood four feet above the ground. Some crossed the Don on boats, rushed the gates and stood inside the yard. Everybody who could see the ring was asked to pay a shilling. Among the crowd was the Whig politician Charles James Fox, who was probably not alone in having travelled half the length of the country to take in the classic horse race and the big fight. The stake was 200 guineas.

Humphries, 'scarlet ribbons fluttering at his knee', drew first blood, cutting Mendoza on the left side of the head, on the right side of his ribs and leaving his ear 'much mutilated'. But Mendoza, who was the slight betting favourite, had the better of him. Humphries' right eye was shut and there was a bad cut over his left eye, while a springing blow (possibly a quick, uppercut type of punch) had split his top lip and left a 'wound as clean as a razor cut by the left side of his nose'. Humphries was finally beaten after 73 minutes and 72 rounds and afterwards Mendoza was carried away on the shoulders of his followers and driven off in a post-chaise. Later he relaxed with a public stroll on Doncaster Racecourse, where the festival may well have been continuing. Afterwards, Mendoza's cousin Aaron lost a violent, hour-long brawl with a West Countryman named Packer.

Humphries' defeat convinced him to retire and his patron Bradyll, showing better grace than others in similar positions, set him up as a coal merchant at the Adelphi Wharf in central London. He died a wealthy man in 1827.

Mendoza mixed with royalty and engaged in sparring tours, also teaching boxing at the Lyceum in the Strand and in Capel Court. He toured Britain as the star act in Astley's Circus and also earned well as a recruiting officer for the English Army. In other words' he helped the Press Gangs. Mendoza enjoyed his fame with a flourish. In Dublin on 2 August 1791, he agreed to meet an Irish amateur named Squire Fitzgerald and, no doubt to the delight of the common folk, forsook his normal professional requirements and fought 'for love'. Mendoza won, of course, but in which of its many forms the reward was taken is unknown.

By the time of the retirement of poor Ben Brain, Mendoza claimed the championship and cemented that with a twice-delayed, but eventually 23-round win over Bill Warr of Bristol (whose manslaughter conviction in 1789 had clearly done him little lasting harm) at Smitham Bottom near Croydon on 14 May 1792. He spent a great deal of his time in touring and enjoying his reputation, stopping off every now and then to replenish his finances with a fight. Sometimes it was even for small stakes – don't forget, there were no real fight promoters then and Mendoza was always a poor businessman – as when he beat Bill Warr a second time in 15 minutes at Bexleyheath on 12 November 1794. Twice he was unable to fulfil a commitment, paying out forfeits of £20 and 25 guineas to Bill Hooper and Warr respectively. Reading between the lines of the rather heroic reports and his own memoirs, it seems as if Mendoza lost his way. It was reported early in 1795 that he was a guest of King George III at Windsor Castle and 'descanted' with the monarch the art of pugilism. Like the great Broughton half a century earlier, soft living was more than likely eating into his youth.

William Hooper

Bill Hooper, incidentally, was a good fighter. A Bristol-born tinman who lived in Tottenham Court Road, he was sponsored by the obnoxious Lord Richard Barrymore, the hated head of a family 'firm' popularly nicknamed Newgate, Hellgate and Cripplegate. The Prince of Wales despised the man as much as ordinary people did. He suggested the Barrymore brothers should not have omitted from the 'company name' that of their sister – Billingsgate! (For those unfamiliar with London, Billingsgate is the site of the famous fish market.) Barrymore, who had scandalously married the daughter of a man who ran a sedan-chair business, was shot dead, accidentally it was ruled, in March 1793. He was in charge of the Berkshire militia who were marching a band of French prisoners from Rye to Dover when they stopped for a rest on top of Folkestone Hill. Barrymore had just returned to his seat in his carriage when a gun in his possession went off. The bullet hit him in the head and he died within minutes. He was succeeded by his brother, known as Cripplegate because of his club-foot.

Hooper was said to have been a fearless, upright citizen until he was influenced by Barrymore, who petted and spoiled him to the point where he became an overbearing bully who forgot the training routines that had made him an athlete capable of battling for three and a half hours with Ben Brain. He turned into a womanising drunk who lost money, health and even the most debauched of his acquaintances. One night he was discovered unconscious on a doorstep in St Giles. He came out of it enough only to make an attempt at his name – 'Hoop ... Hoop' – and was carried to a workhouse to die.

In view of Mendoza's steady demise, his defeat by 'Gentleman' John Jackson, who was always referred to as 'Mister', on 15 April, 1795, was not a surprise to those who could recognise the signs of athletic decline.

It took place near Hornchurch, Essex, at a site where since the days of Henry II an annual wrestling match had been held for the prize of a boar's head. That day, a Wednesday, it had rained so heavily that the surrounding tracks had turned into mud, but plenty of people still made their way through to the field where an old man held on a pole the boar's head, 'tastefully decorated with holly and light blue ribbons and a lemon placed between his ample tusks'. Jackson drew first blood when he knocked Mendoza down right at the start and in the fourth round the much bigger challenger, who was 5ft 11ins and 203lbs, walked through Mendoza's defences and ripped open a terrible gash over an eye. From then on Mendoza was punished and knocked down repeatedly in brief rounds until by the ninth he was very slow. Jackson then grabbed him with his right hand by his long, dark hair, and with the left battered him senseless. Mendoza recovered within the rest time and continued fighting but was soon knocked out. The whole event spanned only 10 and a half minutes.

Seven weeks after fighting for the championship, Mendoza and Jackson acted as seconds in a fight near the New Road in London between 'Mrs Mary Ann Fielding' and 'a Jewess of Wentworth Street', won by the former in 80 minutes.

There were 70 knockdowns – and a prize of 11 guineas.

There was also a bizarre fight on 22 September 1796 at Bradenwell near Erith in Kent between 'Chapman, a young man born without arms' and a Woolwich blacksmith named Knight. After an hour, Chapman fighting with head and feet, won. Knight was ferried away with two broken ribs!

Mendoza quit the ring to run his academy near the Strand and seemed well set. But the need for cash eventually became great enough for him to fight again. He beat Harry Lee in 53 rounds at Grinstead Green, Bromley, on Friday, 21 March 1806 for a purse of 50 guineas, then toured with a circus, giving exhibitions, until he settled down to run a pub in Kensington. He had one last fight, losing in 12 rounds and 15 minutes, one day short of his 56th birthday, to Tom Owen at Banstead Downs on 4 July, 1820. This fight was made to settle an old grudge and must have been a sad spectacle.

He kept the Admiral Nelson in Whitechapel, where he and his wife raised 11 children. His memoirs were the first ever written by a prize-fighter and further set him apart as an extraordinary person. He remained a revered figure as he lived on into old age, eventually dying at 72 in London on 3 September 1836. His descendants still live in the London area.

'Gentleman' John Jackson

Jackson was born on 25 September, 1769, the son of a Worcestershire builder who had moved to London. From a solid, decent family background, he was brought up with impeccable manners, which is why they nicknamed him 'Gentleman'. When he boxed for the first time at 18 it was against his parents' wishes, but a crowd which included the Prince of Wales saw him beat a seasoned fighter William Fewterell (spelled alternatively Futrell and Fewterel) who was also the publisher of the first boxing newspaper. Fewterell, who had not lost in 18 previous ring encounters, was beaten in 67 minutes at Smitham Bottom, Croydon, in June 1798.

Jackson lost his second fight after 20 minutes in the yard of the Swan public house at Ingatestone in Essex against a slow, but strong, 6ft tall brewer named George Ingelston, when he slipped on the rain-sodden turf, dislocated an ankle and broke a bone in his leg. Although he offered to continue strapped to a chair, he was declared the loser. Jackson opened an inn in Surrey, beat Mendoza for the championship and then retired. He opened the sporting centre of the day at 13 Old Bond Street, London, which offered sparring with gloves for the rich and famous, just as Broughton had done half a century earlier. Lord Byron played there, as did the Dukes of York and Clarence. Byron said of him:

'Jackson not only told you what to do, but why you should do it ... Jackson was not unmindful of the fact that art never ends. If there was anything new in the gymnastic, equestrian or pedestrian way, there be assured was Jackson, not merely witnessing the exhibition but examining the means by which the effects were produced. He was consequently often at Astley's and at the Surrey, when Ireland, the jumper, was there, and knew all the famous fencers, funambulists, dancers and riders of his day, and his day was a long one.'

According to Henry Downes Miles' magnificent *Pugilistica*, Jackson's father built the arch 'over the Old Fleet Ditch, near the mouth of the River Fleet, flowing from the Hampstead and Highgate Hills and crossed by bridges at Holborn and Ludgate. This forms the great sewer of Blackfriars from the north into the new Low Level, over which run Faringdon Street and Bridge Street... his uncles were farmers, tenants of the Duke of Bedford and the Marquis of Hertford.'

Jackson even tried to clean up the sport by forming the Pugilistic Club in 1814. It ran until 1824, but its success was limited. Byron, arrogant and patronising, labelled Jackson 'The Emperor of Pugilism' and his status in society was reflected in July 1821 when he provided an 18-strong bodyguard for George IV's Coronation at Westminster. The new king had seen anti-Royalist mobs on the streets of London 12 months before, just as they had been in the dangerous days of 1795, and after banning his estranged, but popular wife, Caroline of Brunswick, from the ceremony, he feared an embarrassing scene. As a young man George had alienated his father and the common people by excluding his wife in favour of his Roman Catholic mistress, 'Mrs Fitzherbert'. As it happened, his subjects did not feel called upon to defend the honour of the 'wronged' lady. The only trouble came from Caroline herself. Dressed in a muslin slip and a silver brocade petticoat, she demanded to be let in. When she was turned back, she screamed furiously: 'Let me pass. I am your Queen. I am Queen of Britain.'

The door was slammed shut in her face, possibly by one of the pugilists. (Before the year was out she would be tried for adultery.) The new monarch was so pleased with the performance of the bouncers at his coronation that he sent them letters of thanks and a gold medal to share. They raffled it and Tom Belcher, brother of the great champion Jem, won it. Sadly, Jackson was lost to pugilism after a man named Elliot, who had backed Sam Martin, the Bath butcher, demanded his stake back, even though his man had lost. Jackson was so disgusted that he had no more to do with the business.

Jackson, who had helped bring boxing to its grandest era, lived in comfort to the age of 76 until, with his favourite niece holding his hand, he died at his house, No. 4 Lower Grosvenor Street West, in Brompton, London, on 7 October 1845. He was remembered, as well as for his fighting and social achievements, as a moderate man who always earned more than he spent. A marble monument was erected in his memory in Brompton churchyard, topped by a lion and with a naked gladiator (with precisely positioned laurel wreath) at one end. The inscription read:

> 'Stay, Traveller,' the Roman records said,
> To mark the classic dust beneath it laid; –
> 'Stay, Traveller,' this brief memorial cries,
> And read the record with attentive eyes.
> Hast thou a lion's heart, a giant's strength?
> Exult not, for these gifts must yield at length.
> Do health and symmetry adorn thy frame?
> The mouldering bones below possessed the same.
> Does love, does friendship every step attend?
> This man ne'er made a foe, ne'er lost a friend.
> But death too soon dissolves all human ties,
> And, his last combat o'er, here Jackson lies.'

Tom Owen from Portsmouth, and born in Portsea on 21 December 1768, claimed the championship after Jackson's retirement on the strength of his victory over William Hooper in 64 minutes and 50 rounds in Harrow in November 1796. Hooper had drawn that 210-minute marathon with Ben Brain, had battered Wright The Carpenter until the poor man's head 'so terribly swelled and his face so much disfigured as scarcely to be known' and had broken the arm of a strong man named Bunner. As well as those dreadful

Mendoza v Humphries: one of a great series of battles.

struggles, he had emerged a no-doubt battered and exhausted winner from a two and a half hour slog with Bob Watson. Hooper was expected to beat Owen, but dislocated his shoulder and, with his size and maybe those long battles telling against him, he lost to a man who seemed nothing more than a raw novice. Egan sneered at Owen as 'a mere tyro of the fist, and one completely ignorant of the rules of the art.' Owen, who ran a pub and was also an oilman – that is, the lighter and maintainer of the street lamps – lost in half an hour to the more scientific and highly respected Jack Bartholomew on 22 August 1797 on Sunbury Common for a prize of a mere 25 guineas.

Owen, who is accredited with inventing the dumb-bell, drifted out of contention and in 1799 lost in 42 minutes to a Jew named Howser on Enfield Raceground for 10 guineas. He was so badly beaten that he was carried to Enfield Hospital to recover. Later that year he was back, taking an hour to defeat Davis, described as a local excavator, at Deptford. A few years later, when second to Joe Berks against Henry 'Game Chicken' Pearce, Owen stifled Berks' cries of submission between rounds by stuffing a handkerchief into his mouth. For outraging even the brutal standards of that day, Owens was thrown into jail for three months for riot and conspiracy. He stayed around the prize-fighting scene and even fought again when he beat Mendoza. He died at Plumstead shortly before Christmas 1843 when he was 74. He was remembered as a civil man, a good companion and a more than tolerable singer. His pub was the Shipwright's Arms at Northfleet.

There were other great public heroes who fell just short of championship honours. Tom Jones, known as Paddington, supposedly had more contests than any other pugilist, most of them in the Hyde Park ring. He was only 5ft 8in tall and 147lbs, but was widely respected. He had a public spar with Jem Belcher at Old Oak Common, Wormwood Scrubs, in 1799 and also fought a draw with the great lightweight Caleb Baldwin, who was known as the Pride of Westminster. Jones died at Paddington on 22 August 1833, aged 67.

Bill Warr of Bristol was brought to London as a man to beat the great Tom Johnson, but was badly exposed. He beat William Wood, the coachman, but twice lost to Mendoza. He was a publican at the One Tun in Jermyn Street, and died in March 1809. He was buried in St James cemetery, St Pancras.

William Wood lost only to the best of his time and maintained his interest in the sport long after he had retired. He died in 1839. George Ingleston, the brewer who had that lucky win over Gentleman Jackson, had his last fight against Bill Warr in 1793 and continued to live in Enfield, where he was widely respected as a hard-working man. Bob Watson of Bristol, who fought Elisha Crabbe for 45 minutes in 1788, lost to Hooper the Tinman in two and a half hours at Langley Broom. He quit the ring in 1791 to become a butcher in Bristol, although occasionally he would give exhibitions. He died in 1837, aged 71. Elisha Crabbe, who beat Death Oliver at Blackheath in 35 minutes before the Prince of Wales in 1788, lost to Watson and Tom Tyne and afterwards was a peace officer based at the Mansion House, headquarters of the Lord Mayor of London. He died suddenly, for reasons unclear, while travelling on the Gravesend Packet on 9 June 1809.

Jack Bartholomew, who carried the Championship of England into the 19th century, was said to be skilful and courageous. The son of a Brentford gardener, he emerged in June 1795, when for a five-guinea purse he beat Jack 'Young Ruffian' Fearby on Hounslow Heath. His win over Owen at Sunbury Common gave him some recognition. He had earlier lost on a foul to William Wood between Harrow and Ealing in January 1797 and then fought a 51-round draw with the brilliant, precocious Jem Belcher on the Uxbridge road for £20 on 15 August 1799, by which time he was employed as personal bodyguard to the eccentric Lord Camelford, whose life was bizarre even by the standards of the English upper classes. While serving in the West Indies, Camelford shot dead one Lieutenant Peterson for refusing to obey orders, was court-martialled and, naturally in view of his position, acquitted.

He retired to civilian life, but fairly soon afterwards set off for Paris with a brace of pistols and a double-edged dagger, intent on assassinating Bonaparte. He got no further than the edge of the English Channel when he was seized as a suspected smuggler. When he admitted his intentions, a charge was brought against him of attempting a capital crime, but which was eventually thrown out because the judge ruled his intentions were patriotic! He became a familiar fight-watcher, usually accompanied by his dog Trusty. The job of personal bodyguard, held at this time by Bartholomew and later by Bill Richmond, entailed following his Lordship, disentangling him from drunken disputes, taking him home when necessary, and indulging him in a light spar each morning.

Bartholomew had been outboxed by Belcher in sparring at Will Warr's house, but pulled off the gloves and asked for a fight for real. Camelford backed him for 50 guineas – and it went on. Bartholomew, who was much better in the ring itself than he was at sparring, gave Belcher an extremely tough fight and very nearly beat him. Bartholomew was arrested the following day for breach of the peace and bound over, which slightly delayed the rematch.

It eventually happened on Finchley Common on 15 May 1800, this time for 300 guineas. Belcher was so badly knocked out at the end of the third round that a black pigeon was released, signalling his defeat to those waiting near his home. However, Belcher recovered in time to stand at the scratch, Bartholomew couldn't finish him off and instead the younger man threw the older with such force that he landed on his head. Bartholomew was severely concussed, couldn't see properly, was disorientated and confused and eventually lost decisively in 17 rounds, by which time he was vomiting blood. To add to his misery Bartholomew was too slow to escape the attentions of the peacekeepers, who arrested him for breach of the peace! Not surprisingly, Bartholomew suffered from the effects of too many violent fights. He died, officially from cirrhosis of the liver, in an alms house in Westminster in July 1803. A man who is undervalued, he was well ahead of his time. He left specific instructions on his death for his body to be subject to a post mortem. With Jack Bartholomew, prize-fighting ended one century and began another. More than that, it moved into the era that historians usually consider was its greatest, its golden age.

Daniel Mendoza at work: one of the most skilful and scientific of champions.

4

BELCHER, PEARCE, GULLY AND CRIBB

Jem Belcher was born to be king. He was the grandson of Jack Slack, who was allegedly the grandson of James Figg. The man who was to become famous as 'The Napoleon of the Ring' was born at St James Back, Bristol, on 15 April 1781, the son of a butcher who married Slack's daughter Mary. His first known, official prize-fight was as a 17-year-old at Langdown Fair near Bath, and at 18 was fast and graceful enough to hold Jack Bartholomew to a draw in London. He was still only a month past his 19th birthday when he beat Bartholomew in the rematch. One of the most naturally gifted fighters of them all, he was mature beyond his years, and because of his youth could afford to walk the wild side more than most. After his second victory over Bob Britton of Bath he toasted himself by drinking a yard of ale.

His brother Tom was also a respected pugilist, and so was his brother-in-law Pardo Wilson. There is also a record of a sister engaging in a prize-fight against another woman which lasted 50 minutes. But at 22 Jem was blind, and at 30 he was dead. So much was packed into such a short time, it's convenient and not altogether inappropriate for historians to see in him, and his greatest contemporary Henry Pearce, lives that parallelled those of the great Romantic poets, Percy Shelley and John Keats, both of whom died young and yet left behind them a magnificent legacy.

The first challenge to Belcher was from an Irish stonemason Andrew Gamble, who himself had on 1 July, 1800, broken the collar bone and jaw of Noah James on Wimbledon Common 'within sight of the gibbet upon which dangled the ghastly skeleton of Jerry Abershaw, the notorious highwayman'. Abershaw had been hanged for murder in August 1795, going merrily to his death with a flower in his teeth and chatting with anyone who had the time of day. As a macabre warning, the authorities refused to allow the body to be cut down, instead hanging it in chains and gibbeting it afresh to rot in its own time.

Four days before he fought Gamble, Belcher survived an attack by four men in Chelsea, all of whom he saw off, without coming to harm. With an estimated 20,000 guineas laid in bets, it was perhaps understandable that this was seen as a deliberate attempt to nobble the young star. No proof was ever at hand, however, and the incident was virtually forgotten once Belcher had dispensed with the game but outclassed Gamble in five rounds and nine minutes at Wimbledon on 22 December 1800 in front of a huge crowd, whose roar was reported to

Jem Belcher

have been heard ten miles away. When pigeons carrying the news of his victory arrived in Bristol, the bells of several churches were rung in celebration. With the proceeds Belcher bought a London house and one of the finest coaches and pairs in the city. Some say it was this fight that convinced the Fancy of his right to be called champion. Beforehand, Belcher was only a narrow 7-5 favourite, but made nonsense of the odds. At the end of round four, Gamble was flat on his face and out to the world, and although he was pushed back by his seconds, who included Daniel Mendoza, it took only one right hand to put him away.

Three times (once unofficially) he dealt with Joe Berks, sometimes written Bourke, who was a truculent, tough, sometimes drunken butcher from Shropshire. Berks struck Belcher at a prizefight at Wimbledon in 1801, to which the champion had been specially invited. The outraged Belcher demanded honour be served there and then in the available ring. When he took almost 20 minutes to overcome the butcher, the watching Lord Camelford considered it a worthy proposition to set them at each other again, in formal conditions, with Berks sober and well-prepared. He put down a stake of 100 guineas and called in Mendoza to train the Midlander. The return was delayed when Belcher was arrested, but they eventually met again at Hurley Bottom, a valley four and a half miles from Maidenhead between the Henley and Reading roads, on 25 November 1801. In another part of the field as the Fancy gathered, a man raced a sow ... hardly heroic stuff, but it must have been chaotic fun.

This time Belcher won in 25 bloody minutes, wearing down the raw but game challenger with careful body attacks. At the end Belcher offered a winner-take-all purse of 300 guineas to Mendoza. Quite properly, Mendoza, who had been a retired and much respected old champion for the past five years and who kept a good house at the Admiral Nelson in Whitechapel, turned it down. Mendoza, however, was never a man to lose an opportunity for publicity and said he would only meet Gentleman Jackson, who had been retired seven years. The inference was plain – and insulting to the young champion. The bad feeling graduated into a public slanging match.

Joe Berks

The third match between Belcher and Berks was delayed twice before it was successfully carried out in a large field behind St George's Chapel, facing Hyde Park, at Tyburn Turnpike, on 20 August 1802. The previous day the two men had argued and scuffled at Camberwell Fair. Berks had a front tooth knocked out! For some reason, possibly because the result was considered predictable, Belcher earned only 30 guineas for a victory that turned out to be unexpectedly savage. Maybe he underestimated Berks, who didn't even make an attempt to box with the champion, preferring to wrestle. His tactics worked so well that after one round it was feared Belcher's neck was broken. Slowly, Belcher picked his defences apart with precise punches and his mouth and face bled. At one point they fell down – and as they got up, the ever-defiant Berks spat a mouthful of blood into Belcher's face. After 14 rounds Berks' features were horribly distorted and he could barely see. Defeat was conceded, but 'butcher' Berks would remain one of the most resilient, and probably one of the craziest of championship contenders. After the fight he was left in a *post-chaise* until the result of the succeeding contest was known, but the neglect caused him no obvious ill-effect. Two days later he won 20 guineas by beating Jack Warr, son of the prize-fighter Bill, in a 100-yard sprint after they had argued about who was the faster in the One Tun in Jermyn Street.

Some time after their second fight Berks and Belcher, along with their chief seconds, were forced to appear before Newbury Magistrates to face charges of unlawful assembly and public fighting. Berks had been unable to raise bail and so had spent three months in Reading jail. They were given what amounted to conditional discharges – and within a month the announcement of their third fight was made! The authorities wouldn't let it drop and in May 1803 all four were charged again 'that being persons of evil and malicious disposition and fighters, duellers, rioters, etc. had staged a duel'. Again, they were found guilty. Again, they were warned to keep the peace. Belcher clashed with the authorities once more when he hired Sadlers Wells Theatre for a pugilistic exhibition. The magistrates reacted by closing the building for the summer.

In 1806 Berks was charged with two accomplices, including an Irish prize-fighter named Jack O'Donnell, with stealing a £5 note and a guinea from a man named William Gee. They were found guilty and sentenced to be transported. Only the intervention of Gentleman Jackson saved Berks from a new life in Botany Bay or some even worse place, and he was last heard of as a non-commissioned officer in the Grenadiers serving under Wellington in Spain.

Belcher's last fight as champion was at Linton, near Newmarket, on 12 April 1803 when he outclassed the declining Jack 'Young Ruffian' Fearby for a prize of 100 guineas. The action was interrupted briefly and with riotous consequences by a local clergyman and a constable, who made what must have been hilarious attempts to curtail the proceedings. They were both hauled away by the jeering mob and slung into a ditch. By round five Fearby was vomiting blood. In the 11th and after a 20-minute battering, he conceded.

Belcher was 22 years old and lord of the sporting world, comparable in history only with Mendoza and the great Jack Broughton. He owned property, ran with the finest of London society and acted pretty much as he pleased. And then one day after training at Gentleman Jackson's he travelled over to Little St. Martins for a game of rackets with a friend. He was hit in the left eye by the ball and blinded. Surgeons had no choice but to remove the eye and in that one terrible moment, his life was thrown into disarray. Benefits were held for him around the country and enabled him to take over the Jolly Brewer in Wardour Street, Soho. And he stuck it for a while, enjoying the deceit of bringing his old Bristol acquaintance, Henry Pearce, to London as a 'dark horse' and watching him become champion. But gradually, as Pearce's reputation grew to rival his own, Belcher became jealous and frustrated. He began to spar with his brother Tom and slowly became obsessed with beating Pearce and regaining his former glories. A one-eyed man should not have been fighting, of course, but these were hard times, when men were responsible for themselves and not each other. Eventually, he pressed so hard that the match was made.

At Blyth, south of Doncaster, or more exactly half a mile outside town on a small piece of common land, on 6 December 1805, the two great fighters met in front of a crowd of 25,000. Pearce was a reluctant 4-5 favourite, but began like a rank outsider as the still boastful and bitter Belcher gave him a boxing lesson and opened a cut on his right eyebrow. The blood streamed down on to the chest of the 'Game Chicken'. In round seven Pearce was rocked by a right hand, but kept slinging wide, arcing punches at the body and arms and inside used his greater size and strength. He headlocked Belcher and hammered him with one hand until the former champion's blood spurted on to the ground. By the ninth Belcher was tired and his arms were dropping. By the 12th Pearce was in complete, if reluctant command. As Larry Holmes was to do with Muhammad Ali 175 years later, Pearce went about his grim business unhappily, refusing to apply the finish with what might have been a kindly ruthlessness. According to Egan he even called out:

'I'll take no advantage of thee, Jem. I'll not strike thee, lest I hurt thy other eye.'

Belcher made a last, defiant rebellion against his fading senses in the 17th but as they came up for the 18th, he admitted: 'Hen Pearce, I can't fight thee no more.'

One of the saddest encounters in the history of pugilism was done. Pearce recovered at the Blue Bell Inn at Barnby Moor, three miles away, and then moved on to Grantham for a victory party the same night.

As ridiculous as it may seem to us, Belcher fought twice more, losing both times to a later champion, Tom Cribb, firstly at Moulsey Hurst, Surrey, in April 1807, and a second time at Epsom Downs in February 1809. Just as he had done with Pearce, he gave Cribb a boxing lesson. Cribb was an inferior fighter to both Belcher and Pearce, but he had a huge heart and immense durability and strength. Pearce, now himself in a steep decline thanks to his inclination towards London's hellish gin-palaces and women of both polite and rough society, was ringside to see his old friend fight Cribb. Belcher's performance was a magnificent piece of defiance. After 18 rounds, it looked as if the old champion was on the brink of regaining the title when he put the bleeding Cribb down heavily. But in round 19, he elected to stand and wrestle and the fight turned against him. In the 20th he broke his left hand and from then on he faded, round by round, until at the end of 41, he had no more to give. And as Belcher sat in his corner weeping tears of frustration and misery, Cribb danced a hornpipe in mid-ring to the cheers of the gathered multitude.

When they fought again, Belcher was a pitiful figure. His health was failing as rapidly as his business, he was sour and morose and no longer filled with the inspiration to train properly. Cribb was a 1-2 betting favourite – and frankly, that was generous to Belcher. Cribb was at his peak and although Belcher outboxed him at times during the first 10 rounds, his end was hastened when he broke an arm on a ringpost. His hands were no longer able to stand up to hitting a man in a long fight and they were cut and battered when he gave in after 31 rounds.

Belcher was simply unable to cope with his ever declining fortunes. He moved to a smaller pub, but that also failed, and some have said he would sit there brooding in silence for hours as custom passed him by. He gambled away most of his possessions, including his £30 gold watch, and was eventually jailed for 28 days after his part in a drunken fracas in Horsemonger Lane. In prison, he caught cold, which turned into pneumonia. His liver, ulcerated by an excess of gin, caused him intense pain. A benefit was held at the Fives Court on 2 July 1811 and he was described by William Oxberry, the writer of *Pancratia*, as a 'decrepit invalid'. Four weeks later, on Tuesday, 30 July 1811 he died at his last pub, the Coach and Horses in Frith Street, Soho. He was still only 30 years old. They buried him at Marylebone after a funeral procession that did full justice to one of the greatest popular heroes of the century. On the Oxford Road so many thronged around that the procession could not move for some time, and as the coffin was lowered into the grave, the distraught prize-fighter William Wood jumped in after it, weeping uncontrollably.

Henry Pearce

The destinies of these Georgian giants were entwined; they seemed to face similar agonies, and all too often they died too young.

Henry Pearce was born in Bristol in 1777. He would fight as a boy in contests set up for bets by his father in local pubs and was, according to legend, never beaten. Belcher knew him and after his accident in 1803, brought Pearce to the capital in secret, presumably to pull off a betting coup when a championship contest materialised. Belcher exhibited Pearce, who always signed himself Hen. and therefore earned the nickname 'Game Chicken', in front of a private circle of London friends against poor Jack Fearby in a ten-foot square bar at the Horse and Dolphin in Windmill Street. He won with gruesome ease and, we are told, blood spattered over each of the witnesses who were backed against the walls. The landlord, afraid that Fearby was dead, hired a woman to wash away the blood as quickly as possible.

Pearce was given the bad-tempered butcher from Shropshire, Joe Berks, to beat up twice – in a room in August 1803, when Berks was under his breach of the peace order and therefore banned from fighting in public, and on a freezing Wimbledon Common in 77 minutes in January 1804. Berks said Pearce was a better fighter than Belcher. Pearce was a modest man, not given in those early days to enjoying too much company. After this second win over Berks he slipped away from the celebrations and was later found by his second Bill Gibbons in a pub in Chelsea, cooking himself mutton chops on the open fire.

He also defeated a Bristol coppersmith named Elias Spree or Spray in 35 minutes at Moulsey (now usually spelled Molesey) near Hampton Court in March 1805, after which he heard his old Bristol friend, John Gully, was locked away in Fleet Debtors' Prison. He was determined to do something about that, but beforehand disposed of Stephen Carte of Birmingham on

Henry Pearce

27 April 1805 in front of a large crowd on Shepperton Common near Chertsey, a Surrey village on the banks of the Thames. The multitude included men and women of fame, notoriety and reputation. There was Alicia Massingham, mistress of Colonel Thornton, and the remarkable Lady Lade, who had been the lover of both highwayman 'Sixteen String' Jack and The Duke of York before she settled down to marry Sir John Lade; and also there was the Duchess of Bedford, who had made her reputation by admitting to her husband gambling debts of £176,000. Lord Eardley brought along his mistress, Bella Prior. After disposing of the outclassed Carte, Pearce sat on a bale of straw to watch Tom Belcher fight Jack O'Donnell and the great lightweight Dutch Sam win a marvellous battle with Bob Brettle.

Pearce's greatest victory was against his acquaintance from his Bristol days, John Gully. He had staged an exhibition with Gully in debtors' prison, as a result of which a sporting gentleman named Fletcher Reid had settled Gully's debts and obtained his release. Gully and Pearce fought for real at Hailsham, Sussex, which was then a small village on the Sussex Downs, on 8 October 1805, Pearce winning a magnificent battle in 64 rounds lasting 77 minutes. Because the men knew each other so well suspicions of a 'cross' had been rife in London, and the fight had already been postponed once, but Gully performed so well that by round 20 Pearce was cut and almost blind in his left eye. However in the 23rd Gully was caught as he fell by a tremendous blow on the side of the head. As he lay on the ground Gully vomited. It was obvious from that point on that he could not win, and yet his courage kept him coming back up for more. The last blow landed on Gully's throat and he was temporarily unable to breathe. At the back of the crowd of 10,000 people, the Duke of Clarence, later William IV, watched from a horse. On the same day, at the same place, Tom Cribb beat the first of the great black fighters, Bill Richmond, in 90 minutes.

The Game Chicken's last fight was his merciful battering of Jem Belcher, but by then his own health was giving rise to concern. His marriage was a disaster, his wife was 'a shameless and abandoned woman, who embittered his life and ruined his home', according to Egan, who may have been prejudiced. Egan blamed this woman's 'infidelities' for Pearce's eventual, fatal dependence on gin. Whatever the cause, he sank quickly. A Leicestershire man named Ford boasted he would beat Pearce for a glass of gin, but the champion wasn't in town at the time. The incident probably meant little in itself, but was indicative of the swinging of opinion.

By 1807 he was a drifter, giving exhibitions from town to town, with a new wife in tow. In Bristol he seemed for a while to be living more temperately and on Clifton Downs he gave a hiding to three gamekeepers named Hood, Morris and Francis, whom he found 'insulting' a woman. In the town itself in November 1807, he also rescued a servant-girl who was trapped in the attic of a burning shop, belonging to a silk mercer named Mrs Denzill, in Thomas Street. His heroism was commemorated by a local journal:

'Oh, glorious act! Oh, courage well applied!
Oh, strength exerted in its proper cause!
Thy name, O Pearce! be sounded far and wide,
Live, ever honoured, midst the world's applause;
Be this thy triumph! Know one creature saved
Is greater glory than a world enslav'd.'

But by 1808 the dreadful, blood-flecked coughs of tuberculosis had set in. It was sheer folly to travel to Epsom Downs from Oxford to watch Belcher fight Tom Cribb in the mid-winter, but he did. Afterwards the 15-mile freezing journey to London, to a friend's pub, the Coach and Horses in St Martin's Lane, broke his resistance. He could barely walk unaided when a benefit was held for him on 11 April 1809. Only 19 days later he was dead. He was 32. He was buried, as he had asked to be, next to Bill Warr, who had boxed Daniel Mendoza three times 20 years before and who had only recently died of consumption. The two of them lay in St James Churchyard, St Pancras. *Pugilistica* recorded that he went bravely to his death, without terror, 'expressing a wish to die in friendship with all mankind'.

Pearce's epic struggle with Gully in Sussex had taken place just a fortnight before the Battle of Trafalgar, in which the British fleet lost Horatio Nelson but defeated the combined Spanish and French navies. It was a euphoric time. And it seemed that just as England ruled the waves, and therefore the world, England's prize-fighters reflected and symbolised its greatness. Gully, Pearce, Belcher and Tom Cribb became national heroes.

John Gully

Gully was a butcher's son born in the Rose And Crown at Wick on the Chippenham road seven miles out of Bristol on 21 August, 1783. A story existed, perhaps apocryphal, of an occasion at Lansdown Fair when 'Sixteen-

String' Jack, who apparently weighed around 18st, beat a man called only the 'Flying Tinman of Bath', and then boasted that he would send anyone else from Bath home in a cart if they so much as had the courage to challenge him. Gully, after consulting his father and brother, threw his hat into the ring. It was 'Sixteen-String' Jack who had to be ferried away in a cart, 'an almost unrecognisable lump of battered humanity'. When Gully was a teenager his father died and he took on the tricky business of running the family shop. Not surprisingly he soon owed hundreds of pounds and, after being pursued by creditors to Bath and then London, he was installed in the Kings Bench prison at Fleet (later Fleet Street) from where many young and good men never returned. It was a strange jail, not especially miserable in its day-to-day life, but simply a place that no-one had the freedom to leave, and therefore a hell in disguise.

Luckily for Gully his stay in jail lasted only a year before Pearce, who remembered him from the Bristol fairgrounds and pubs, engineered his freedom. On release he was taken to what amounted to a training camp two miles outside Egham in Surrey and conditioned for what turned out to be his losing fight with Pearce. On the Game Chicken's retirement, Gully was reckoned to be the best man in the country, although several others were prepared to argue the case. He cemented his claim when he met the Lancashire

John Gully

rogue Bob Gregson at Six Mile Bottom near Newmarket on 14 October, 1807. Among the crowd were the Duke of York, half a dozen Lords including Byron, the Marquis of Tweedale and an assortment of the gentlemen of The Fancy. Gregson, from Heskin, near Chorley, was 29 years old (Gully was 24), 6ft 1in and 216lbs (to Gully's 6ft and 192lbs). He was another of those crazy, larger-than-life characters that boxing seems to attract. He was 'a rough and tumble fighter, steamboat captain, infantry officer, innkeeper, poet laureate of the ring and even in the company of laureates, where the standard of badness is high, probably the worst poet that ever lived'.

It was a vicious fight with Gully's face swollen and blackened, his eye and ear cut, and Gregson's face a grotesque, rainbow coloured mess of bumps and bruises. Eventually Gully's right eye shut and neither seemed capable of rising above their own exhaustion. In the 36th round Gully dragged up one final punch to the throat and Gregson fell for the last time. At the end Gully also collapsed and for some hours seemed in danger of dying. Gregson recovered more quickly and demanded a rematch. Gully's left arm had been permanently damaged and it was thought that he would lose the return, which took place on a private estate belonging to Sir John Sebright near Market Street, Woburn on 10 May, 1808.

A crowd of 20,000 turned out in spite of decoy attempts designed to throw peacekeepers off the scent. A local landlord charged two guineas a head for sleeping space on his floor and the crowd which poured in from London and the surrounding districts so alarmed the locals that it was rumoured a French invasion had occurred. The Dunstable Volunteers turned out, bayonets fixed, to fight for England's honour! The *Morning Chronicle* recorded the chaotic scene along the roads and tracks to the fight:

> 'Broken down carriages obstructed the road; knocked up horses fell and could not be got any further; a guinea a mile was offered for conveyance, and many hundreds of gentlemen were jolted in brick carts for a shilling a mile.'

At the end of the sixth round, after Gregson had shouldered Gully in the eye, only a sharp draught of brandy brought Gully around and to the scratch mark with two seconds to spare. Gregson was on top for 20 rounds but Gully lasted better and after 28 rounds spread over an hour and a quarter, Gregson was beaten. Gully again collapsed and Gregson was carried across to him, barely conscious, to shake hands. This was a normal precaution when a death was feared, a sort of prize fighter's last rites, a gesture that could be offered in evidence, should a manslaughter trial occur.

Gully came round, thanked the crowd for their applause and, shortly afterwards, announced his retirement. The following day he was serving drinks in his pub, the Plough in Carey Street. He is still one of the few champions who have known enough about their own limits to stop at the right time. Gregson lapsed into unconsciousness, was carried to a nearby pub, and it was three days before he could leave for London, where he lay at the Bowling Green in Highgate for some further time recovering. Incredibly, he returned to fight Tom Cribb for the championship five months later.

Several sizeable offers were made for Gully to make the proverbial 'just one more', but at 25 he restarted his business life by running the Plough Inn, became a shady bookmaker – the Prince of Wales was rumoured to be among his customers – and made enough to become respectable. 'Betting men' were elusive creatures who moved in haunts known only to a few and who gathered their knowledge through a complex network of spies and side-of-the-mouth informers. Gully's tendency towards silence and confidentiality no doubt helped him make his way, for living on one's wits as a commissioner of bets, especially when dealing with such well-heeled clients, was precarious. A story was told within Gully's family that relations between him and George IV cooled after he had galloped past the monarch at Ascot Heath without doffing his cap.

He was once fined £200 for horsewhipping his partner Robert Risdale, who was known to be some way less than honourable. He bought into a racing stable at Newmarket in 1812 and won £40,000 by betting on two of his horses, bought the Ackworth Park estate south of Pontefract in Yorkshire, and Hatton Colliery. He became M.P. for Pontefract in the 1832 Reform Parliament and that summer his horse St Giles (memories of the old days, perhaps) won the Derby and he made another £60,000.

> 'You ask me the cause that made Pontefract sully
> Her fame by returning to Parliament Gully.
> The etymological cause I suppose is
> His breaking the bridges of so many noses.'

This was the sneering verdict of one James Smith upon Gully's election to the House which, it was said, he did for a bet. Whatever it was that prompted him to do it, he stayed long enough to dispel any thoughts that he took the position lightly.

'The quiet, gentlemanly-looking man in the blue surtout, grey trousers, white neckerchief, and gloves, whose closely buttoned coat displays his manly figure and broad chest to great advantage, is a very well known character. He has fought a great many battles in his time, and conquered like the heroes of old, with no other arms than those the Gods gave him,' wrote, in *Sketches of Boz*, a young Parliamentary reporter named Charles Dickens.

Gully, who seems to have supported the forward-thinking Reforms of the day without making much in the way of speeches, stayed in the House until a spell of ill-health forced him to resign. His first wife died young and he remarried an innkeeper's daughter. Charles Greville paid him this tribute:

'Totally without education, he has strong sense, discretion, reserve and a species of good taste which has prevented, in the height of his fortunes, his behaviour from ever transgressing the bands of modesty and respect, and he has gradually separated himself from the rabble of bettors and blackguards, of whom he was once the most conspicuous, steadily asserted his own independence; and acquired gentility, without ever presuming towards those whom he had been accustomed to regard with deference.'

Greville also wrote of Gully's delicate hands and coarse face. After resigning his seat in the Commons, Gully lived as a country squire, winning the Derby twice more, with Pyrrhus the First in 1846 (when he also won the Oaks with Mendicant) and with Andover in 1854. He failed in a bid to return to Parliament and at 76 publicly shook the hand of Tom Sayers, who was 'still bearing the scars of battle from Heenan's raw fist'.

Gully bought shares in the Hetton Colliery in Durham while living at Ackworth Park, and was still the owner of an estate and colliery at Wingate when he died on 9 March 1863, by which time he was 79 years old and worth about £100,000. At one time he bought Marwell Hall near Winchester, but after giving up his horses he moved north again to keep an eye on his colliery businesses and lived then at Cocken Hall near Durham. Shortly before his death he moved for the sake of convenience to a house in Durham itself and was buried at Ackworth in ground over which, he had previously determined, that 'no man shall ride roughshod'. We are told the carriages of half Durham and Yorkshire formed the funeral procession. He had 24 children – 12 from each marriage – one of whom was killed serving his country in the 1857 Indian Mutiny. Ten survived him.

Cribb v Molineaux

Tom Cribb is further proof that there was something in the Bristol water. He was born in Hanham, a mining village five miles outside the city, on 8 July 1781 and at 13 trod the well-worn road to London, where he worked as a docker and coal-heaver, developing his 5ft 10in frame to a peak weight of around 196lb. Twice he had serious accidents, once falling between two barges and once slipping while hauling a 500lb crate of oranges. After the second, he was spitting blood for days. An unconfirmed story also existed that he spent some time at sea in the wars against France.

Cribb was the stuff of legend, who came at a time which Englishmen would want to remember as they sat around their tavern tables smoking and drinking before a roaring fire. These were the days of Trafalgar and Waterloo, of an old England before what historians would call the Industrial Revolution, an England of wide open spaces and tiny hamlets. Cribb was, in fact, not as good as the old-timers would have had us believe, relying on an awkward style, his strength, courage – and, occasionally, foul tactics. He was slow and cumbersome, but his spirit was capable of moving all those who saw him fight.

He took 90 minutes to grind down the 5ft 6ins, 42-year-old black

American, Bill Richmond, on the day Pearce beat Gully at Hailsham in 1805 and 18 months later needed 41 rounds to dispose of the one-eyed Belcher at Moulsey Hurst. He won more quickly second time around but Belcher had broken his arm. In between fights Cribb would blow up to about 224lb. Captain Robert Barclay, the first of the great trainers, said of him before he fought Tom Molineaux for the second time:

'From his mode of living in London and the confinement of a crowded city, he had become corpulent, big-bellied, full of gross humours and short-breathed, and it was with difficulty that he could walk ten miles.'

Nevertheless, these were pugilism's great years. In the 1850s George Borrow was to recall the days 'when a pugilistic encounter between two noted champions was almost considered as a national affair; when tens of thousands of individuals, high and low, meditated and brooded upon it, the first thing in the morning and the last at night, until the great event was decided'.

On 3 January 1805, Cribb took 76 rounds to beat George Maddox, who was nearly 50 at the time, and although he beat Tom Blake, also known as Tom Tough, and a Jewish boxer who enjoyed the glorious ring name of Ikey Pig, he was drunk when he lost to George Nicholls of Bristol in 52 rounds in July 1805. He was given a boxing lesson for a time by Richmond, who was middle-aged, outweighed and shorter, but eventually his youth and strength brought him through. Richmond, who was billed as The Black Terror, was the son of a Georgia slave owned by a preacher. Bill knocked out three drunken English sailors in a bar and was given a job as a footman by the British general Earl Percy before coming to England to go to school in Yorkshire. At one time he was apprenticed to a cabinet-maker in York, but his inclination towards the Prize Ring overtook his other ambitions. Richmond retired from boxing in 1815 and was a respected, if underpaid, teacher until his death in December 1829 at the age of 66.

His fighting apprenticeship over, Cribb fought Bob Gregson for the championship and 1,000 guineas in a 30ft ring at Moulsey Hurst on 25 October 1808, only five months after Gregson had lost for the second time to Gully. As usual, when his duties as head of the British Army didn't interfere, the Duke of York was present, as was Lord Byron. Gregson was seconded by Jem Belcher and Bill Richmond, Cribb by John Gully and Bill Gibbons. Gentleman Jackson refereed. They brawled head-to-head for round after slow, gruelling round. Cribb was so exhausted by the start of round 21 that he only just made it to the scratch-line, yet from somewhere he found the inner resolve to press on and in round 23 he tossed Gregson to the ground. Gregson landed with his legs buckled beneath his 16st bulk and was unable to stand, let alone fight. Gregson retired to his pub, the Castle in Holborn, otherwise to

Tom Cribb: the stuff of legend, and a star in the golden era of pugilism.

be known as Bob's Chop-House, after a benefit held at the Fives Court.

In 1810 a dinner was held in his honour on the premises – tickets a guinea each – and Gully, Richmond, Jackson, Cribb and Tom Belcher were all among the party. It ended with an impromptu fight for a £20 purse between Cribb's younger brother George and Dan Dogherty. Cribb 'bled copiously and his head was much disfigured by the hits he received, and at the end of an hour, being quite exhausted, gave in'. Gregson was a bad businessman and was forced to relinquish the pub in 1814. He attempted to start a sparring school, but that did not take off, and instead left to try his luck in Dublin, where he made a better living. In 1819 he embarked on a sparring tour of Ireland along with Dan Donnelly and George Cooper, but later was landlord of a pub named the Punch House in Moor Street, Dublin. That failed too and he was virtually penniless when he returned to live out his last days in Liverpool, where he died in November 1824.

At the end of the Cribb-Gregson fight at Moulsey Hurst, Jem Belcher spat angry words at the new champion, whose lack of skill led him to believe he could come back and regain the title, even if he did have only one eye, and even if Cribb had already beaten him once. Accordingly, the match was made and Cribb beat him again. Pierce Egan called the closing stages 'piteous' and 'dreadful' with Belcher, his hands bleeding and his arm broken, taking a hiding.

Pugilistica records an anecdote of Cribb and Gully taking a stroll through a country village, both in ordinary smock coats, when they saw a man beating a pig. The animal was taking such a vicious hiding that the fighters asked him to stop, upon which the man and four or five of his companions gathered around them menacingly. A free and frank exchange of views followed, and eventually the pig-beater was daft enough to have a swing at Cribb, who swatted him down. 'His nob was materially shook and the claret tapped in masterly style,' says the source. Cribb and Gully went on their way and it was only later that the villagers realised who had passed through. No doubt the pig-beater boasted of having been dropped by the greatest ring hero of their time for the rest of his life!

Cribb took over a sporting tavern named the Union Arms in Panton Street, London, and fought Tom Molineaux, the celebrated black American, at Copthall Common near East Grinstead on 18 December 1810. Molineaux, said to be an ancestor of the world light-heavyweight champion of the 1930s, John Henry Lewis, had been born on a plantation belonging to the Molineaux family of Georgetown, Southern Carolina. Legend had it that he had fought for his freedom against another slave, won and travelled to England, where Bill Richmond found him, penniless and searching hopelessly for the American ambassador. This is no more than unsubstantiated anecdote, but may have been true. He was thought to have been born in 1784. By his teens he was working in New York as a porter in the docks, and sailed for England in 1809.

Molineaux, at 5ft 9in and around 200lbs, was a fine fighter who knocked out Tom Blake, also known as Tom Tough, in eight rounds in August 1810, near Margate in Kent. Another reference to him was made in *Sporting Magazine*:

> 'On Tuesday, 24 July (1810), a bull was baited in Tot-hill Fields, and as is usual on such occasions, the amusements concluded with a boxing match ... The combatants were a Bristol man, one of the old nursery, and a strong, athletic American black of the name of Molineaux ... who had lately arrived in this country.'

Molineaux won in an hour. His match with Cribb fired the public imagination, especially after Cribb had originally refused it, only for the abrasive American to call him a coward. 18 December was a terrible winter's day. Rain turned the last five miles of the road leading to the common into ankle-deep clay, yet still a crowd of around 20,000 arrived, including old champions Belcher, Jackson and Mendoza. They saw the unthinkable happen – Cribb was outworked and outhit and seemed exhausted by the eighth round. At the end of the ninth Cribb looked in deep trouble. He was knocked down by a dreadful blow to the throat, and looked incapable of making it back to scratch, as the crowd settled into a stunned hush.

It was then his second, Joe Ward, pulled one of the most brilliant and cruellest strokes in prize-fighting history. He claimed Molineaux was holding bullets or stones in his hands and poured out insults, calling for the referee to check. The American was confused and angry and in the freezing winter, with his fists stiff from cold, it took time to prove him innocent. As all this went on, Gully brought Cribb round and the champion used his unfairly bought time to recover his wits. Slowly the fight turned. Cribb's legendary stamina began to tell and the wind and rain bit deep into Molineaux's resolve. Cribb also fouled shamelessly, at one time biting Molineaux's thumb to the bone. And by round 38, exhausted, numb with cold and thoroughly discouraged, Molineaux collapsed. Cribb was too exhausted to celebrate.

Cribb retired, but Molineaux claimed the championship, having issued another challenge to the champion within a week of their fight. This was more than any decent Englishman could stomach and the 30-year-old West Countryman was forced by public opinion to postpone the easy life a little longer. He was trained by Captain Barclay, who took him off to his family seat at Ury, near Stonehaven in Kincardineshire, Scotland, where he was drilled into shape. Barclay gave him three initial doses of medicine and for two weeks allowed him to walk as he wished, hunting for magpies and pigeons in the woods on the estate. Gradually he stepped that up to regular exercise, walking between 10 and 20 miles a day. He developed that into 18-20 mile walks with top speed runs of a quarter of a mile. In five weeks Barclay worked Cribb down from 224lbs to 205lbs, and then ground him into top shape with sparring, 'sweats' and strenuous exercise. By fight time he weighed 187lbs. Barclay, whose reputation as the first significant trainer was sealed by this fight, was so satisfied with their work that he gambled 10,000 guineas on Cribb, who was a 1-3 favourite. While the champion had been putting in his work, Molineaux had remained in London and enjoyed himself.

This time a throng estimated at 15,000 travelled to Thistleton Gap, near Wymondham in the tiny county of Rutland, on 28 September 1811. Not a bed could be found for 20 miles around. The Marquess of Queensberry was among the scattered nobles and aristocrats. Again Molineaux, in this land of fair play and honest hearts, may have been nobbled. He wasn't endowed with too much common sense, admittedly, but someone knew of his weakness for good food and strong ale. For breakfast on that late summer day, Molineaux was primed with a complete boiled chicken, an apple pie and, more importantly, a half-gallon of porter beer. Even in an age when Englishmen drank ale instead of water, this was excessive. He tucked away everything with relish. Molineaux was on top in the early stages, closing Cribb's eye, which was 'big as a goose's egg' until it was lanced by his second Gully. Cribb's conditioning and Molineaux's breakfast ensured that the championship stayed in England. 'The black was fat' and slowed under Cribb's body attacks. Cribb then switched to the head and broke Molineaux's jaw. In the ninth Molineaux fell 'as if dead' from a left swing and did not make it to scratch in half a minute. Cribb, who was enjoying himself, invited him to go on, and prolonged the torture until he grew bored and ended it in the 11th. Gully and Cribb danced a Scotch Reel of victory on the 25-foot stage. The following Sunday, Cribb passed through Stamford in a baroville-and-four decorated with his colours, called on Molineaux at Grantham and passed on to London, where the roads were blocked by welcoming crowds.

Cribb retired again and England's prize-fighters agreed he should be called 'Champion' for the rest of his life. On 11 December 1811 a silver cup worth 80 guineas was presented to Cribb at the Old Castle tavern in London, when a banquet was held in his honour. He had one last fling when, nearly 40, he defeated Jack Carter in a room fight in Oxendon Street on 1 February 1820, which he won in one minute. 'Insolence punished,' sniffed the reporter for *Bell's Life*. Eventually he declared his successor to be Tom Spring. In March 1821, the *Sporting Magazine* carried the notice:

'To All England. 'The Championship'. Tom Crib (sic) having been called to the bar, which now so completely occupies his time, – but to be brief on the subject, he has in consequence, entirely resigned the whole of his practice in the ring to Tom Spring, his adopted boy:-, the son, therefore, wishing to tread in the steps of his father and not to lead a dull, inglorious life! anxiously seeking the path of glory – informs all those heroes whom it may concern that for three months he is open to all England, for 100 to 200 guineas a side.'

Cribb's pub, the Union Arms, was apparently a boisterous but orderly house. More than once he had to cope with an idiot who wanted to make a name for himself, but given the potential for trouble, there was little. He did find himself in court once over an incident involving a German dwarf, John Hauptman, whom he employed as a waiter, having found him penniless in the street. When Cribb was away a drunken hackney-cab driver named Beckett insulted the 3ft 4in tall Hauptman, and had his 10-year-old son thrash him. Cribb was so angry that he took the matter before the magistrate. Beckett blamed 'brandy and water' for his lack of respect and agreed to pay Hauptman a sovereign for his pains.

Cribb also survived a terrible accident near Stockwell in December 1822 when he was thrown by a horse and knocked unconscious for half an hour when the animal fell on him. Doctors bled him at the scene and he was carried home to recover. This prevented him attending the funeral of Hickman The Gaslighter, another top fighter who died tragically young (at 37) when the chaise he was driving overturned on Finchley Common. Eventually Cribb had to give up the Union Arms because of debts – he had lent money which had not been repaid, and also had to look after a sick relative as well as his own family. It must have been a great sadness to him that it was necessary for his friends at the Pugilistic Club to stage a benefit on his behalf at the National Baths in Westminster Road on 12 November 1840. At the time he was living with one of his sons, a baker, in High Street, Woolwich. Nevertheless, as sorry as his circumstances became, Cribb was one of the relatively few pugilists of his generation to grow old. He was 66 when he died, after a lingering illness, on 11 May 1848. A monument in the shape of a lion was erected in his memory in Woolwich churchyard. The plinth was inscribed simply: 'Respect The Ashes Of The Brave'.

By contrast, the ill-used Molineaux never found a peace more lasting than the bottle. He was forever the black that Cribb thrashed twice. The fact that he had outpunched the great man for most of the first fight was forgotten. A rough fighter, he was not above fouling if he had to, but then he had a good teacher in Cribb. In 1813 he beat Stephen Carte for 100 guineas near Banbury for £25, and in May 1814 he twice fought Bill Fuller in Scotland. The first fight was interrupted after eight minutes, but the second was a 'tedious mill' near Glasgow which lasted for 68 minutes and contained only two rounds.

Molineaux was eventually declared the winner. But in March 1815, he lost in 20 minutes and 14 rounds to George Cooper at Corset Hill near Edinburgh. Cooper was a tough, experienced fighter from Stone in Staffordshire who had been taught by Paddington Jones and Richmond. Molineaux's flaw seemed to be that he was not sufficiently endowed with either intellect or commonsense. Men like Tom Belcher and Richmond are said to have thought little of him, even though they were effectively his managers. It is likely they saw in him only the means to make money – and allowed him to do what he liked before a contest. He took to drinking too many pints of stout and ale every day. *Pugilistica* paints a picture of a good man whose natural generosity was terribly abused:

> 'Molineaux was illiterate and ostentatious, but good-tempered, liberal and generous to a fault. Fond of gay life, fine clothes and amorous to the extreme ...'

Eventually he went to Ireland, supposedly for an exhibition tour. But he was penniless and interested only in the means of finding the next drink. His once formidable frame was wasted and he was able to present no kind of imitation of the fighter he once was, even for the most imaginative and forgiving of audiences. At the invitation of two black soldiers who had befriended him, he found a roof in the barracks of the 77th Regiment at Galway, and it was there he died of liver failure in 1818 at the age of 34.

Cribb v Molineaux: Tom so nearly became the first American world champion.

5

THE FANCY, THE PATRONS
AND PIERCE EGAN

Pierce Egan, boxing's first serious scribe and historian, captured the spirit of his time and formed the reputations of pugilists from Figg to Cribb, and onwards until he more or less withdrew from the sport in the late 1820s. His exact origins are uncertain, but more than likely is that he was born in Ireland in the first half of the 1770s. He was well read, but mostly self-educated, and like most newspapermen was more interested in the telling of contemporary stories than in burying himself in the classics of Ancient Greece and Rome. He was a merry-making, hard-drinking raconteur who struggled to make ends meet and keep his family secure. In the early 1800s he was working as a compositor for Joseph and George Smeeton, the former of whom died in a fire at the family printing house in 1809. George Smeeton's publications included the *Eccentric Magazine*, and while circumstances are unclear, it seems likely that he responded to the popularity of pugilism by offering the job of writing *Boxiana* to Egan. Volume One of the classic series was released by Smeeton from his premises in St Martin's Lane, Charing Cross, in 1812. It was immediately a rapid seller, and while Egan's name was not on it, his authorship was generally acknowledged.

The success of *Boxiana* helped Egan, who wrote for the *Weekly Dispatch* and apparently helped boost its sales. The arrival of a literate working class – a blanket term, but nonetheless not inappropriate – was still some way off, but the work of the Methodists in Sunday Schools increased the chances of an ordinary man or woman being able to read or write. This in turn provided a market for those who wanted to write about contemporary life and who were blissfully unaware of Latin, Greek and the workings of Homer, Virgil and the great bank of classical philosophers and playwrights. Leaflets, newspapers, religious tracts suddenly cascaded into the market place. Boxing was reported in *The Morning Post* and in *The Times*, although the latter generally disapproved of the sport. Executions were given extensive coverage: the processions to Tyburn had been discontinued in 1783, but there were still huge crowds for hangings outside Newgate jail in Egan's time. Newgate had been ravaged by fire during a riot in 1780, but was rebuilt and was considered a fine building. A description of the jail remains in the sensational accounts of the *Newgate Calendar*.

'Malefactors under sentence of death are secured in cells built expressly for that purprose; there are five upon each of the three floors, each vaulted, in height about nine feet to the crown of the arch, and about nine feet in length, by six in width. In the upper part of each cell is a small narrow window double-grated. The doors are four inches thick. The strong wall is lined all round with planks, studded with broad-headed nails. In each cell is a barrack bedstead. It is observed that prisoners who had affected an air of boldness during their trial, and appeared quite unconcerned when sentence was pronounced on them, were struck with horror, and shed tears, when they were brought to these dark and solitary abodes.

'Condemned felons are executed in front of the prison, on a large moveable scaffold (called the New Drop), which is kept in the Press Yard for this occasion. The malefactors stand upon a false floor, and when their devotions are finished, on a signal being given, the floor suddenly drops, leaving the unhappy sufferers suspended in the air.'

In Egan's heyday there were around 100 executions a year in London, and when the celebrated forger, Henry Fauntleroy, was hanged in 1824 the crowd was estimated at 100,000, with reserved seats costing £1. Pierce also made some serious money by his enterprising interview with a condemned murderer, John Thurtell of Norwich. Thurtell and three accomplices killed a gambler, William Weare, who had just returned from a good day at the St Leger race meeting at Doncaster. They put the body into a sack and tossed it into 'green slime' at Elstree. Egan, who knew Thurtell as a fringe member of the pugilistic community, talked to him in jail and published the conversation. It was sensational work.

He wrote the amazingly popular *Life In London* and in 1832 the *Book of Sports* – but by that time he had little to say about boxing. There were other publications, including a life of George III and a guidebook of Bath, but it was for *Boxiana* that he remained best known.

Egan put out a reprint of his old Volume One with a new Volume Two in 1818, this time with his own name on the title page, and a third volume in 1821, all of these published by Sherwood, Neely and Jones. However, he then fell out with the publishers over the production of a fourth volume. Sherwood took him to court, arguing that the company held the copyright. Egan contested that they did not and won a landmark decision. His argument was no doubt celebrated by his fellow writers: 'Although I sold the plaintiffs my book,' he said, 'I did not sell them my brain.'

Sherwood, however, beat him into print with its own Volume Four of *Boxiana*, which is generally understood to have been put together by Egan's bitter rival, John Badcock, who wrote under the pseudonym Jon Bee. This forced Egan to delay his own Volume Four until another publishing opportunity arose through George Virtue of Paternoster Row. This took the shape of a new series, with the three early books reprinted, along with two new ones to make Volumes Four and Five, between 1828 and 1830.

A full set of *Boxiana* should realistically comprise Egan's five books and the 1824 rogue edition of Badcock. Later reprints were issued through neighbouring publishing houses, but the text remained unaltered, even if some of the illustration plates were omitted. The six-book series remains a jewel for any boxing memorabilia collector and, providing the reader can handle Egan's quaint style, is hugely entertaining.

Egan's popularity inevitably declined as fashions changed, but he was a figure of considerable influence – and one who is neglected by literary critics who no doubt consider his offerings too 'low-brow' for serious study. Yet writers as great as Dickens and Thackeray almost certainly read him avidly. His last published work was a throwback to fondly remembered days with his friends of the Fancy. He called it *Every Gentleman's Manual, or a Lecture on the Art of Self Defence*. Egan was in his 70s when he died in Islington, north London, in 1849. He was buried in the sprawling Highgate Cemetery. The exact location of his grave has now been lost, but in his time he was responsible for the charting of boxing history. He had some eccentric ways and his opinions must not be taken as wholly representative, but his legacy is a marvellous picture of a sporting culture at the height of its popularity and influence.

Egan dedicated the first volume of *Boxiana* to 'Captain' Robert Barclay Allardice, who trained Gully and Cribb, and who was a pioneering fitness theorist. He sparred and took part in the sport of pedestrianism, which remained popular throughout the 19th century. Barclay, we are told, once achieved a target of walking 1,000 miles in 1,000 successive hours. In other words for almost six weeks, he walked at least one mile in every hour, without sleep. Why? Who on earth knows. To us it's eccentric, not to say downright stupid, but then it probably seemed like an interesting test for body and mind. It cannot have done Barclay too much harm: he was 75 when he died in 1854 after being kicked on the head by a horse.

Barclay was a vital figure in that he made sure Cribb, who was not naturally inclined to train, was fit to fight. Cribb's role was vital to the English embracement of pugilism because of his two defeats of Tom Molineaux. He was also the source of a conversation which helps explain just how men saw the act of settling a dispute with their fists as perfectly natural. Barclay recalled a pugilist complaining loudly to another man: 'Why won't you fight I? I never did ought to offend yer.'

The patrons, of course, came from the ranks of the wealthy. We have dealt with most: the Prince Regent and his accolytes, a Lord or two here, a fake Colonel there. At pugilism's height, wherever there was money to be flashed around, there was somebody only too willing to flash it. Sometimes, they lasted a long time: the politician, William Wyndham, for example, became a boxing fanatic after suffering what we might now call trendily a near-death experience in 1780, when hit by some kind of sudden illness. He recovered, jettisoned his previous intellectual, quiet ways and vigorously pursued his pleasures. His diaries show he was ringside at more than 20 major fights. While he survived and used his position to defend prize-fighting with great enthusiasm, others figured only briefly: Barrymore died young, and the dandy 'Colonel' Harvey Aston was shot dead in a duel. George Hanger, a friend of the Prince of Wales, learned his boxing from the top class pugilist, Sam Martin of Bath, and lived a chequered life, which included patronising boxers. He married a gypsy, published a pamphlet on the art of rat-catching, spent time in debtors' prison and dealt in coal and diamonds.

The Pugilistic Club was formed after discussions at John Jackson's premises in 1814. It had initially 120 members whose annual fees helped pay boxers. The idea was to cure the sport of the curse of fixed fights. It attempted to provide a much-needed stability in the sport and its policy of employing an official ring-maker, the mercurial and somewhat seedy Bill Gibbons, unwittingly helped in the long-term standardisation of rings. Pugilistic Club members wore blue and yellow waistcoats with buttons engraved with the initials 'PC' . They carried dark blue ribbons on their hats, and some of their less aristocratic members were used to maintain order at ringside.

Gibbons was paid two guineas a day to organise the minute details of a big fight and to provide the ring. Egan didn't like him, and it was said he could not be trusted. Some suspected him of double-crossing even the fine intentions of the Pugilistic Club by fixing fights himself. As well as being wrapped up in boxing, Gibbons was part of a smuggling chain dealing in fine veils and lace shawls. At one point the law caught up with him, and to keep in favour he paid £200 to the court in respect of tax avoidance. Egan described Gibbons as rivalling 'the beautiy of one of his own bull-dogs' and talked of his protruding teeth, and his habit of slouching with his hands in his pockets. It was said, probably mockingly, that his dying words were his habitual phrase 'Burn my breeches'.

Egan described the Fancy at the Tom Spring-Jack Langan fight in 1824:

'It was a union of all ranks, from the brilliant of the highest class in the circle of Corinthians, down to the Dusty Bob gradation in society; and even a shade or two below that. Lots of the Upper House, the Lower House and the Flesh House. Proprietors of splendid parks and domesnes; inmates from proud and lofty mansions; thousands from the peaceable cot – and myriads of coves from no houses at all; ... it was a conglomeration of the Fancy.'

The Pugilistic Club, because of its fees, could appeal only to the moneyed, but its ideals were perceived as worthy of support. The Daffy Club was established at the Castle Tavern, Holborn, when Tom Belcher was licensee in 1814, and catered for the less well off. It had no ambitions beyond the support of pugilism and certainly could not engineer the kind of funding needed to back fights. However, it played its part as a gathering place for boxing fans. Daffy, by the way, was one of the nicknames for gin. Boxing pubs abounded in the heyday of the sport, and remained a lure to the young for many years. Dickens was said to frequent the ale-houses of the city, while Branwell Bronte, the brother of novelists Charlotte, Anne and Emily, travelled to London to study at the Royal Academy in the 1830s, only to spend his money in the Castle Tavern.

Gradually, as times changed, these establishments lost their connection with boxing, although one or two of the old places are still standing. One example is the Lowndes Arms, just off the Kings Road, which was built in 1825 and had the prize-fighter Alec Reid as an early landlord.

Serious problems began to afflict the sport from 1824 with the closure of Jackson's rooms in Bond Street and the landmark judgement at Kingston Assizes of Mr Justice Burroughs, whose ruling on a fight between Jem Burns and Ned Neale made it plain that boxing with the bare-knuckles was outside the law. Burroughs said the contest, organised by the Pugilistic Club in December 1824 at Moulsey Hurst, one of its regular venues, indulged the propensities of the vicious and encouraged gamblers. Frankly, it sounds more like the opinion of a politician rather than the sober proclamation of a judge, but the effect was obvious. Earlier that year writers had debated the pros and cons of boxing in *The Weekly Dispatch*, *The Times* and *The Public Ledger*. The abolitionists were winning.

However, we race ahead too fast.

6

A NEW GENERATION

Boxing had been practised in Ireland for most of the 18th century, without developing into an organised business. In the 1730s, Philip Skelton, Rector of Templecarne, hired a boxer named Jonas Good as a bodyguard against drunken pilgrims! During the 18th century Irish boxers – Peter Corcoran, for example – had travelled to England and earned fame and occasionally fortune in the ring. Michael Ryan, who lost to Tom Johnson, was the first major Irish boxing hero, but the greatest of them all was a 6ft, 14st Dublin carpenter, Dan Donnelly. He boxed only three times, claimed he trained by restricting himself to 25 whiskeys a day, was supposedly knighted by the Prince Regent, and was dead at 32.

The ninth of 17 children born in Townsend Street in Dublin, legend has it that Donnelly became a prize-fighter when he punished a local thug who insulted his father. In his first official fight at the Curragh of Kildare on 14 September 1814, Donnelly trounced Tom Hall of the Isle of Wight in 15 rounds. His second fight, when he beat the Englishman, George Cooper, on the Curragh in December 1815 is the stuff of legend. Donnelly was outboxed by the waterman from Stone in Staffordshire but turned the fight with a right hand that broke Cooper's jaw. The site is known as Donnelly's Hollow, his footprints as he left were preserved in the turf, and 'pilgrims' have created a path alongside them. A five-feet high monument is still there, containing a description of Donnelly's career and, at the Hideout pub in nearby Kilcullen a glass case contains, or at least did until fairly recently, the champion's right arm! It was cut off when his grave in a Dublin cemetery was raided and was at one time used for scientific research in Edinburgh. Not until the 1950s did it find its way home.

Donnelly was landlord of several Dublin taverns – but drank too much himself and ran up debts. His answer was to travel to England to seek out prize fights. His drinking was the stuff of legend, and he had contracted some form of venereal disease by the time he stepped in against Tom Oliver at Crawley Downs on 21 July 1819. Donnelly won, but took 34 rounds and 70 minutes to do it, ending the fight with a sickening 'cross buttock'. He was unimpressive, and no moves were made to match him again. He gambled and drank away his purse money. The story goes that when his wife arrived to take him home, he had only £2 in his pockets. He was billed to appear at Donnybrook Fair in 1819, but was on a drinking binge and didn't bother to show up. And it was in his pub in Dublin that he died suddenly on 18 February 1820. His demise was greeted by a clutch of romantic elegies which sealed his reputation.

Jack Scroggins, born John Palmer in London on 29 December 1786, was one of the toughest men of his age. He was only 15 when he defeated Bill Walters in 65 minutes at Brentford in 1803, but it was not until a decade later that he reached his peak. He stood only 5ft 4in and when properly fit was a solid, stocky 152lbs, yet was content to give away whatever physical advantages were necessary in order to box. A quarrelsome little man who would readily back his words with his fists, he was press-ganged into the Navy, but got himself invalided out and was once locked up for hitting a peace officer. He wasn't particularly skilful, but his grit and bravery were all-consuming. He won 19 fights in 19 years, but twice lost gruelling marathons with Ned Turner and was also beaten by Jack Martin, who was known as the Master of the Rolls because he was a baker, in 1818. He also earned a 100-guinea purse by defeating Jack Church in 58 minutes in August 1816. Scroggins drank far too much and claimed, later in life, that he had drunk 40 glasses of gin a day for 20 years. He fought for the last time against Gipsy Cooper in 1822, but was still healthy enough to deliver a speech in praise of Ned Turner on his old adversary's death in April 1826. Gradually he became a bar-fly, living off his memories and his wits, helped out by those who remembered him in better days. Cribb would feed him sometimes at the Union Arms, but he was a hopeless case long before he died, aged 48, on 1 November 1836.

Jack Randall was known as 'The Nonpareil' and was born of Irish parents in St Giles, London, on 25 November 1794. His finest hour was at Crawley Hurst in December 1818 when he beat the top class Ned Turner in a fight that lasted two hours and 20 minutes. Incidentally, Randall's fight with Jack Martin, a brilliantly executed victory and demonstration of sheer ring skill, at Crawley Down, 30 miles from London, on Tuesday, 4 May 1819, was attended by such a sensitive soul as the Romantic poet John Keats, who was there to help himself overcome his grief at the death of his brother, Tom. Randall was a wonderful boxer, but out of the ring, his is a depressingly familiar story. He ran a pub, but drank himself to death on 12 March 1828 at the age of 34. While on the subject of poets, by the way, the 'country

Dutch Sam

poet' John Clare from Helpston in Northamptonshire spent the last 23 years of his life in a mental asylum during which at one point he believed he was a prize-fighter, either 'Boxer Byron', Tom Spring or the later hero Ben Caunt. In his notebook at St Andrew's Hospital in Northampton, Clare, whose father was a wrestling champion and farm worker, wrote: 'They're feeding me up for a fight, but they can get nobody able to strip to me.'

Dutch Sam (real name Sam Elias) took over the mantle of Daniel Mendoza as the hero of England's Jewish community. He stood around 5ft 6½ in, and weighed between 130lbs and 133lbs, yet could punch like a middleweight. He was born on 4 April 1775 in Petticoat Lane, Whitechapel, in London's East End, and fought between 1801 and 1814, when he lost to Bill Nosworthy, a fighting baker. Sam had a high forehead and curly hair and a muscular upper body. He was a fast, hard puncher, who reportedly had more than 100 fights at a time when most boxers had less than 20.

He once claimed to train on a medicinal diet of three glasses of gin taken three times a day – some way short of the perilous claims of Donnelly and Scroggins – and some say he was one of the finest fighters, pound-for-pound, that the Prize Ring ever produced.

Sam beat Paddington Jones in 1801, and in 37 rounds at Wood Green, north London, also beat Caleb Baldwin. In 1806 at Virginia Water near Egham he defeated Tom Belcher in 57 rounds, and the following year at Lowfield Common near Crawley in Sussex and then at Moulsey Hurst he beat him twice more. However modest his drinking habits appeared, he nevertheless died young, at only 41, in the London Hospital on 3 July 1816, and was buried the next day in the Jewish cemetery at Whitechapel. In spite of his moderation, gin was held mostly responsible for his demise.

George Maddox was born in Tothill Fields, the parish of Westminster, in 1756. He didn't start fighting until he was 26, when he took on Symonds The Ruffian at Datchet near Windsor, and gave Tom Cribb a gruelling battle of 76 rounds and 130 minutes when he was 49! Five years further on and he fought Bill Richmond, losing after an hour because he was exhausted. Maddox had talent and lived a quiet life, returning after each contest to earn a regular living as a costermonger – that is, a street-dealer who usually sold fish, fruit or flowers – with donkey and cart. The poor man lived cleanly – and therefore it was a terrible, undeserved irony that he met a particularly filthy end. While trudging along to market before dawn one day in 1809, he fell into an open sewer and smashed his thigh. Somebody did manage to haul him out but the terrible streptococcus bacterial disease set in and his flesh was eaten away until he died a dreadful death in St Thomas' Hospital.

Caleb Baldwin, known as The Pride of Westminster, was a brilliant lightweight who was born Caleb Stephen Ramsbottom in a house close to Westminster Abbey on 22 April 1769. He may have been boxing as a 16-year-old and certainly fought Paddington Jones at Hurley Bottom after the Mendoza-Warr battle in May 1792. After half an hour an unresolved dispute meant the fight was ruled a draw. On Wimbledon Common in 1800 Baldwin accepted the open challenge of an Irishman named Kelly and won in 15 minutes. His adolescent exploits had apparently been long forgotten, for it seemed before this fight he was known only to his friends who regarded him as 'good with the mufflers'. He beat Jack Lee, the butcher and considered a rising hopeful, in 23 minutes at Hurley Bottom in 1801 and two years later defeated Jack O'Donnell for 50 guineas a side in only eight rounds on Wimbledon Common. But in 1804 Baldwin lost to Dutch Sam in a hard fight near Highgate in 1804, after which Caleb's friends claimed he was out of condition. An attempt to make a rematch came to nothing – Dutch Sam pulled out of the agreement and forfeited his deposit. That remained the only defeat of his career.

A happy little man, Baldwin was considered an honest, brave and scientific fighter, who went on to become a first rate teacher. At a benefit arranged for him and the veteran 'Old' Joe Ward in 1817, Baldwin had a spar with Paddington Jones, whom he had boxed for real a quarter of a century before. He does not appear to have been especially short of money and was only too willing to offer his services in exhibitions for the more needy. He died in Westminster on 8 November 1827, aged 58.

Tom Belcher was Jem's younger brother and fought from 1804-13 with a brief comeback in 1822. Always smart and well-dressed, he organised sporting dinners after taking over the Castle Tavern in Holborn from Bob Gregson. A boxing man to the core, he had to restock the Castle after Gregson's failure, but did so and worked hard to make it profitable. He was known as a moderate, good-tempered man who confined his gambling to special occasions and was always ready with a welcome to his customers – in short, a natural landlord. His pub also housed the Daffy Club, as we have already said. In the ring he had 13 battles, won eight, drew one with Dutch Sam, and lost four. He was born in Bristol in 14 April 1783 and followed Jem to London when he was 20. In 1828 he sold the thriving Castle to Tom Spring and retired, moving back to Bristol in his later years and dying there at the age of 71 on 9 December 1854.

Ring fatalities were mercifully rare, but one did happen in June 1809 at Hackney when James Ayres knocked out William Dormer with a blow which landed just below the left ear. Dormer got up, but collapsed again and died. Ayres and his second, William Robinson, were tried at the Old Bailey for murder. Ayres was convicted of manslaughter, imprisoned and branded on the arm with a hot iron. Similarly, Thomas Clayton, who killed Jem Betts in a bout in 1817 near Reading, spent six months in jail.

The Prize Ring's hold on the nation's sporting men seemed to tighten by the year. London abounded with 'professors' of boxing, the members of the Pugilistic Club strutted their stuff at ringside, and thousands travelled miles to be at good class contests. For a battle between Jack Carter and Tom Oliver in 1816 at remote Gretna Green, just across the Scottish border, almost every man in Carlisle made the journey north. Egan wrote: 'A horse, chaise, cart, or any sort of vehicle whatever, however dirty and despicable was not to be procured at any price.' And on a rainy day in February 1817, the Austrian Archduke Nicholas was treated to a trip to prize-fights – 'a tedious 70-minute affair between Fisher and Crockey, and a better 35-minute fight between West Country Dick and Charley Marten'.

England was a place of rapidly changing moods, a land of contrasts in behaviour and taste between old and new. The traditional, barbaric sports nestled readily with the new-fangled games like cricket and pedestrianism. When compared to cock-fighting, coursing, hunting, and the ritualised torturing of tethered animals, pugilism was a kind of halfway house that suited those of both tastes. But by and large the mass of Englishmen and women were interested in relatively basic entertainments. They enjoyed the public horror show of an execution and would gather in large numbers for all kinds of sporting events. Occasionally, the very size of a crowd would cause a catastrophe. For example, at a bull-bait in Rochdale in November 1820, a large crowd saw dogs attack the bull on a six-foot cord for three hours. Eventually, the parapet of a bridge that was supporting some of the crowd collapsed. Boulders 'about a yard in length and thick in proportion' crashed down on to people standing below, followed by those who had been on the bridge. Five people were killed on the spot, four more died from their injuries and many more were injured. One woman had both of her thighs broken. A young man had his arm completely severed.

Generally, a code of behaviour was maintained by public consent. For example, cock-fighting establishments often had a cage which was suspended by a pulley from the roof. Anyone unable to meet his or her gambling losses was forced into it and hoisted up to the ceiling for the remainder of the proceedings, where they were fair game for verbal and missile assault!

Disease was rife. *The Sporting Magazine* solemnly recorded a case of rabies: 'After 32 hours' extreme suffering, a young man in the service of R. Sheriffe, Esq., of Diss, Norfolk ... died of hydrophobia.'

The unnamed man had washed and cleansed the wound of one of his master's hunting spaniels which had been bitten by an infected terrier.

An obituary of Mr J.J. Braysfield, a wealthy eccentric from Camberwell, illustrates how much a part of London life pugilism had become.

> 'Almost from his infancy, he was an attendant upon all the fairs, boxing matches, races and diversions of every kind round London, from the ring made by the first class amateurs, of the Fancy, down to the weekly badger baiting in Black Boy Alley. He was no less a constant attendant upon the execution of criminals.'

The *Sporting Magazine* of December 1811 had also carried a report of what it declared to be 'Amazonian Boxing'. Two women, Molly Flower and Nanny Gent, fought to settle a family dispute for the price of a pint of gin and a new shawl on Wormwood Scrubs on 12 December. Flower won after a 20-minute struggle, and the writer was impressed:

> 'Both were good hitters, and they were worse hit about the head than is witnessed amongst many second-rate pugilists. Nanny jibbed a bit in the twelfth round and gave in from a dexterous hit down in the following round.'

Participation in the Prize Ring was open to all social classes, although the rules that apply now were just as relevant then: in other words, those who needed to fight for a living far outnumbered those who fought for fun or love. They also tended to do better.

On 5 December 1820, a forty-something gentleman amateur by the name of George Williams fought the professional, Joshua Hudson, at Moulsey Hurst. Williams was highly thought-of among his well-heeled friends, while Hudson, from London's teeming East End, was a happy-go-lucky character who was sometimes in shape, sometimes not. Upon entering the ring, we are told that Williams 'bowed in the most graceful manner, and there was a superior air about him altogether'. He began by cutting Hudson's eye in the first round, but by round three was given no chance. 'He went down quite distressed ...' The *Sporting Magazine* writer recorded that by round five 'the claret was running down in torrents, and Williams was brought up to the scratch in a most distressed state.' Hudson floored him and although Williams was pushed up for the sixth, one more blow was enough to end it. Hudson, who fought with a shoulder injury, took only nine minutes to put the gentleman in his place. 'The swell found out the difference between sparring and fighting ... Williams was taken away in a *post-chaise*, almost insensible, and did not come exactly to himself for 40 minutes.' Hudson's own limits were soon afterwards exposed by the top class pugilist, Ned Turner, who beat him at a 'turn-up' in a pub without receiving so much as a scratch.

Turner was a steady boxer, said to have boxed out of a left-handed stance, who was involved in a fatality in his first ring appearance. On a wet October morning before a small crowd at Moulsey Hurst, he beat a lightweight named Curtis in 66 rounds spread across 85 minutes. At the end Curtis collapsed unconscious, and when time was called he was still sitting on his second's knee with his head lolling to one side. He was carried to an inn at Hampton where he was bled ... and, not surprisingly, died shortly afterwards. Turner was sentenced to two months in Newgate Jail for manslaughter. He was visited regularly by prize-fighters and friends and came out to follow his career in the ring. He boxed Jack Scroggins several times and others like Cy Davis and Jack Martin.

Turner was born in Crucifix Lane, Southwark, on 8 November 1791. His parents were Welsh, from Montgomeryshire. His southpaw stance enabled him to defend himself well and he emerged from his battles relatively unharmed, but he was an asthmatic, which weakened him. When news came that his health had deteriorated seriously, a benefit was arranged for him on 18 April 1826, but he died the day before at the home of his cousin, Mr Baxter, a Smithfields hat-maker.

Before we come back to Tom Cribb's successor, Tom Spring, we should spare a few more words for Bill Richmond, the first black and first American fighter of any note. Richmond was born in the area of Staten Island, New York, called Richmond – known locally as Cuckolds' Town – in August 1763. After being taken into the protection of the English Army at the age of 14 and brought to England, he learned to enjoy cricket as well as fighting. However, it was not until 1804, when in his early 40s, that his abilities were fully appreciated. No doubt his nationality and colour presented him with considerable disadvantages in terms of advancement within the sport, but some also said he did not take it as seriously as he might have done when he was young. At one time he was a bodyguard to the infamous Lord Camelford. He boxed until 1818, by which time he was an elderly man, but he always kept himself in good condition by teaching other fighters the finer points of the trade. He died in the Horse-Shoe Tavern in Titchbourne Street, Haymarket, three days after Christmas 1829.

Tom Spring

Tom Spring, christened Thomas Winter, was born at Fownhope near Hereford on 22 February 1795. At 12, inspired by tales of the glorious

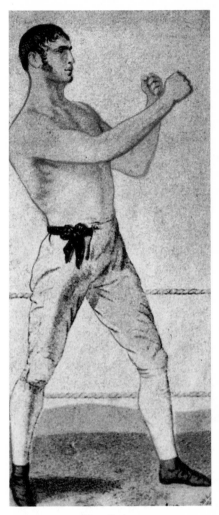

Tom Spring

heroism of Nelson, Trafalgar and the Napoleonic Wars, he tried to run away to be a drummer boy in the Army – but his father caught up with him and condemned him to a safer adolescence on the family farm. At 17 he was working as an apprentice to a butcher, but combining his trade with boxing ... and over the years the butcher became one of his proudest supporters. He stood 5ft 11½ in tall and weighed around 185lbs, and quickly developed a reputation as a thoughtful, neat boxer with plenty of courage. Eventually he became one of the greatest of all tacticians who stuck rigidly to a plan once he found it worked and was terribly difficult to shake from a fighting rhythm.

At Mickleham Downs near Leatherhead on 1 April 1818, the 23-year-old Spring drew large crowds to the first big fight of the season as he beat Ned Painter, from Stretford, near Manchester, who had begun as a 4-7 favourite, in 31 rounds and 89 minutes. People climbed into fir trees lining the site to watch. A contemporary report described Spring's style: '... his body far back, and his length of arm rendered him difficult to get at.'

At the end of six minutes of sparring, Spring staggered Painter with a blow to the throat and he went down, the back of his head slamming into a ring stake. He seemed 'completely stupified' and his cornerman Tom Belcher lifted him up 'with the heaviness of a log ... a swelling, the bigness of an egg, had now risen on his head and the skin on his shoulder was cut'. Yet Painter fought on for more than an hour and 20 minutes until he was too exhausted to box and gave in.

Four months later they fought again for 100 guineas a side at a place called Russia Farm, near Kingston-upon-Thames, and Painter, an accomplished ring technician in his own right, won in 42 rounds and 64 minutes. Painter knocked Spring down and cut his eye with a tremendous right hand in the first round. Spring's injury was a nasty one, with the blood running in streams, and he seemed concussed from the punch, but he slowly recovered until the ninth round when a blow to the ear had him staggering off-balance and bleeding again. Still he fought back, showing enormous determination, although by the 31st he was virtually finished. For the last ten rounds he stood and took his punishment, finally crumpling to the floor for the last time from another blow to the ear. The Fancy applauded him for refusing to give in. When the call to scratch came, he was still out. Painter formally announced his departure from the ring at the Fives Court in September 1818 with an exhibition with Bill Richmond, but aspersions were cast against his character – somebody in the London 'fraternity' put it about that he had deliberately lost the first fight with Spring.

An attempt for another match with Spring fell through, but Ned's supporters did manage to arrange one with Tom Oliver close to North Walsham, 16 miles from Norwich, where the outcome of the contest is said to have dominated conversation in every sporting pub. It was such a major event that a stage 100 yards long was built to accommodate the more gentile spectators, while others piled into 60 wagons set back from the ring. Painter satisfied his backers, and himself, by knocking out Oliver with a punch to the temple in the 12th round.

Afterwards Painter returned with his friends to the village, while Oliver, who was astonished when he regained consciousness to find the fight was over, dressed and sat down on a bale of straw to watch the next contest. He told friends that all he remembered was a shock of lightning. Both, we are told, were so well that they ate a hearty breakfast the following morning. This time Painter retired for good. Although he was originally from Manchester, he had gone to London and presented himself to fellow Lancastrian Bob Gregson at the Castle, and embarked on a career in the ring from 1813. Among those he beat early in his career were an Irishman named Coyne, 'Gamekeeper' Alexander and a serving soldier named Shaw, at which point Painter was on a kind of day-release from the Fleet Debtors' Prison. He also beat a black fighter named Sutton in Norwich, where he was a popular visitor, and after winning his return fight with Spring he left London to live in Lobster Lane, Norwich, where he began a new life as a publican at an inn called the Anchor. He left it in late middle age, moving to a house in the Market Place, dying on 19 September 1853, aged 56.

The defeat by Painter actually enhanced Spring's reputation and he went on to beat Jack Carter, who had been claiming the championship since 1817, in 115 minutes and 71 gruelling rounds on Crawley Downs in May 1819. The crowd was '100 feet deep', including Archduke Maximilian of Austria and the French ambassador, 'in their gilded coaches'. Spring and Carter were both cautious boxers and for the first hour and a half did very little, but then Tom took over. Carter went down so heavily in round 54 that some gamblers were offering a guinea to win a shilling on Spring. Carter recovered a couple more times but by the 70th was confused and, as weary as Spring was, he put Carter down and out in the next. The general verdict was that Spring's skills were far superior, and if he had punching power to match them he would surely have won in half the time.

After a good rest, during which he enjoyed a sparring tour with Tom Cribb, on a stormy morning on the Downs near Epsom in May 1820 he won easily in 18 rounds over Bob Burn. Spring was unwell, but went through with the fight. Burn had impressed in sparring at the Fives Court, but was out of his depth and the future champion eased back instead of seriously hurting him.

Next he beat Tom Oliver, the Battersea Gardener 'who was famous for his sweet peas and nectarines', in February 1821. Fighters and Fancy were chased from two sites on the west road out of London and eventually found a spot called Newman's Field at Hayes.

Sporting Magazine captured the scene:

'The string of carriages for miles winding down the road – the horsemen galloping and leaping over the hedges, the pedestrians all on the trot, and the anxiety displayed on every countenance to arrive on time ...'

Spring asked Oliver, as they shook hands, how he was and the Londoner answered happily: 'Pretty bobbish. Very well.'

Spring outboxed and outhit him as he pleased to win in 25 rounds and 55 minutes. Oliver fought with extraordinary courage, battling on in spite of suffering several terrible falls, and disputing every exchange as best he could. Those who had the ability to assess a man on the basis of his technique rather than his ability to attract hero-worship knew that in Spring they had a fighter to match any in memory, especially his father-figure Cribb, but his light hitting made it hard for the general fans to warm to him. No doubt the majority still hankered for a return to the great days of Belcher, Gully and Pearce. Some even insulted Spring and called him names – 'lady's maid fighter', 'china man', 'light tapper'. It was also said he couldn't make a dent in a pound of butter.

In March 1821 Spring challenged all-comers in a newspaper advertisement but received no takers. As he awaited his next fight he took over the Weymouth Arms in Weymouth Street, Portman Square. A strange incident followed when Spring was arrested and charged as an accessory to the death of a pugilist named James Smith following a contest near Brighton in April 1823. Spring's defence was that he was not at the fight, but the justices did not believe him and bound him over to keep the peace for 12 months.

On 20 May 1823 when Spring fought Bill Neat, another man who considered himself champion, at Finkley Down, near Andover, Hampshire, the roads from Gloucester, Newbury, Winchester, Bristol, Southampton and London were filled with travellers making their way to a hill at the back of the down. Eventually there were 'upwards of 30,000 spectators ... among them numerous well-dressed females'. Spring took only eight rounds and 37 minutes to win, and some suggested a fix, but this was vehemently over-ruled by the *Bell's Life* writer, who said Neat broke a forearm. After three rounds Spring told his cornerman Ned Painter: 'It is as right as the day. He can't hit me in a week.'

Neat informed his second, Tom Belcher, after the fourth that his arm was broken, by the sixth he was showing great signs of distress and when time was called for the ninth, Neat got up and shook hands with Spring, explaining he could not box on because of his arm. Afterwards Spring visited him as he lay in bed after the bone had been set by a surgeon, and gave him £10. This was an especially sweet result for Spring, who had forfeited to Neat the previous year when his backer, Elliott, withdrew and died soon afterwards.

On New Year's Day, 1824, £600 stakes were laid over a sporting dinner at Tom Cribb's house for a fight which had already been made and prepared for, between Spring and the new Irish star, Jack Langan from Clondalkin, just outside Dublin. And six days later, on Thursday, 7 January 1824, a crowd which some put as high as 50,000 watched the fight at a muddy and partly waterlogged Worcester Racecourse, where the grandstand was extended with extra wings and scaffolds – with appalling consequences. After Spring's arrival in Colonel Berkeley's *barouche*-and-four but before that of Langan, part of the overloaded wooden structure collapsed. Fifteen hundred people were thrown to the ground, but with surprisingly few casualties. People also watched from the masts and rigging of the tall ships on the River Severn.

'Swells were seen sitting down in the mud more coolly than if lolling on a sofa.'

More of the stand broke during the second round, this time it was said but not, as far as I can tell, proven that one person died, and the boxing was halted until the chaos subsided. Certainly, more than 20 people were seriously hurt, most of them with broken bones. After an argument about a belt which Spring always wore, and the champion had agreed to remove it, they got down to business. Langan cut an impressive physical specimen, but some said he looked too drawn at 172lbs, conceding a stone in weight and a couple of inches in height. Langan smiled and cocked a thumb to his nose during the early sparring and his cornerman Josh Hudson called out: 'Fight away, Jack, he can't hurt nobody.'

Langan bloodied Spring's lip and fell on top after a cautious first round which lasted nine minutes. The slow pace continued in round two, with Langan's nose bloodied before the interruption caused by the collapse of more of the grandstand. Spring seemed to have settled on a slow, wearing-down, 'hit and not get hit' policy. By round six Langan's left eye was closing, but Spring was hurt when he fell heavily on his head. In the following round the whips were hard at work preserving the space of the ring as the crowd thronged ever closer and Spring damaged the knuckles of his left hand on the Irishman's hard skull. Langan had his successes with throws to finish rounds, but made little significant impression on the champion's defences and for long periods it was tedious fare. By the 19th there were calls from spectators of 'Go to work, Tom!' The champion replied calmly: 'All in good time.'

Langan remained cheerful and even helped Spring up after throwing him through the ropes to complete round 21. By the 28th, with an hour and a quarter already gone, Langan seemed to be having the best of it, and round 31 ended with Spring landing on his head again. Langan's strength and ability at throwing worried the champion's supporters, but when Langan laughed at him 'You have done nothing yet' in the 38th, Spring repeated: 'All in good time. I shall do it at last.'

Slowly, the crowd edged forward and by round 48 the fighters had little room in which to work and whenever they took steps to the side or back, they were jostled. The outer ring had long been broken down, and only those closest to the front could see anything at all. Spring had no room to use his skills, and his cornerman Tom Cribb threatened to flatten anyone in his way, while one of Langan's seconds cracked an over-enthusiastic aristocrat over the head with a *shillelagh*. 'There's no difference here,' he said. 'Lords are no better than commoners. I can't distinguish them one from another!'

Spring had to fight now, because of the lack of room – and soon proved he could when he wanted to. Nevertheless, he was shaken badly by a throw on to his back, with Langan landing on top of him, at the end of round 65. He ploughed on, however, and by the 73rd Langan, outreached and outboxed, was fading. He was floored by a solid right hand to the centre of the head in the following round, and in the 75th his face was covered in blood to the point where someone cried out: 'Take the brave fellow away!'

Langan called back: 'I will not be taken away. Who dare say so?'

But his resources were spent. His head lolled on the shoulder of his seconds after the 76th and Spring hit him repeatedly until he fell in round 77. He was still unconscious when time was called and Hudson gave in for him. He awoke after another half-minute and wanted to fight on:

'I am not beaten – clear out the ring – I can fight for four hours.'

The fight had lasted two hours and 29 minutes. It was recorded as a 77th round finish, but contemporary writers said it was impossible to be absolutely sure because of the crush. By the end they had only five or six square feet in which to fight.

A return was arranged, the details ironed out over several meetings at formal dinners, and after first selecting Warwick, it was eventually settled that Birdham Bridge, just outside Chichester, the capital of Sussex, would be the site, Tuesday, 8 June 1824 the date. People poured out of London to stay either in Chichester itself, or in Bognor, Brighton or Portsmouth. Langan arrived with a black silk handkerchief around his neck, the gift of a lady he met at a local inn. She had offered him a green one, but he refused modestly. 'I am not of importance enough to make it a national affair ... it is merely to decide which is the best man.'

The woman, it is said, told him before they parted: 'You are Irish. Colour is immaterial to a brave man. Glory is your only object. Go, then, and conquer!'

Spring was cool, confident and relaxed, while Langan again seemed in perfect condition. Once more, it was a long, drawn-out contest with high skills on both sides. Gentleman Jackson, acting as 'Commander-In-Chief', was so impressed during round three that he called out: 'Beautiful!'

Spring's sprightliness for a heavyweight made him extremely hard to hit cleanly on the head and more than made up for his light punching. By round seven, Langan was bloodied and groggy, but although Spring went to work far more quickly than in their first fight, the Irishman withstood the blows and battled grimly on. After 45 minutes and 20 rounds it seemed Langan could not last much longer, but appearances deceived. Langan refused brandy, telling his seconds to keep it cool for he might need it later on. And damage to Spring's right hand also meant he could not hit with full force, even though he was able to stay in control, which in turn led to another gruelling war of attrition with Langan's grim determination astonishing even hardened fight watchers.

By the end of round 36 he fell as if exhausted, but told Tom Belcher in his corner: 'I will not give in. I shall win it.'

Belcher had to carry him to the scratch for the 38th, yet he recovered his strength and milled on. By round 47 Belcher was claiming that Spring's hands were so badly damaged that he couldn't hurt a mouse. Langan took brandy and water for the first time. In round 54 Langan had a sudden moment of superiority, but couldn't sustain it and fell like a log from a clean blow in the 56th. Yet again, he recovered and rallied, but there were cries of 'Take him away' as he went down to end round 58. Every round seemed to be his last, and yet he continued to come up to the scratch and try to fight. Jack Randall said at ringside: 'I never saw such a fellow. He'll fight for a week. He don't know when to leave off.'

There became a kind of horrible stalemate, with Langan too tired and groggy to land with a good blow, and Spring's hands so damaged that he could hardly make a fist. Langan seemed angry with his body for not answering his call, and he consistently refused to be taken away by Belcher, who was himself under increasing pressure to rescue him. At the end of round 74, this huge-hearted Dubliner turned away those who were pleading with him to stop: 'I will fight. No one shall take me away.'

By round 76 he was running on instinct alone and he finally went down from an open-handed push to the face. He had fought for an hour and 49 minutes. Even before he left the ring Spring was asked to promise never to fight again because of the damage he had suffered to his hands. He agreed and told Langan as soon as the loser recovered his senses: 'Jack, you and I must be friends to the end of our lives; and anything that is within my power, I will do to serve you.'

Before the crowd dispersed £50 was collected for Langan, which was afterwards increased to £150.

Spring, who complained of bruising from his falls as well as the badly broken hands, was put to bed in the Swan Hotel in Chichester, bled and then lowered into a warm bath. His face had swollen, yet he was cheerful and calm. Langan was given similar treatment at the Dolphin, and complained that his preparations had been disrupted by the journey, but took the defeat well. By the evening, Spring was out of bed. He visited Langan, leaving £10 in his hand, before being cheered out of town the following morning in an open *barouche* in the company of his backer, Mr Sant. Spring, who had been running a pub named the Booth Hall in Hereford, took over the Castle Tavern in Holborn when Tom Belcher gave it up. Spring ran it until his death from heart disease on 20 August 1851, aged 56. He was buried in Norwood cemetery.

Langan enjoyed a successful benefit at the Fives Court in the Haymarket nine days after the second Spring fight, then travelled to Bristol and by steamer to Tenby in Wales, before returning to Ireland to visit his family. A doctor told him a shoulder damaged in his last fight would need a 12-month rest, and he never completely recovered from the injury. In sparring tours with Spring and Peter Crawley, he discovered he could no longer punch properly because of the pain. Langan settled in Liverpool, and ran an inn where:

'... every Irish harvester got two days' free lodging from him ... with plentiful porridge, potatoes and beer, a nightcap of potheen and a straw bed, but had to leave his sickle or shillelagh outside.'

He was a fine story-teller and a good singer, and proved a lively, hard-working and friendly landlord who ran a clean house. He moved on to take bigger premises, which he called St Patrick's, at Clarence Dock in the city and made enough money to retire, when his health began to fail, to a house he bought in

Five Lanes End, Cheshire. When he died on 17 March 1846 – St Patrick's Day – at the age of 47, he was worth £30,000.

Tom Cannon, called the Great Gun of Windsor, claimed the title when Spring retired. The son of a Windsor waterman, he was born at Eton in 1790. He was a good all-round sportsman, who particularly enjoyed cricket and rowing, and earned his wages as a fisherman and a bargeman. In 1814, he was caught fishing in protected waters and fined £5, but didn't bother to pay and left to live in Newbury. Nobody seems to have chased him for the money. He had occasional fights from 1809, when he gave away height and weight to a soldier named Tom Anslow and beat him in a little over half an hour.

Years on, in 1817, he also beat a professional of little ability named Bill 'Dolly' Smith, who also worked as a horse-keeper, at Shirley Common near Windsor. Smith was a strange one: he stood only 5ft 5in tall and scaled 158lbs, and lost almost every fight he had. Cannon didn't compete in the ring again until, after watching Josh Hudson and Jem Ward fight in 1823, he got the taste for it. He issued a public challenge to either man, Hudson accepted and Cannon beat him on 23 June 1824, officially at Yateby in Hampshire, but in a field near Everfield churchyard on the boundaries with Berkshire and Buckinghamshire.

Before the fight Hudson's supporters moved among the ringsiders offering up to 3-1 to Cannon's friends, but found few takers. However, Cannon upset those odds decisively when he outclassed Hudson in 17 rounds taking only 20 minutes. Hudson was fat – when he stripped, somebody compared him to Falstaff – and was blowing even by the second round. Cannon roughed him up, and although Hudson dug as deep as he could, he had made a terrible mistake and knew it.

The supposedly raw novice could fight – and, worse for Hudson, knew how to box. Cannon took several hard blows, but his desire and grit brought him through the rough patches. Hudson could barely put up his hands by the 17th and a blow to the side of the head stretched him out. Hudson challenged him to a return when they met at the Fives Court six days later, and a match was eventually fixed for 23 November 1824 at Warwick Racecourse. Cannon, who stood 5ft 10in and weighed 183lbs, was again in top shape, while Hudson was 20lb lighter than before at 192lbs. Plainly, he had taken the job seriously ... but to his amazement was still not good enough. This time the fight ended in 16 rounds with the man from Windsor cleaning up around £1,000 after betting heavily on himself.

Cannon had an eye closed by the eighth, and blood ran from a gash on his cheek in the 11th, and yet still he won. There wasn't much in the way of science about the way he went to work, but he could fight and box tolerably, and allied to his tremendous determination and fitness, these were attributes enough to see off Hudson. Afterwards, Cannon was ferried to the Regent Hotel in

Cannon v Ward at Warwick in 1825 ... Tom Cannon lost the championship in a ferocious ten-minute fight with Jem Ward of Bow.

Leamington, where he recovered surprisingly quickly, while Hudson was put to bed at the Castle Inn at Warwick.

Cannon claimed the title and at a sparring exhibition at the Fives Court in which he and Hudson re-enacted their Warwick fight, he was billed as 'Champion of England'. He also went on tour, won a 200-yard race with one Squire Smith at Shepperton, but lost at both billiards and wrestling to a Mr Carney, laughing after losing at the latter that he did not understand the game. Plainly, he had a good time, but his claim to the championship was disputed by Jem Ward – and on a scorching day, on 19 July 1825 at Warwick, he lost his title in a ten-minute battle that was terrible in its ferocity and a strange contrast to most of the slow, drawn-out wars of attrition that were a feature of the time. Cannon, who was by then 35, was picked up in the 10th round and slammed against the boards, Ward falling on top of him. Spring, Cannon's second, blew brandy up the champion's nose, but couldn't revive him and 'Squire Osbaldeston pronounced Jem Ward champion of England'. After the fight Ward, who was known as the Black Diamond, was too weak to walk, a condition that cannot have been helped by the local doctor, who bled him straight after the fight. (Squire Osbaldeston was one of the most famous sporting men of his generation, whose memoirs were discovered and published in the 1920s and remain a much sought-after eye-witness account of the age.)

Cannon made money in a stage show at the Coburg Theatre with a piece called 'The Fight at Warwick', but drifted out of contention as a championship contender when he lost to Ned Neale in half an hour at Warfield, Berkshire, in February 1827. After that he retired, aged 36, and was set up in a London tavern, the Castle in Jermyn Street. Although he did good business at the start, his custom drifted away and instead he took a job tending swans. His health eventually failed because of repeated attacks of gout and rheumatism, and depressed by his failure and ill-heath, he shot himself dead on Sunday, 11 July, 1858. He left a widow, who was helped to manage by donations from some of Tom's old boxing friends.

Jem Ward

A clever painter and natural musician who played the flute and fiddle, Jem Ward was also a brilliant boxer who was probably the best of the fighters who followed Tom Spring. His reputation is forever spoiled, however, because of a misguided decision to throw a fight early in his career. Born at Bow on Boxing Day 1800, and the eldest of seven children, he was star of a sparring club in Bromley in Kent when still a teenager. He earned his money then as a coal-whipper, but made what amounts to a professional boxing trial at the Fives Court in January 1822. He passed and went on to beat a moderate performer named Dick Acton in six rounds covering less than a quarter of an hour at Moulsey Hurst in June 1822.

Then he disgraced himself when he plainly took a dive against a man named Abbot, again at Moulsey Hurst four months later. Ward claimed he had been warned 'not to win' when talking to his second Eales during the fight, and eventually even though Abbot could hardly stand, it was Ward who slumped down and then failed to make it to the scratch for the 23rd round. The umpire could not swear to a 'cross', but added that 'there was wrong conduct somewhere'.

Meetings of both the Daffy Club and the Pugilistic Club were held, Ward burst into tears and admitted he had faked his defeat but said he had been told to do it by his backer for a payment of £100. The Pugilistic Club shunned him and he was ostracised for a while, but gradually he was allowed back into the boxing community. When he did return to London he lost to Josh Hudson, but did well enough to be given another chance. This time he was

Jem Ward

impressive in defeating Phil Sampson of Birmingham in 25 rounds and 50 minutes. He was so skilful that some veteran observers said he reminded them of the great Jem Belcher. The general opinion was that if he behaved himself he could go on to become champion.

Tom Cannon beat Josh Hudson to earn recognition as champion, and Ward was ready to issue his own challenges. Jack Langan was his first target, but the Irishman was unable to box because of his shoulder injury. Instead, he fought Phil Sampson again at Perry Lodge, on the estate of the Duke of Grafton near Stony Stratford on Buckinghamshire's northern border with Northamptonshire, on a rainy winter's day, 28 December 1824. Sampson tried, but was outclassed. After 37 minutes and 27 rounds his friends took him away.

Ward was the first champion to receive a Championship belt (Cribb's was a personal ornament) which was strapped around his waist at a benefit for one Harry Holt at the Fives Court, which was in St Martin Street in Leicester Fields, on 22 July 1825, three days after his victory over Cannon.

'I have got it, and I mean to keep it,' Ward said proudly. He also shook hands with Cannon, who said he had been beaten by the heat more than any punches he had taken. Ward wanted to take time off, and four days after receiving his belt he announced his intention to spend a few months on a sparring tour that would make him unavailable for serious combat for seven or eight months.

'In the interim, the various aspirants to the championship may contend with each other, and I shall be happy, at the expiration of the time specified, to accommodate the winner of the main,' he wrote in a letter to *Life In London*.

It was in fact 17 months before he boxed again ... for £100 a side against Peter Crawley of Stoke Newington, on Tuesday 2 January 1827 near Royston Heath in Cambridgeshire. Royston was convenient because in the case of intervention by the law-keepers, there were two county borders near at hand. However, many of the Fancy missed the fight because of confusion over the site. Tom Oliver and Tom Cannon had negotiated an excellent place on private land at Haydon Grange Farm, but Bill Gibbons felt slighted because the choosing of the venue was his job, and decided on Royston Heath. A substantial number, including John Jackson, travelled out of London and descended upon Haydon Grange Farm, only to find nothing happening. Others from the court missed it because they felt it prudent to stay in London to await the imminent death of the Duke of York. (This was Frederick, 'the Grand Old Duke of York' of the nursery rhyme. He was the brother of King George IV.)

Crawley, who was known as Young Rump Steak because he was a butcher, was an 11-5 outsider, and had a slight weight advantage at 180lbs to 175lbs. He was also suffering from a hernia, which almost certainly meant he had to rely exclusively on boxing and ignore the wrestling throws that were such a vital part of the business, but at 26, and after several years of learning to fight, was at his peak. Ward began brilliantly, knocking Crawley down and cutting his right eye with a countering left hand. As he came to scratch for the second, the challenger's eye was lumpy, but he ended a good round with a right hand to the forehead that put Ward on the turf. Ward was dazed and almost unable to see, but his second Josh Hudson shook him and he gathered his senses.

It was a scientific fight with plenty of blocking and stopping, and when Ward broke through Crawley's defences with a right to the body, Crawley stood back and smiled in acknowledgement. The round ended when Ward slipped over on his hands and knees as he tried to avoid a blow. Crawley merrily threatened to hit him on the behind. In the fourth they got down to business, trading punches and bringing loud applause. 'Claret,' reported *Bell's Life*, 'was freely drawn from the conks of each'. When Ward was sent staggering to the ground, the crowd broke through the outer ring and it took time for order to be restored. Both were bleeding from mouth and nose by round five, with Hudson urging the champion on from the corner:

'Fight, Jem! Fight, my boy!'

They went down in a heap, Crawley on top, to end the session. They seemed tired, the blood flowed copiously – and in the seventh it seemed to have turned the champion's way when he threw Crawley heavily with a cross-buttock 'which not only shook Peter, but the very earth on which he fell'. Odds on a Crawley win were offered – and not taken – at 10-1. He was greatly distressed as he came to the scratch, his mouth hanging open, but Ward was also suffering and did not follow up his advantage.

Eventually they began to trade blows again, and it was Ward who seemed the weaker of the two. The ninth was torrid again as, after a short spar, they ignored defence and slammed punches at each other's heads. The end came when both fell, with Crawley again managing to land on top. Crawley smiled as he came up for the 10th and once again they moved around the ring, punching without a break. They punched themselves out, but Crawley somehow kept the left hands eating into Ward's grotesquely battered features. Both men were in a terrible state as they came up for the 11th, but while Ward still tried to force the fight, he was the nearer to exhaustion and when Crawley connected with a heavy left to the mouth, the champion fell flat on his back, his hands on his belly, senseless. His seconds picked him up, but he was unconscious and could not come up again. After 26 raw minutes, it was over. Crawley, as shattered as he was, stood looking at Ward as if allowing his achievement to sink in. He tried to shake hands but Ward was out cold, and eventually the new champion walked to his waiting *chaise*.

As gamblers do after a shock result, one man claimed to have won £530. Some of those who had lost whinged about a fix, but the claims were absurd and not taken seriously. In defeat, Ward had finally freed himself of his reputation as a cheat. He was still unconscious when he was laid to bed at the Red Lion and a doctor said his pulse was very weak. However, at 6 p.m., four and a half hours after he had been knocked out, he came round, immediately recognised his friends at the bedside and complained of a headache.

Once back in London, Ward began to talk of regaining his title. He blamed himself for his defeat, saying he had underestimated Crawley and fought with him instead of being more cautious and boxing in his normal, sensible manner. Two days after the contest, Ward appeared at a benefit for Harry Holt and Ned Baldwin, his face still badly cut, swollen and bruised. However, Crawley was also there – and stunned the Fancy by announcing his retirement, saying fame was his ambition, not money, and his win over Ward had brought him all that he needed. He ploughed his winnings into a pub, the Queen's Head And French Horn, in Duke Street, West Smithfield.

Peter was a popular man and his business was well supported. His father, who was a fine musician, would sing and play there, and generally Crawley's house was well ordered. Like many other fighters, he had to put up with the occasional ridiculous challenge from drunken guests and, even in later life, refused to back down from an insult until an apology was offered. When he refereed a championship fight between William Perry, the Tipton Slasher, and Harry Broome in 1851, he stripped off his coat after Perry, whom he had disqualified, yelled abuse at him. They had to be parted before the old champion attempted to prove he still had enough of his youth left to hand the Black Countryman a lesson! Crawley also found time to teach boxing to amateurs and kept his pub to the end of his life, which came at the age of 64 on 12 March 1865.

Ward had planned to hand over his championship belt to Crawley, but when he heard the retirement speech, he refused, saying he would not give it to a man who had no intention of defending it. He reclaimed the championship and began looking for a suitable opponent. A fight proved difficult to set up, and then Ward was lucky to escape serious injury when he and a 16st sparring partner, Bob Burn, fell headfirst from a ring at the Tennis Court in Windmill Street after a rail (forerunner of the rope) broke. He was fortunate to land on top, and apart from a sprain in the neck was not hurt. This did, however, further delay moves towards making a fight.

Finally, the Fancy met at the Castle Tavern and arranged a match for the championship between Ward and 38-year-old Jack Carter, who was just out of jail after serving a sentence for stealing a £5 note on the London to Oxford coach. Carter's backer pulled out, however, and the fighter himself had to put up a £50 stake for the opportunity. Ward was not amused by the small purse, but realised he needed to box competitively again and the deal was agreed. They fought at Shepperton on 27 May 1828, Ward winning in 17 rounds and 32 minutes. Carter bled from the lip by the second round, was cross-buttocked heavily in the fourth and never really looked like winning. He was groggy by round six, his left eye was shut by the ninth and the other bleeding, and by the 13th there were cries for him to be pulled out. He went down almost as soon as the following rounds began and at the start of the 17th the time-keepers, Tom Spring and Peter Crawley, entered the ring to plead with him to give in. He refused, and even when he was flattened again and the referee joined in the requests for him to stop, Carter said he could fight on. 'There's nought the matter with me,' he said. His seconds, however, knew the truth of it and gave in on his behalf, a decision that met with general approval.

Ward fought for the last time, outclassing Simon Byrne of Ireland before a crowd of 20,000 at Walcote, also written at the time as Woolleycut and Willycuts, three miles out of Stratford-on-Avon, on 12 July 1831. They fought for £200 a side. It seems a halcyon scene now. Imagine the ground wet with morning rain, but with a summer sun shining through. 'The assemblage was immense...waggons and carts which had been collected soon found an abundance of customers.'

Ward came in at 1.10 p.m., accompanied by seconds Peter Crawley and Harry Holt, his colours 'blue and bird's eye'. Byrne, in Irish green and yellow, with Spring and Tom Reynolds in his corner, walked to the ring five minutes later. It took three-quarters of an hour to agree on the referee, but the fight started at four minutes past two. Ward, 5ft 10ins and 173lbs, with not an extra ounce of flesh on his bones, was outweighed by a stone, but Byrne was too fat. Ward controlled the fight from start to finish with lefts to the head. He also used right uppercuts to soften Byrne's resistance. Byrne landed only two or three decent left hand counters in the entire 33 rounds and to the disgust of the crowd, often went down without being hit. Blood poured from his nose and mouth by round 33 and his seconds pulled him out with the clock on 77 minutes. Ward 'gave an active bound and left the ring'.

His career was over – and in his last fight he had 'only exhibited a little blood from his teeth', while poor Byrne was carried bodily to his carriage.

Ward toured America at one time, but no bouts were recorded and he faded from the scene. He lived long, but his last years were spent in the Licensed Victuallers' Asylum off London's Old Kent Road. He was 83 when he died on 3 April 1884.

There were other first rate fighters who drew substantial followings in the 1820s. Ned Neale, mistakenly described as Irish and given the name O'Neil, was actually from what *Pugilistica* described as 'the pleasant village of Streatham in Surrey'. Born 'of humble but respectable' parents in March 1805, he fought from 1822 until he retired in 1828 to take on the Rose and Crown at Norwood. At his peak he was one of the best of his generation who beat men like Edward Baldwin, also known as White-Headed Bob, in 1824, Jem Burn and Phil Sampson of Birmingham. Attempts to match him with Jem Ward came to nothing, and he lost a second fight with Baldwin in 1828 only a month after they fought an 84-round draw (which was curtailed by the magistrate).

His last bout before retiring was a one-sided thrashing of an Exeter publican named Roche, who was more wrestler than boxer, at North Chapel cricket ground in Sussex, 44 miles from the centre of London. Roche, who had completed his training at headquarters in the 'charming retreat of Edmonton', had a big reputation in his part of the country but turned out to be considerably older than expected and flabby at 196lbs. Neale was in perfect shape at 170lbs and after 30 minutes of uneven fare, he invited Roche to stop. The Devonian was only too pleased. Badly battered around the face, he was taken to a nearby inn and bled. Only one of his pre-fight 'friends' remained with him, and whoever this man of honour was, he paid the doctor a shilling to perform the bleeding.

After a spell of public baiting, Neale came out of retirement to fight his tauntor, Young Dutch Sam, at Ludlow in 1829. Although still only 24, he had endured several long struggles and was already fading. He lost in 71 rounds and 101 minutes... and in a rematch in 1831 was beaten again. His last fight was another defeat, this time against Tom Gaynor, whom he had dealt with decisively several years earlier. Neale was an honest, hard-working man who kept the Rose and Crown until his death in 1846.

Jem Burn

Jem Burn, who lost to Neale after a brave struggle lasting six minutes short of an hour at Moulsey Hurst in December 1824, was from a Darlington fighting family. His two uncles were both prize-fighters and although as a boy he was apprenticed to a skinman – a skinner of animals, popularly known as a 'skiver' – his eventual destiny was not hard to predict. He found his way to London, to the Rising Sun in Windmill Street, Piccadilly, to be exact, where his uncle Ben held court, and was welcomed into the city's fighting community. Early sparring sessions showed he had talent and some went so far as to predict he would be champion one day, especially after he outclassed an Irishman known only as Big O'Neal at Chertsey Bridge near Staines in 1824. The end sounds heart-rending:

'(Round) 31. O'Neal was quite abroad – he could not see his opponent, and, in making a hit at the air, stumbled forward on the ground.

'32, and last. On time being called, O'Neal left his second's knee, and turned away from the scratch. He was completely blind. Over in fifty minutes. Langan gave in for him.'

Burn's display so delighted one Sir Bellingham Graham that he gave the fighter five sovereigns. His progress was halted by his defeat by Neale, however, and he never reached the top. Phil Sampson beat him, and although he defeated Pat Magee from Liverpool, he won and lost against Ned Baldwin and then lost to Neale a second time. He had married a prize-fighter's daughter, Caroline Watson, in 1826 and settled to a life of a sporting man at the Queen's Head in Windmill Street. Pugilistica records almost surreptitiously:

'Many an M.P. slipped away from St Stephen's, and many a smart guardsman from a Belgravian dinner-party, to give a look in at Jolly Jem's snuggery; an inner sanctum, communicating with the sparring-room, and set apart for "those I call gentlemen," as Jem emphatically phrased it.'

Burn's mantelpiece carried the following inscription:

'Scorning all treacherous feud and deadly strife,
The dark stiletto and the murderous knife,
We boast a science sprung from manly pride,
Linked with true courage and to health allied -
A noble pastime, void of vain pretence -
The fine old English art of self-defence.'

In his later years Burn moved to the Rising Sun in Air Street, Piccadilly, and kept an equally happy house. Eventually he was confined increasingly by gout and died of a stomach illness in 1862.

Ned Baldwin, White-Headed Bob, was from Ludlow in Herefordshire. He moved to London to fight when nearly 20 years old, and learned his trade well enough to become a teacher as well as a first rate exponent inside the ring. He was considered better than Jem Burn but not as talented as Ned Neale – and put his defeat in his first fight with Burn down to not having fully recovered from measles, which had struck him low for most of 1826. There was probably little to choose between them. Although Baldwin won the return fight, it took him 85 rounds. The contemporary report is chilling:

'... Jem fell at the stake, completely doubled up from exhaustion. Belcher tried to bring his man to the scratch, but he could not stand, and 'time' being called, Bob was proclaimed the conqueror, in exactly one hour and a half, amidst the warm congratulations of his friends. Jem remained for some time unconscious, while Bob stood up shaking hands with his admirers, and was carried off in triumph.

'Belcher was, of course, dreadfully mortified. He accused Jem of laziness, for not going in to finish before; and charged the time-keeper with calling time too quickly at last, when Jem was distressed, while he gave additional time to Bob, when he most wanted it. This was denied; and, in fact, the irregularities in time-calling, as we have already stated, were not attributable to the time-keeper, but to those who assumed his prerogative, and thereby created much confusion. Some time elapsed before Jem could be removed from the ring, but on comparing punishment, the odds were fearfully against Bob, who, we think, was more punished than in his last battle. His wiry frame, however, added to the uncommon pains taken by Curtis and Ward, brought him through, and, in fact, as it were, he performed a miracle.'

Baldwin had lost to Neale in 1824 after a spell of loose living – when they were first matched, Baldwin's backer withdrew him because he felt the fighter was not well enough to box. Their last meeting in 1828 was White-Headed Bob's last fight, after which he took a benefit at the Tennis Court and moved into the Coach and Horses in St Martin's Lane. He was indisciplined and reckless, lived life beyond its limits, and was dead of some form of excess at the age of 28.

Young Dutch Sam was the ring name of Samuel Evans, undoubtedly one of the finest fighters of this or any other time. He did not box for the championship, but was unbeaten in nine years from 1825 until 1834. Born on 30 January 1808, he was the son of the ring genius of the previous generation Dutch Sam, whose death in 1816 left the boy more or less homeless. After living on his wits for the rest of his childhood, he worked for a baker and then a printer and by the age of 17 was a prize-fighter. He outclassed Ned Stockman for a £20 purse in July 1825, emerging without so much as a scratch in 36 one-sided minutes, and expressed surprise when he was declared the winner. 'Is it over?' he asked. 'Why, I'm not hurt in the least. I could fight an hour longer.'

From then on, he moved up in class steadily and beat everyone who agreed to take him on: Harry Jones, known as The Sailor Boy; Tom Cooper, The Gipsy; Jack Cooper, The Slashing Gipsy; Dick Davis, The Pet of Manchester; and others. After beating Tom Gaynor in 17 rounds near Andover in Hampshire on 24 June 1834, no matches were made for him in the next four years.

He was to have made a comeback in 1838, but was arrested and bailed for acting as a second to his friend Owen Swift in a tragic fight following which Swift's opponent, 'Brighton' Bill Phelps, died. Evans fled the country and stayed in Paris, where one Jack Adams was attempting to run a boxing academy. It was strictly against French law – and Evans found himself arrested again, and this time, although once again absent when the hearing was held, was sentenced to 13 months in jail for the simple act of taking part in a sparring session with Swift. He returned to England and was arrested, slung into Hereford jailhouse and stayed there until a jury found him Not Guilty. However, there was also a little matter of assaulting a policeman, a case which had hung over him from earlier in the year, resulting from a melee at the Royal Standard pub in Piccadilly. The policeman, apparently, interrupted a late night drinking session and Evans flattened him. For this he got three months. When he emerged from jail, he attempted to settle down. By now 32, he married a publican's daughter and took over, first, the Black Lion in Vinegar Yard, Drury Lane, and then the Old Drury Tavern in Brydges Street, Covent Garden. He tried hard, but his health failed and he died of tuberculosis on 4 November 1843, aged 36. He was buried at Kensal Green, in his wife's family vault. One disapproving obituary, while doffing a due cap to his abilities as a boxer, regretted his ability to live on the edge.

> 'His temper was cheerful, and he possessed a flow of natural humour which rendered him an agreeable companion in social circles. A reckless disregard to his own interests, and an unhappy disposition to mix in those scenes which constitute what is called 'Life In London', and in which he was often the companion of sprigs of nobility, to whose wild vagaries he was but too much inclined to pander, led him into scrapes from which he had some difficulty in escaping .... He died calm and collected, surrounded by several of his friends, who while they pitied could not but condemn the headlong folly which had distinguished his passage through his short but eventful existence.'

That, I think, is an obituary worth dying for!

There were other leading men. Tom Gaynor, the Bath Carpenter, fought for ten years. His last battle was against Young Dutch Sam in 1834, by which time he was chronically ill. He was dead before the year was out. Alec Reid, known as the Chelsea Snob, boxed throughout the 1820s, and Tom Brown, who answered to Big Brown, actually went so far as to claim the championship when Tom Spring retired. Phil Sampson was a button-maker in Birmingham before he took up prize-fighting in 1819, and did so well that he stuck at his new trade for the next dozen years. He fought most of the best including, twice, Jem Ward, but overstepped the mark when he threw a punch at Tom Spring in a booth at Epsom races. A row flared up, and the next night Sampson challenged him to a fight for £300 a side. Spring accepted, but Sampson, by then realising the stupidity of his behaviour, apologised. They shook hands, broke open a bottle and drank themselves into friendship.

Dick Curtis from Southwark was a supreme lightweight, who stood 5ft 6in and scaled only 126lbs – a featherweight by today's standards. There was also Barney Aaron of Aldgate, and Jack Perkins, a 140lbs man who was the first to beat Curtis.

Even as the 1820s drew to a close, the decline of prize-fighting was accelerating. The sport has always had its opponents. To those involved, the problem was probably barely noticeable at first – when fights did not draw big crowds, or command space in newspapers, it may have seemed a temporary thing, a lull between heroes of the stature of Belcher, Cribb and Spring and the next great man, whoever he would be. But slowly the years rolled on and pugilism, heroless and increasingly disreputable, went out of fashion.

Fights happened, of course, and the Championship of England passed on from fist to fist, but the decline was slow and painful. As boxing had always relied on the mood of the country, the mood of the country depended to a large extent on the character of its monarch, far more so then than in the 20th century. And Queen Victoria, who ascended to the throne as a young woman in 1837, was to gaze over the nation in her austere, disapproving way for more than six decades. Her personality reflected perfectly the serious mood of the new moralists. Boxing could not be stopped, but it could be heartily disapproved of. It could be driven into the unfathomable depths of society, into the places where supposedly respectable men and women would not walk, or if they did, would never admit it. Boxing, in other words, returned to its own.

7

SLOW, PAINFUL DECLINE

James Burke

By 1833, and in the wake of the retirement of Jem Ward, James Burke, a squat, muscular 22-year-old Thames waterman claimed to be champion. Already, however, the game was a poor imitation of what it had once been, and its popularity nosedived even further because of a major ring tragedy. Burke, who was from St Giles, boxed Simon Byrne near Ascot Racecourse – and the Irish challenger, who had previously lost a marathon struggle with Jem Ward and had beaten Phil Sampson of Birmingham in another terribly hard fight, died without regaining consciousness after being knocked out in 98 torrid rounds lasting three hours and 16 minutes. The irony was not lost on the Fancy. Only three years earlier Byrne had been arrested for manslaughter following the death of an opponent, Sandy M'Kay.

Burke was a natural entertainer who dressed and made-up like a clown to charm the crowd before the fight. He was also partially deaf and struggled under a speech impediment – hence his plain nickname 'Deaf 'Un'. In the ring, he accumulated experience and was cunning enough, but relied heavily on his strength and fitness to compensate for the limitations in his skill. In round 19 against Byrne he was on the point of defeat, but his second revived him by biting clean through his ear. At the start of the 98th round Byrne's handlers carried him to the scratch mark, but he was unconscious and fell to the ground as soon as they let him go. He was probably already lapsing into a coma. Three days later he was dead.

Burke was cleared of blame, but opposition to pugilism increased and he travelled to the United States of America, only to find hostility even more marked. When he did find a place 'uncivilised' enough to permit prize-fighting, he was not expected to win: in 1837 he fought Irish-born Samuel

James Burke

O'Rourke, who had been his major sparring partner, in New Orleans. In the build-up O'Rourke was adopted by the local Irish community.

After three rounds Burke let fly at O'Rourke's second Mick Carson, who had apparently pushed him and threatened to 'slit his gizzard', and the mob broke down the ring. The Englishman fled for his life on a horse, armed with a knife handed to him as he fled. O'Rourke was paraded as the winner through the streets of New Orleans, where his drunken supporters rampaged in an orgy of violence that ended with the mayor calling out the militia, the Washington Guard. Burke eventually reached the safety of New York, where he had friends and where prize-fighting was more established. The incident was reportedly grimly in the *Charleston Courier:*

> 'For some two or three days past, large numbers of our population have been thrown into considerable excitement by handbills posted in bar-rooms and at the corners of streets that a pugilistic combat was to take place yesterday between two prize-fighters, Deaf Burke, an Englishman, and O'Rourke, an Irishman. The fight took place at about one o'clock, at the forks of the Bayou Road. Some two or three rounds were fought, to the particular advantage of neither of the belligerents. The second of O'Rourke, happening to come within hitting distance of Burke, received a severe blow from the deaf man. This was the signal for a general scrimmage in which the Irishmen joined O'Rourke, attacking Burke and his friends with fists and sticks .... Burke was followed by a crowd of Irishmen with shillelaghs, dray-pins, whips and other weapons. A well-wisher, seeing him pass, handed him a bowie knife, and another gave him a horse, on which he escaped to New Orleans. The man who handed Burke the knife was cruelly beaten by friends of O'Rourke, and we fear killed.'

On 21 August 1837 Burke beat Tom O'Connell in the tenth round of a less eventful battle at Hart's Island, near New York, which attracted the attention of sportsmen from as far away as Baltimore and Albany, as well as, grudgingly, a writer from *The New York Herald.* He justified his interest with a gravity and pomp that no doubt served adequately the consciences of the literate members of his city's population:

> 'Although we regret and detest such exhibitions, our duty as chroniclers compels us to make public what otherwise we should bury in oblivion... The British people are particularly fond of this exhibition, and there are some good consequences attending it. Three or four do not fall upon and beat a single individual. The single man when struck down by his opponent is permitted to rise and put himself, as it were, in something like a state of equilibrium ... and when the party combating cries 'Hold, enough!' no bowie knife enters his vitals. With all its disadvantages, therefore, and demoralizing tendency, it may be doubted whether the spirit emanating from it may not be productive of benefit among the lower classes.'

No doubt, this kind of moral wrangling passed over the head of Burke, who had long ago sorted out for himself why he wanted to fight for a living. Soon afterwards, he returned to England, and reclaimed the championship.

Big fights were not easily set up. Once Burke was lined up to defend his title against Bendigo, whose real name was William Thompson, but the match fell through. In the meantime the champion appeared in pantomime and stage tableaux, until the deal was finally clinched for the Bendigo fight in the Leicestershire village of Heather in February, 1839. Bendigo, a left-hander from Nottingham who fought out of the right-foot-forward southpaw stance, was too fast, too clever and too able a wrestler for the out-of-condition Burke, who was eventually disqualified for butting in the tenth round, after 24 minutes. The offence was relatively rare in those days, but is plainly reported:

'10, and last (round). The Deaf Un, greatly distressed, still came up with a determination to produce a change if he could by in-fighting. He rushed into his man, hitting left and right, but receiving heavy jobs in return. He forced Bendigo with his back against the ropes, and, as he had him in that position, deliberately butted him twice, when both went down in the struggle for the fall. Jem Ward immediately cried 'Foul!' and appealed to the referee, who refused to give any decision till properly appealed to by the umpires. He stepped into the ring, where he was followed by the umpires, when he was again appealed to, and at once declared that Burke had butted, and that therefore Bendigo was entitled to the victory – a judgment in which, it is due to say, the umpire of the Deaf Un, although anxious to protect his interests, declared in the most honourable manner he must concur .... With regard to the butting, of which we have no doubt, our impression is that it was done intentionally, and for the express purpose of terminating the fight in that way rather than by prolonging it to submit to additional punishment and the mortification of a more decided defeat ...'

In modern boxing parlance, Burke swallowed it! In the build-up to the fight Bendigo had narrowly escaped serious injury or worse when a storm wrecked the house in which he was lodging in Crosby near Liverpool. He clambered out of his bedroom window only ten minutes before the roof fell in.

Burke, who had been suffering pain from a knee injury for some time before the Bendigo fight, did not have the necessary stamina to undergo a serious contest and so fouled out. Afterwards, he returned in good health to Appleby and then moved on to the village of Atherstone in Warwickshire, where 'football kicking' was taking place. He stayed the night in Coventry and caught the mail train to London the next morning. He was not badly hurt, but his arms were a mass of bruises, relics of his attempts to block Bendigo's blows. Bendigo was back in Nottingham by nightfall, claiming the championship, although *Bell's Life* made its position plain:

'He has to conquer Caunt before he can be proclaimed Champion of England.'

Caunt was the giant Ben Caunt from Hucknall, a hamlet west of Nottingham, who was by then living in London and with whom Bendigo had a celebrated series of battles. When Bendigo beat Burke, he had already won and lost against Caunt in 1835 and 1838. In spite of their rivalry, they would not meet again until 1845.

Meanwhile, Burke fought Nick Ward in 1840, and two days after it ended because of a mob invasion he was deemed the loser on a foul. This defeat cost him all claims to the title, while Ward, the younger brother of the old champion Jem and a scientific boxer of considerable ability, was catapulted into contention. Ward was from St George's in London's East End, born on April Fool's Day, 1811, and a product of the sparring schools of the capital. Frankly, he preferred sparring with gloves to raw action and had disgraced himself in an 1835 bout with one Sambo Sutton at Finchley by quitting in the 12th round. Today we would probably acknowledge Ward's concerns as perfectly sensible, but in his own time he was scorned for 'lack of bottom'. Or as Bell's Life put it, 'he has a very strong antipathy to punishment which can be avoided'.

Ward's first fight was an 18-round win over John Lockyer at Moulsey Hurst in February 1835. Then three months later came the defeat in a hastily arranged match with Sutton, an eccentric character whose party piece was to stand on his head and perform some kind of dance-and-song routine for an hour while consuming copious amounts of whatever alcoholic inspiration was closest to hand. After walking out on the fight, Ward admitted he was not cut out to be a fighting man and returned to the sparring houses. He did not box again competitively until 1839, when he scraped past Jem Bailey, an Irishman from Norwich, in a fight that was held in two separate places because of police interference. It ended after a total of 33 rounds in Woking when Bailey was ruled to have hit Ward while he was on the ground. Bailey was furious and attempted to continue, but Ward would not retaliate, removed his colours from the cornerpost and claimed his 'triumph'.

This background was hardly one to inspire confidence in his chances against Burke, even though the Deaf Un was by now suffering from a chronic knee problem. Nevertheless, at Lillingstone Lovell, a village west of Stony Stratford in Buckinghamshire, on the private estate of one Colonel Delappe, Burke and Ward met on a chilly, rainy day on 22 September 1840. Shortly before 1 p.m. Burke cast his hat into the ring and claimed victory by forfeit because Ward had not arrived at the appointed time, or as he said 'in the absence of Young Nick, not Old Nick'. For those who weren't raised in the fear of Old Nick, he's the Devil himself.

Ward and his seconds and friends were 15 minutes late because they took a one-horse cart, which made painfully slow progress through the wet, marshy byeways leading to the site. Finally, however, the fight began with Ward a surprisingly sound favourite at 4-7. Ward looked in tremendous shape, while Burke was also in a better state than when he had lost to Bendigo. The former champion wore green and white breeches made out of the cloth of the 'drawers' he had used in most of his previous 15 wins in the prize ring. Physically, they were well matched with Ward at about 178lbs, probably seven or eight pounds heavier. As always Burke smiled as the contest opened, while the younger, unproven man was more tense and serious. Burke took his time, aware of Ward's long left leads and picking them off with his arms as they came. 'It won't do, Nick,' he grinned.

Although Ward bloodied Burke's cheek, the first round lasted 37 boring minutes, and as *Bell's Life* recorded, 'excited general displeasure from its want of animation'. Other pugilists were calling out their complaints. Jem Burn asked for a pillow, and Tommy Roundhead yelled at Burke to get on with it because he had a leg of mutton ordered for 11 p.m. The moans were ignored. Burke bled from the mouth and Ward a little from an ear, and by the time they had been fighting for 50 minutes the crowd's irritation was increasing.

'Why don't you go and fight?' came one call.

'I'm ready,' said Burke. 'Why don't he come?'

Ward wouldn't 'come' because he knew that the longer the fight lasted, the better his chances. Burke's knee was not up to a long, tough struggle – and Jem Ward called to his little brother: 'The day's long enough, take your time, Nick.'

At one point in round three, Ward dropped his hands, stood off, scratched his head and rubbed his chest. He fought in flurries, then simply moved Burke around and kept him using his leg. By round five, the tactics were beginning to work. Burke 'was evidently distressed and not firm on his pins'. The old champion had a cut on an eyebrow by round six, and by the eighth his left eye was swollen. By the 11th round, two hours had elapsed, and at last something went right for Burke – he cracked a right hand on Ward's nose and bloodied it. Maybe because of a sudden onset of hail and rain from the 12th, the fight at last opened up and Burke had the worst of it, until in the 17th round he was thrown into the ropes. They propped him up, but Ward hit him with heavy right hands until he went down, with his friends yelling for a foul.

The umpires disagreed, and Burke was picked up and put on his second's knee, while it was sorted out. The crowd had rushed forward and in the crush there was considerable confusion, with claims that Ward had gone over to his opponent's corner and begun an 'overtime' fight, but if it happened it died down and eventually the referee was produced. He ruled that Ward had won fairly.

Three years later, flat-nosed and with his face bearing the scars of his trade, Burke beat Bob Castles at Rainham Ferry, Essex, when he was ill with the tuberculosis which killed him, with a little help from drink, on 8 January, 1845. He was still only 35.

Ward fought Caunt on 23 February 1841 for £100 a side at Crookham Common near Newbury. A thin layer of snow covered the frost-hard ground and a chill east wind swept across as the crowd gathered and the fighters stripped. Ward, as usual, was serious and quiet, while Caunt, a 4-5 favourite, was relaxed, even nonchalant and openly happy. A 6ft 2½in, 15st giant, he was from a boxing background. His father had been employed as servant and sparring partner by Lord Byron. Unlike Burke, who was content to let Ward go at his own pace, Caunt bundled forward straightaway and made him fight. It was a much better affair with Ward using all his speed and ring cunning and Caunt swinging his heavy blows and attempting to 'give him the benefit of a Nottinghamshire hug'. But to the frustration of the crowd, it ended in only the seventh round when Caunt, who 'came up fresh as a sucking bull' at the start of it, clouted Ward twice on the side of the head after Nick had slipped to his knees to avoid fighting on the inside. The foul, claimed for the blow struck while Ward was down, was allowed, and the referee quoted both Broughton's Rules and the new London Prize Ring Rules to put a stop to the arguments of Caunt's backers.

In spite of the disappointing ending, the broadsheet ballad celebrated the event as if it were another Cribb-Molineaux. So when did salesmen ever worry about minor details like facts? The ballad ended with the gloriously rousing chorus:

> 'Yet hurrah for the Ring and the bunch of fives!
> Like a giant refresh'd the Ring revives,
> It awakens again to vigorous life
> To scare the assassin and crush the knife:
> Then welcome to earth as the flowers in spring
> Be the glory renew'd of the Fighting Ring,
> And over each British boxer brave
> Long may the banner of fair play wave.'

The Prize Ring Rules, produced in 1838, were little more than an expansion of those drawn up by Broughton. They insisted that a man must walk to the scratch-line unaided, rather than be placed there by his seconds, which put a stop to men who were unable to fight being allowed to take further punishment. This came five years after the ring tragedy involving

Burke and Byrne when the latter was placed by his seconds on the scratch when those closest to the action suspected he was still unconscious. The new rules also stopped spiked boots, and the list of fouls was explained more clearly. For example, they catered officially for the disqualification of fighters who went down without being hit. While this had been the practice for some time, it had not been considered a factor when Broughton's Rules were agreed in 1741. Specific problems appertaining to outdoor fights – for example, what happened when darkness fell and the bout was still in progress – were also incorporated.

Ben Caunt

A rematch between Caunt and Ward, whose claim to be considered champion was best of all, was inevitable. And within a week it was agreed in principle at the Black Lion pub, run by Young Dutch Sam in Vinegar Yard, Brydges Street, off Drury Lane. The fight went off on farmland belonging to a Mr Pratt at Long Marston on the Warwickshire side of the border with Oxfordshire on 11 May 1841, less than three months after the wintry fight at Crookham Common. The Fancy descended on the scene, most finding it easier to walk than take carts and horses along primitive tracks and roads. Among those in Caunt's corner, which was led by Tom Spring, was his cantankerous, aged uncle, Ben Butler, described in *Pugilistica* as 'a man well stricken in years, and a cross-grained old curmudgeon to boot'! As in the first match, Caunt was smiling and chatting happily as the preparations took their course. Ward had the great lightweight Dick Curtis for a counsellor, with another top man, Harry Holt. Caunt was unusually light at 202lbs, and was suspected of having over-trained, even though he had needed time off when he turned his ankle on a stone while out walking.

But while Caunt had no spare flesh at all, Ward was surprisingly heavy at 188lbs, which led to rumours that he had not prepared himself properly. Before the fight, a subscription among the followers of the Prize Ring in London had raised enough to provide a new leather and purple velvet championship belt to be presented to the winner, which would then be passed down from champion to champion. Presumably, Jem Ward had kept the old one as his own. When the belt was presented, Caunt looked at his opponent and said: 'This is mine, Nick.'

Ward, as always a cautious man, would say only: 'I hope the best man may win it and wear it.'

Before the fight began, both smiled, Ward a little more abstractedly, and the pattern was pretty much the same as first time around with Caunt barging forward when he could and attempting to use his strength and punching power, with Ward basing everything on what was probably a left jab. This time there was no early, controversial finish. Caunt was too good, too strong and too much of a natural fighter for Ward, who grew increasingly negative and timid as the rounds went by. Ward's skill merely prolonged the end until the 35th round. *Bell's Life*:

'Ward was kidded up once more by his second and bottle-holder, but it was clear that all the King's horses and all the King's men could not draw him to the scratch with anything like a determination to protract the combat. Caunt let fly right and left at his mug, and down he went for the last time. His brother ran to him, but it was all up; and as the only excuse for such a termination to the battle, Nick pretended that his ribs were broken ... Caunt was thus proclaimed the conqueror, and 'The Champion of England', amidst a general cheer and expressions of contempt towards Ward – so strongly emphasised that the usual collection for the losing man was omitted by Holt, who shook a hat with a few halfpence he had himself dropped into it, and then put them in his pocket with a laugh. We examined the supposed fracture in his ribs, but could discover nothing beyond severe contusions ... Nick was immediately conveyed to his omnibus, where he became prostrate in mind and body, exciting but little sympathy in the breasts of the general body of spectators. The fight lasted 47 minutes.'

After having the belt strapped around his waist, Caunt vaulted the 4ft 6in ropes, went to see Ward and exchanged compliments with his brother Jem, and then raced 'a Corinthian' across a stretch of ploughed land for the prize of a bottle of wine!

Ward retired after that disgrace, ran pubs in Liverpool and London, until he died suddenly at the King's Head in Compton Street, Soho, aged only 38. He suffered some kind of lung failure.

Ben Caunt

Ben Caunt was born on 22 March 1815 in Hucknall Torkard, near Nottingham. While some said he was originally a navvy, he always claimed to have begun his working life as a gamekeeper. Certainly, he was an excellent shot. He was only 20 when he fought Bendigo for the first time near Appleby House, on the Ashbourne Road halfway between Nottingham and Birmingham. Bendigo conceded five inches in height and more than three stones, but had moves slick enough to overcome the disadvantages. For his part, Caunt was strong, determined and courageous, but had nothing like the skill needed to deal with a crafty, artful dodger like Bendigo, who scored in fast bursts and then dropped from the first light punch he took. At the end of the 22nd round, the bleeding, embarrassed and thoroughly racked-off Caunt ran over to Bendigo's corner, yelled 'Wilt thou stand up and fight fair, thou damned hound?', and sent him and his second sprawling on the turf with a single back-hander. Caunt was disqualified.

It was a hollow victory, but it attracted a good deal of publicity. And by the time they fought again in 1838, Caunt was 23 years old and much wiser in the ways of the prize-fighting world. He beat the popular Nottinghamshire man William Butler in August 1837 and another giant named Boneford three months later. Bendigo had also been winning, beating in turn Bill Brassey of Bradford, Young Langan of Liverpool and Bill Looney. The match was finally made for 3 April 1838 and sited at Skipwith Common, four miles outside Selby in Yorkshire. Bendigo stayed at the White Swan in Askern, while Caunt was accommodated at the Hawke Arms, about two miles further up the road that ran between Doncaster and York. The sporting crowds sweeping up from London and Nottingham dismayed the unsuspecting locals. A story is told that one old lady asked what the fuss was about and was told there had been a rebellion in West Riding and they had all been driven across the River Ouse for sanctuary. The ringmaster, Grear, actually found a place too remote, on a riverbank well off the track. Thousands who had made the long trek missed the fight because they couldn't find it!

This time Bendigo and Caunt slogged it out for 75 rounds, once interrupted by a magistrate who, when completely ignored, gave up and left. Caunt's left eye was closed in the first round by a southpaw left, yet they fought on for another 74. At one time Caunt claimed the fight on a foul, appealing that Bendigo had kicked him as he lay on the ground. This was not allowed, and Bendigo seemed to have the edge when he slipped over in round 75 just as Caunt rushed forward. He was deemed to have gone down deliberately without taking a blow, and this time Caunt's claim for a foul was upheld. It was a tame way to finish and Bendigo's supporters claimed he slipped by accident because of the new rule restricting the use of adequate spikes on the boot. Caunt refused to go on, and when he tried to leave on a horse, was pulled off it. Eventually, with the help of his own fans, he was able to leave on foot. Badly battered and bruised from the 80-minute battle, he was forced to walk the four miles to Selby, where his injuries were tended.

* * *

William Thompson (Bendigo)

Bendigo was one of triplets, nicknamed Shadrach, Meshach and Abednego – hence Bendigo – after the Biblical story of Daniel In The Lion's Den. They were the youngest of 21 children, born to a redoubtable Nottingham woman on 11 October 1811. In later life Mrs Thompson had a habit of bringing down her weighty fist on the bar of her local pub and declaring that in her triplets she had the greatest mechanic, the greatest fool and the greatest fighter in England. Mothers have a right to be biased, but I wonder what the middle one did to be condemned so utterly!

The Thompsons had a tough time. They were raised in the workhouse following the death of Mr Thompson. Young William emerged to sell oysters on the streets of Nottingham, and also spent some time in a factory. For fun, and subsequently for extra money, he also boxed. He had an engaging, extrovert personality, and always attracted good crowds, boxing from 1832, when he was still only 20. By the time of his first fight with the novice Caunt, he was 23 and had come through around a dozen battles. He continued to box regularly, and even after losing the rematch with Caunt, claimed to be champion of England on the grounds that James Burke was out of the country and the second Caunt verdict was an injustice. When he beat Burke in Leicestershire in 1839, Bendigo's argument was strengthened, but he was then forced into temporary retirement by a freak accident to his knee-cap when giving a public exhibition of acrobatics. He fell badly when somersaulting.

Caunt beat Bill Brassey, otherwise known as John Leechman, at Six Mile Bottom near Newmarket in 101 rounds on October 26, 1840. Four years

William Thompson

earlier Brassey had lost 'a severe contest of 52 rounds' with Bendigo on the Doncaster road nine miles out of Sheffield. Caunt then lost to Nick Ward on a foul, which gave Ward his reason to a serious championship claim, but beat him in a return, and toured America, giving exhibitions. He refused to fight Charles Freeman, who stood anything from 6ft 6in to 7ft tall depending on the source, even for a purse of $10,000, but instead brought the American home as his protege. Then Bendigo, by now fit again and with the backing of the old champion Jem Ward, came out of retirement, disputing Caunt's claim with typical fervour.

Bendigo and Caunt, who was by now the landlord of the Coach and Horses in St Martin's Lane and was supported by Tom Spring, met for the third time near Stony Stratford, Buckinghamshire, on 9 September 1845. Bendigo won on a foul in the 93rd round. They drew a tremendous crowd, as one broadsheet balladeer recalled, probably within 24 hours:

'On the ninth day of September
Eighteen hundred and forty five,
From London down to Nottingham
The roads were all alive;
Oh! such a sight was never seen,
Believe me it is so,
Tens of thousands went to see the fight,
With Ben Caunt and Bendigo.'

Caunt trained in Barnet, shedding 42lb from the 238lbs he scaled when going about his day-to-day business in the pub, while Bendigo worked ferociously under the guiding eye of Jem Ward at Crosby, near Liverpool. The supporters of both men descended on the sleepy station at Wolverton. After being refused permission to hold the fight at Stony Stratford, they moved over the border to Lillingstone Lovell on the border of Buckinghamshire and Northamptonshire, which is close to where the Silverstone motor racing circuit now stands. The atmosphere was ugly even before the fight began at 3.30 p.m. on a blazing afternoon – Bendigo's rowdier fans ignored the 24-foot outer rope and broke through to the edge of the 12-foot ring, and were allowed to stay. (In the 'old', respectable days, they would have been forcibly removed.) The fight itself was the usual fare between these two: Caunt impassively plodding in, trying to get close enough to use his strength to slow and weaken Bendigo, who flitted in and out, around him, snapping away like a terrier, then dropping to the ground whenever he was clipped on the head or body, always taking care not to absorb too solid a whack.

As it wore on, the inner ring became so crowded, it ceased to exist in any effective way. One of Caunt's supporters even lashed out at Bendigo – and Tom Spring, in Caunt's corner, took a crack from a stick in the hands of one of the northern fans. In round 85, after which two hours had elapsed, the referee, the famous old sporting gentleman, Squire George Osbaldeston, was forced to take refuge from the mob inside the fighting ring itself. Only pleas from Jem Ward persuaded them to let him resume his position. The Nottingham supporters seemed to have been the main trouble-makers and ringside reports illustrate a scene of frightening confusion with blows from fist and club being launched almost indiscriminately as the bout continued. In round 92 Bendigo struck Caunt below the beltline and the big man crumpled to the earth. Osbaldeston said he had not seen the punch land, and ruled that the fight continue.

With Bendigo's fans in increasingly angry mood, it ended dubiously in the 93rd round. Caunt floored Bendigo, but as he returned to his seconds for the interval, the Nottingham man jumped up and raced after him. Caunt sat down, plainly under the impression the round was over – and immediately Bendigo's seconds, Ward and a colourful character known as Holy Land Pink (presumably because he lived in the area of Aldgate in east London known as Holy Land) appealed for a foul on the grounds that Caunt had gone down without being hit. By now Osbaldeston wanted no more of the dreadful situation he had put himself in and readily agreed that Bendigo had won, upon which the new 'champion of England' was carried away in celebration. News of the anarchic nature of the fight was greeted with horror by pugilistic fraternity and society alike. Osbaldeston, who said he regretted ever having anything to do with the day's events, washed his hands of it and showed no interest whatsoever in altering his verdict, which therefore was deemed to stand. *Bell's Life*, the major literary supporter of the Prize Ring, went so far as to call it 'a disgraceful and disgusting exhibition ... a blow has been given to the boxing school from which it can never recover'.

The *Illustrated London News* of September 27, 1845, set down the general tone of disgust:

'For years the practice of pugilism has been one revolting to mankind, degrading to all the honourable and honest feelings of human nature. For years it has ceased to receive the countenance of gentlemen, save of the few who hoped, by their tolerations, to rescue it from the fat that was closing around it. At last it has passed its climax. A recent exhibition – with an illusion (sic) to which we will not pollute our page – has placed the Ring in a position to damage the character of any man who shall hereafter be known to endure a prize fight. We heartily rejoice that the crisis is come and over. We believe the system called Sporting has materially served the national character – we believe that it has ministered to, as well as served, the manliness of teste and pursuit for which the citizens of Great Britain are everywhere distinguished, and we are right glad that the first and chief cause of offence against it has been removed for ever.'

It hadn't, of course. Fighting for a prize, be it a bull with golden horns or a bag full of folding money, has a way of surviving, which remains the one practical argument against each generation of abolitionists. The enthusiasm of the Victorian moralists certainly diminished and altered it, but far from killed it.

By this time England had an earnest and well-organised police force, but prize-fighting was a constant source of frustration to the new breed of law-enforcer ... and in turn to any member of the wealthy classes who did have the inclination to attend. Fights could not be officially policed, as pugilism was not technically legal, and with royal patronage gone, the sense of lawlessness increased. With the advancement of the railway system, travellers could move at higher speeds – and could therefore disperse more quickly from the scene of any crime they might have committed. As always, prize-fights were chaotic events, but now, as the Bendigo-Caunt fight amply demonstrated, they had a dark edge to them. Underworld scores could be settled among the anonymity of the crowds, pockets could be picked more safely than ever, and not surprisingly the support of relatively decent, upstanding and, more important, influential sporting men declined. Gradually boxing retreated to the seedy clubs of the major cities, to the gipsy camps and temporary quarters of railway navvies and canal workers.

It should be pointed out that boxing was not alone in courting sporting scandal in these early Victorian years. For example, the 1844 Derby was the subject of a major gambling scam when a moderate colt named Running Rein, backed down from 20-1 to 10-1, won the race by three-quarters of a length. Running Rein turned out to be a far better, physically similar horse named Maccabeus. Even more scurrilous, in a race designed to find the fastest three-year-old in the country, Maccabeus had already passed his fourth birthday! The horse was disqualified and the man held responsible for the switch, the jockey Levi Goodman, had to flee the country. In the same race, a horse named Leander was leading until it broke a leg when Maccabeus bumped into it at top speed. Leander was put down, but when examined was found to be at least four years old. The image of racing was severely damaged by the whole mess.

Nevertheless, boxing's name suffered again in July 1850 when Paddy Gill of Coventry defeated Tommy Griffiths, who then died. It transpired that Griffiths had been asked to take a dive, but refused, upon which a poisoned sponge was placed in his mouth after one round. Gill was tried for manslaughter and acquitted.

After collecting his purse of £400 for beating Caunt in 1845 Bendigo retired, leaving the championship situation confused once more. He returned on 5 June 1850, as a veteran of 38, and won a controversial, hollow, 'foul' decision over 26-year-old Tom Paddock of Redditch. The fight, which took place at Mildenhall in Suffolk, about a quarter of a mile from the village railway station, ended in the 49th round, in just short of an hour. Bendigo had drilled himself into excellent shape at 163 ½ lbs, and was a 1-2 betting favourite, but took a sustained hammering from a man who was leagues beneath him in terms of skill, but had the strength and unbridled enthusiasm of youth to push him on relentlessly for round after round.

Bendigo was tired and feeling his years, but Paddock was over-anxious and reckless and in the 49th round let fly with two punches after the old champion had slumped to the ground once more. Paddock was disqualified when he had the fight won. The decision caused an uproar and immediately it was announced, Paddock lost his temper and gave Bendigo another smack. Both sides argued that their man was winning. Paddock's supporters said, not unreasonably if the fight report is an honest source, that Bendigo was almost too tired to go on, while Bendigo's people countered that Paddock fouled on purpose to get out without losing face. The referee was a target for abuse from the Paddock fans, one of whom, known as Long Charley Smith of Birmingham, cracked him on the head with a bludgeon. Tom Spring prevented any more assaults on him, but although Long Charley legged it as fast as he could, the Paddock faction's view was that the official deserved his bruised skull.

Paddock took a special train to London, his face swollen and with a broken right hand. Bendigo retired to the Railway Tavern and waited for the 'express train' to Nottingham, which pulled into his home city the same night. What would we give, a century and a half later, for a public transport system that would take us in one ride from Mildenhall in Suffolk to Nottingham on the same day! Bendigo stepped off the train to be greeted by a huge crowd who knew only the bare result of the fight. A band played the hymn 'See The Conquering Hero Comes' and after acknowledging his people, this most charismatic of champions took refuge in his brother's house where his injuries were tended. He never boxed again.

For all his athletic prowess, Bendigo was a wild drinking man and a rough handful when he wanted to be. He was repeatedly in trouble with the law in his home city, and it was when he was locked up for the 28th time for breach of the peace that he was the subject of a religious visitation. The Damascus Road of his life arrived during a sermon by the jail chaplain on the story of David and Goliath. Bendigo, deeply moved, repented his sins and became a fire-and-brimstone evangelist who drew crowds almost as large to his open-air pulpit as he had done to his fights. He had a quaint, old-fashioned way of speaking and, dressed in a black frock coat, hat and gloves, would let forth lengthy sermons, as was the fashion, on the sins of the flesh, gambling and the demon alcohol.

Apparently, he saw no conflict with this public stance and his private habits of knocking back the odd quarter-pint of gin and having a serious flutter on a pigeon race. His legend was such that he had a town named after him in Australia (it's about 100 miles north of Melbourne) as well as a racehorse and an alcoholic drink. One of the great characters in boxing's chequered history, he died at the age of 68 in August 1880, from internal injuries after falling down a flight of stairs at home in Nottingham. A suitably melodramatic memorial of a sleeping lion on a pedestal was erected in the city in 1891. The unveiling ceremony drew huge crowds, and no doubt the old rogue would have heartily approved of the extravagant inscription:

'In life always brave, fighting like a lion,
In death like a lamb, tranquil in Zion.'

Caunt also retired after the third Bendigo fight, and seems to have cut a respected figure. In 1842, he was presented with a cup by admirers in the Newcastle-upon-Tyne area, which as the inscription explained was 'a token of respect for his abilities as a pugilist and his conduct as a man'. He also had to cope with a terrible tragedy when a fire broke out at the Coach And Horses on a day when he was away visiting friends in Hertfordshire. An 18-year-old servant, Ruth Lowe, his nine-year-old daughter Martha and his six-year-old son Cornelius died in the blaze.

Caunt made one last step into the prize ring in September 1857 against Nat Langham of Hinckley in Leicestershire. Langham was married to a relation of Caunt's wife, and also ran a popular pub, the Cambrian Stores, which was near to Ben's. They were business as well as sporting rivals. Bad feeling between the men led to the fight on the banks of the Thames at Tilbury. After 60 inconclusive rounds, lasting an hour and a half, they had boxed themselves to a standstill, and while they were prepared to hold on until darkness fell, they eventually agreed to call it a draw and end their differences. Langham then changed his stance and said he was under the impression that the fight would be re-started on another day, but it never was. Caunt took

Nat Langham

to pigeon-racing for a hobby, but early in 1860 he caught a severe cold on his lungs when out for a long, cold winter's day's racing and never completely recovered. His lifestyle didn't help his health – long hours and late nights in a smoky bar – and he was only 46 when he died of pneumonia on 10 September 1861.

The unremarkable, confused years, the Dark Ages of Pugilism, had set in. The London Prize Ring Rules were revised in 1853, but they were really only another updating of Broughton's guidelines, more detailed but by no means revolutionary. They did not go far enough to provide prize-fighting with a solution to its unpopularity. Fist-fighting would adapt, as it always does, to the demands of the society in which it operates, but for the time being, few seemed able to grasp what those demands were. Sport and society were evolving side-by-side, but as the major cities expanded and trouble-areas became more deeply entrenched and impenetrable, the desire for a more respectable way of living increased.

The London of the middle years of the century nurtured an underworld as tough and squalid as any in history. The tiny alleyways and passages that coursed away behind the frontages of main thoroughfares like The Strand were home to thousands of obscure, almost lost spirits. People were born, grew up, lived and died packed together in filth, even the most sensitive of souls among them hardened into hustling for some kind of edge or protecting fiercely whatever tiny remnants they held as precious. There were stories of women who slept sitting up, cradling infants to keep them safe from the rats which crept amongst the human wreckage in constant search of a feast. People slept in the stifling, stinking heat, sometimes 20 or 30 to a room, unaware of the basic dignities. Life, in spite of the earnest reforming movement that developed from the 1830s onwards, remained ugly and base for so many who had the misfortune to be born in the wrong place.

However, attitudes outside these horrific warrens were changing. Although there was much that remained barbaric, people gradually became more sensitive to their fellows ... and to their animals. While slaughtering for food was still primitive and cruel – sheep, for instance, at the underground slaughterhouse near St Paul's were thrown into a deep pit in order to break their legs and make them easier to knife to death – public opinion increased against the sports whereby animals were tortured for the pleasure of the paying punters. Bull and bear-baiting were banned in 1835 and cock-fighting in 1849. Dog-fighting and, of course, field sports like foxhunting and hare-coursing continued unchecked.

Legislation had its effect. Gambling dens were virtually ruined by the Gaming Act of 1845, and bookmakers' high street shops were outlawed by Act of Parliament eight years later. (On-course, or rather on-site, gambling remained untouched on the grounds that it would have been too unpopular with those influential enough to alter the course of a general election.) Basically, man's sense of what was and what was not decent sport was changing. For so many centuries an enactment of a life-and-death struggle, sport was now a more complex, blurred reflection of it. Now victory, either for an individual or a team, was often enough to satisfy the spectators. Blood, whether animal or human, no longer had to be shed as a pre-requisite for high entertainment. The process was gradual at first but, with the will apparent in Victorian life, increased in momentum as the century moved on.

Cricket matches had been played between counties since the first half of the

18th century, and the MCC had been formed in 1787. Athletics competitions had developed from around 1810 onwards, the Henley Regatta was first held in 1839 and seven years later the rules of association football were drawn up at Cambridge. By 1860 the Open golf tournament had begun. The revolution in sporting manners was unstoppable and even public hangings, for so long considered a necessary deterrent but which were often accompanied by a wild, raucous party attracting thousands of revellers, some of whom camped overnight to get the best vantage points, were barred by the Capital Punishment Act of 1868.

But again we leap too far ahead. There were other pugilists whose stories remain worth the telling.

8

THE TIPTON SLASHER

William Perry, forever remembered as the Tipton Slasher, was the first Black Countryman to hold the title 'Champion of England'. Born on 21 March 1819 in Tipton, Staffordshire, Perry grew up in the industrial heartland west of Birmingham from which Queen Victoria is said to have averted her gaze as the Royal train sped north. Perry worked barges and was also a navvy. He had a deformity in one leg, the origin of which is uncertain, but by the age of 16 was in London, working around Battersea and Chelsea. Already he had a reputation as a competent fighter.

His first official contest was against a young Irishman named Barney Dogherty. The plans were rumbled by the police, who prevented them beginning on Wimbledon Common. Perry won the first seven rounds opposite the Ship public house at Mortlake before they were moved on again. The police kept up with them well enough to foil plans to continue the bout at Barnes, but eventually it was completed on Lechmere Common near the King's Road. Quite how the law-enforcers lost their scent is unclear, but it doesn't say a great deal for the standards of detective work in the 1830s! Perry was too good for Dogherty, who was apparently a slow and very awkward fighter, and seven more rounds were enough to persuade the Irishman's friends to retire him. Perry impressed the critics, however, and reports declared him to be 'a scientific, hard hitter ... not to be sneezed at'.

Perry left London to return to the Black Country without taking part in a major fight, but made his name in his home area on 27 December 1836 when he beat a well regarded Birmingham professional, Ben Spilsbury, in 19 rounds. He was still not much more than a boy, but his followers called him 'The Tipton Slasher' and he was usually to be found training and living at the Fountain Inn in the village. In November 1837 he beat Jem Scunner, from nearby Gornal, in a fight that was spread over two days following an argument over a foul claim on the first, but which ended with Scunner unconscious after 31 rounds. When Jem Burke returned from the USA and reclaimed his championship, Bendigo was unavailable because of his serious knee injury and Caunt was still in the States. Perry was the man chosen to fight Burke in 1842, but the Slasher's backer failed him and Burke's man claimed all but £15 of the stakes already lodged.

Caunt then returned with a giant, 22-year-old American 'sparring partner' named Charles Freeman in tow. Caunt refused to risk himself in proper combat against the big man, but Perry, always carefree and unworried by the possibility of taking a whack or two, saw no problem in the match. He accepted confidently even though he knew he would be conceding up to a foot in height and nearly 70lbs in weight.

Freeman was hyped as the most formidable fighting machine ever seen, but then as now those who promoted prize fights were sometimes only loosely acquainted with the art of telling the truth. Freeman was big, strong, durable and extremely brave, which in the 1840s, when prize fights were sometimes a matter of who could stick to the task for the longest time, was a substantial help.

Freeman and the Slasher fought an incredible marathon beginning on 6 December 1842 at Sawbridgeworth in Hertfordshire. The first England-America contest since the celebrated Cribb-Molineaux battles of 30 years before, it created huge interest ... and attracted surprisingly little from the law. Freeman and his friends were confident enough to ignore the traditional back-roads route and travelled by the main highway from London in a carriage lent them by the self-styled cleric 'The Right Reverend Bishop of Bond Street' stocked with refreshments, including roast fowl. However, the organisers bungled.

On a winter's day, the fight did not begin until after 4 p.m., with the late afternoon closing in. For a big man Freeman was surprisingly nimble, but could also punch, and after feeling his power early on, the Slasher boxed defensively. He did cut Freeman on the left eyebrow in the sixth, but showed sense enough to keep out of his way in the early stages. Perry could fight well enough, but by now also knew the Bendigo-type trick of timing a drop to the turf to make it look as if he had gone down under either pressure or from a blow. Freeman had a confident, light-hearted air about him and wagged his finger and grinned when Perry went down deliberately during an exchange in round 14. *Bell's Life* reported that with 23 minutes and 21 rounds gone, all of which had ended with Perry on the floor, neither man had suffered any real damage.

And so it went on, Freeman trying to fight and Perry conserving his strength and going down whenever it seemed sensible. By the 35th round, the light was failing rapidly and Perry's vociferous Black Country fans were getting out of hand, interfering with the umpires' job. In the 45th round, an appeal to the referee for a foul was rejected on the grounds that the official could no longer see, but his perfectly reasonable suggestion that the fight be adjourned until the next day or called a draw was rejected by both sides. The fight was absolutely nonsensical, and even the meticulous *Bell's Life* writer gave up reporting after round 50. 'The men were only visible from the light colour of their skins and drawers,' he grumbled.

There was a suggestion that as the strange affair progressed, Perry tried to lure Freeman to fight in his corner where his unruly supporters had crowded in, but to his immense credit the American remained calm and refused to be intimidated. Finally, by round 70, and at half-past-five, the wintry evening fog settled on the scene and the referee jumped into the ring and placed himself between the fighters. Both men claimed they were robbed of the verdict and agreed to begin again at noon the following day.

After the parties had returned to London, it became obvious that more time would be needed to organise the 'continuation'. After one attempt in Essex had been foiled by a police superintendent named Captain Robinson, it was a fortnight before they could sort out the arrangements. Eventually, they all boarded a steamer named 'Father Thames' and chugged off beyond Gravesend to Cliffe Marshes. Freeman had plainly done no work since the first meeting, for he sat in the weighing-chair at 264lbs, while Perry seemed if anything thinner and paler. They began, or continued, depending on the point of view, at 13 minutes past midday on 20 December 1842, a full fortnight after darkness had spoiled the first attempt. The tactics were the same, although Freeman seemed to have the better of it most of the way and, unlike in their first meeting, Perry seemed demoralised from time to time. Finally, in the 37th round, with 39 minutes on the clock, Perry rushed in, hit Freeman on the shoulder with a right hand and dropped to the floor. The American's corner claimed a foul, the referee agreed – and the marathon was over. Perry was still fresh, apart from what sounds like a cauliflower ear and a cut finger. He denied falling on purpose and wanted to carry on, and his backer Johnny Broome was so frustrated that he wanted to set up a battle between Perry and Caunt. Nothing came of it.

Instead Perry embarked on a series of fights with Tass Parker of West Bromwich. The police stopped the first one after 67 rounds, the second in February 1844 lasted 133 rounds, at the end of which Parker was disqualified for going down without being hit, and The Slasher won the third in 27 minutes in August 1846. Freeman, meanwhile, was never able to develop his reputation. In 1844, when still only 24, the big man died of consumption.

Bendigo's retirement left the championship position confused, and his comeback victory over Tom Paddock in June 1850 was so hollow that it enhanced the reputation of the 26-year-old from Redditch rather than that

William Perry

of the old champion. Consequently, when Perry and Paddock were matched on 17 December 1850, it was generally agreed that the winner would be recognised as champion. The exact location of the ring was an even more heavily guarded secret than usual, but those who wanted to be there boarded a specially chartered train at Waterloo. After being chased out of Hampshire by the police, they settled on a spot on Woking Common. The day was drawing to a close by the time arrangements were completed, but the moon was full, and at 4.30 p.m. they began. *Bell's Life* said Perry won the toss for corners and was therefore able to 'place his back to the rising moon, so that his toothless mug was in the shade'.

Paddock, who had seemed a burly figure when fighting Bendigo, was the smaller man here. Too small, as it turned out ... and not good enough, which amply demonstrated just how far Bendigo had declined. By the third round, the outcome seemed so obvious that the odds on The Slasher had been slashed to 1-2. By the fourth Paddock was in pain from a damaged right shoulder, and the fight continued as a one-sided spectacle, several times Perry turning down the chance to appeal as Paddock fell without being hit. By round 22, the light was actually improving as the moon rose higher, and Paddock was shaken badly by a punch to the nose which bloodied his face. In the 27th, Perry floored Paddock in his own corner, but as he turned to cross the ring, the Redditch man jumped up, ran after him and clouted him around the ear, which was more than enough to get himself disqualified.

At 31, Perry was finally acknowledged as the best boxer in the country, although Bendigo stubbornly refused to hand over the championship belt, which he claimed had been given to him as a present. Instead, he agreed to fight Perry for £500 a side, but then backed off when Perry lodged a £50 deposit with the editor of Bell's Life fixing his side of the match. That finally ended all claims Bendigo retained to the championship.

Perry did not reign long. His old trainer Johnny Broome put up his young brother Harry as first challenger, but by now even the act of watching a prize-fight was becoming a test of patience and endurance. The fight did not capture the imagination of the public, and even the 'fight trade' had little interest.

Betting was minimal. It was agreed the fight should happen at Mildenhall in Suffolk, where Bendigo and Paddock had boxed, but they arrived at the site to discover that the field they remembered so well as a perfect natural arena was under plough! They moved on to another spot and a reasonable-sized crowd eventually drifted there, including soldiers stationed at nearby Newmarket.

It took more than an hour and a half to agree on the referee, which must have increased the tedium for spectators, some of whom must already have been tired. Finally, they settled on the old champion Peter Crawley, and with Perry a 1-2 favourite, they began at a quarter to three, more than six hours after most of the crowd had set out. Broome was a couple of inches shorter, but had a perfect physique, and was plainly unafraid of the champion, who had sneeringly referred to him as a boy. Perry, suntanned and hard, but also toothless and with his deformed 'K-leg', cut an aged figure alongside the 24-year-old who stood in front of him. Jem Wharton, one of the prize-fighters present, yelled out: 'Go to him, Tipton, he's afraid of you!'

Perry attacked, but Broome was far from intimidated and threw him heavily in the third, landing across him. The Slasher was badly concussed and

Perry v Broome

his seconds carried him by arm and leg to his corner to revive him. By the fifth he had shaken off the effects, but Broome drew first blood from the nose in the seventh and already the odds had switched around to evens. Unlike many more eagerly anticipated battles, which turned out to be flops, this was gruelling, exhausting action. By the ninth Perry's forced grin fooled nobody. By the 11th his left eye was lumpy, his lip was cut, but both men were breathing heavily. The fight continued to be close until it ended controversially in round 15. Perry locked Broome in a hold with his left, and let go with a right as the young man slipped to the floor. He was technically down when the punch landed on his head and Crawley disqualified him. The Slasher was outraged, and Crawley was the target of sustained verbal abuse from Perry's supporters.

Eventually, after removing his coat in a bid to fight Perry himself, the portly old-timer was hurried away. The general view was that while Broome had done the better work, Perry was still the fresher of the two and might well have gone on to win. Perry refused to accept the result and continued to declare himself champion, but the disqualification stood. The claim of the Slasher gained ground, however, when a rematch was made and Broome forfeited. Attempts to match him with Aaron Jones and Tom Paddock were similarly foiled, and he concentrated on his 'other life' as a publican in Spon Lane, Tipton. In the end he was out of the ring for six years.

Eventually, he came back, still claiming the championship, to fight little Tom Sayers from Brighton on 16 June 1857, by which time he was 38 years old. Like many a ring veteran, Perry refused to accept the possibility of defeat against a man whose achievements did not yet match his own. Boxers are sometimes the worst matchmakers of all ... and so it proved here. The Slasher backed himself heavily, but was outwitted by one of the great British sporting heroes of the 19th century.

Perry was four inches taller, and his frame had spread with age to 202lbs, while Sayers was only 154lbs. They both talked sense beforehand, with Perry saying he would not make the mistake of chasing the little man, but would stand his ground and wait. Sayers said Perry was washed-up and could not stay the pace he would set him. They set out on a boat from Southend in a gale-force wind, with 200 selected passengers, many of whom were sea-sick. The first attempt to land was thwarted by the distant presence of the police, but they finally disembarked at the Isle of Grain in Kent, almost directly due south of Southend, and where, astonishingly, a large crowd suddenly began to assemble. Word had obviously leaked out over the general destination of the boat but quite how so many as the 3,000 reported to have watched found their way to the Isle of Grain (which is not in fact an island, but the end of a small peninsula in the Thames estuary) is mysterious. Most people probably braved the waves in small boats, and it's something of a surprise that there were no reports of any casualties.

It was a long, grim, slow and horribly one-sided fight, with few decisive highlights. Perry began as if he expected it to be easy, but the years of inactivity had robbed him of his timing and accuracy. He lumbered forward and Sayers was more or less able to anticipate everything he did. Sayers drew first blood with a sharp blow to the mouth in round two, which astonished the Slasher, who hesitated as if puzzled and then charged in, his arms whirling like windmill sails. Sayers avoided them easily, smacked him between the eyes and danced away laughing. Later in the round, Perry's nose bled and his pre-fight game plan of letting the little man come to him was lost. He rushed in, which suited Sayers perfectly. Sayers landed a cracking left to the cheek, which split the skin, and soon afterwards the older man returned to his corner to have the blood wiped from his face. Eventually, Perry did land heavily enough to put Sayers on the floor. The success encouraged him, and he was smiling again by the start of the third. In laboriously describing the blow-by-blow action, the *Bell's Life* writer clearly enjoyed himself in stretching his prose:

'The Slasher stopped two more well-intended ones, and then got home on the side of Tom's cranium; Sayers returned heavily upon the proboscis, once more turning on the tap. Tom now dodged, and then got home heavily on the damaged cheek – a tremendous hit, and again did the home-brewed appear. The Slasher retired to be cleaned, and came again viciously, but Sayers pinked him on the smeller, receiving a slight return on the top of the nob.'

That these were tough men is hardly worth repeating, but the sheer time for which they slogged away was incredible. The first seven rounds of fighting were spread over one hour, 15 minutes. By round nine Perry was fading rapidly and Sayers was as agile and accurate as he had been from the start. Whereas the first five rounds had ended with Sayers on the floor, Perry had gone down at the end of the sixth, both had fallen in the eighth and the ninth saw the dazed and badly shaken veteran wobbling and staggering down. He dragged himself up just in time for the 10th, and gamely attempted to throw punches, but had nothing left. After a left to the cheek, and a right that sliced his upper lip, the Slasher fell for the last time and was carried to his corner. Although they got him round in time, his main backer, Owen Swift, stepped into the ring to retire him. Perry protested but the sponge was thrown up to signal the end, and 'Old Tipton', as he was known, wept profusely.

As they waited for the boat back across the by-now calmer Thames, Sayers led a collection for Perry which raised £22. The Slasher's championship had gone for good, and so had everything he owned, for he had gambled too heavily. He had to give up his pub and, although collections amounting to

£125 helped him restart, he never recovered his fortunes, later dealing in old iron and from time to time giving boxing exhibitions or sparring with the gloves to help aspiring youngsters.

At a race meeting at Handsworth, he tried out the 'Strength Test' machine on the accompanying fair – the one where customers hit a pad with a sledgehammer and hope to ring a bell at the top of a pole. As he swung the hammer, the proprietor saw him and yelled in panic: 'Not you, Mr Perry, not you!'.

Too late. The Slasher's blow buckled the iron supports, splintered the wooden pole and sent the bell flying! They held a collection for the owner ... but by then Perry had moved on to Morris Roberts' boxing booth. Roberts was offering two-pence to anyone who could stay the distance with either of the booth champions, one of whom happened to be one George Gough, who had, at some time in the past, insulted Perry behind his back. Roberts' spiel ground to a spluttering halt as The Slasher answered the call and tossed his silk-lined topper into the ring. 'Come, come, Mr Perry,' pleaded Roberts, to the amusement of the gathering crowd.

> 'You can't expect George to stand up against the champion of all England. That doesn't stand to reason, that doesn't. Now does it, Mr Perry.'

But the challenge had been made and met. Perry wanted his tuppence worth. And so, having smashed the strength machine, Perry proceeded to enjoy himself in teaching George Gough a rather harsh lesson.

The grand old man died suddenly at his home, the Old Toll House, halfway between Bilston and Wolverhampton, on Christmas Eve, December 1880. He was 61. The cause of death was given as alcoholism and pulmonary congestion. The coroner was informed by Perry's son, William, of Gibbet Gate, Bilston, who was present at the death. He was buried in St John's church at Kate's Hill, Dudley, in a grave marked by a simple iron plate. In 1925 a public subscription provided a granite slab tombstone. The legend of 'The Slasher' has endured. In the early 1990s it was claimed that the remains had been removed from Dudley and reburied secretly in Coronation Gardens, Tipton, where a memorial stone was erected, near a lifesize bronze statue of the old champion. A newspaper article quoted one of those involved, who said the body had been moved by 'local lads who decided they wanted to return him to Tipton', adding:

> 'The skeleton hadn't decayed that much because of the lead-lined coffin and the grave was restored, so there was no evidence of it having been disturbed.'

According to the vicar of St John's, however, there was no indication to believe that any such activity had occurred.

Harry Broome

Harry Broome, who was born in Birmingham in 1826, stood 5ft 10½ ins and weighed 168lbs in his prime. His elder brother Johnny was a fine fighter just short of championship class. Johnny ran sparring sessions at his pub in Piccadilly in the heart of London, and it was there that Harry learned his trade as a teenaged lightweight. Gradually, he filled out, and won his first significant battle against Fred Mason, known as the Bulldog, in October 1843. *Bell's Life* was impressed. Harry, it said, had 'courage, combined with perfect self-possession and a fair share of science. He is quick on his legs, and possesses the happy knack of using both hands with vigour and effect. He never once lost the control over his own actions, and between the rounds nursed and husbanded his strength with the cunning and calmness of a veteran'. Not a bad review for a 17-year-old novice. By the time he fought Perry for the title in 1850, he was a seasoned 24-year-old who knew his business inside-out.

In 1844 he fought a London middleweight, Joe Rowe, for 81 rounds spread over two hours 21 minutes, at which point the mob invaded the ring and prevented a result. Broome broke his right thumb in, he said, the fourth round, and the hand was seriously damaged by his use of it over the succeeding 77. In a rematch in May 1845, Broome defeated Rowe in 27 rounds at Eynsham near Oxford. In 1846 a fight with Birmingham rival Ben Terry ended in another mob invasion, but again provided Broome with more experience.

He beat William Perry controversially in 1850 to lay claim to the championship, which the Slasher disputed. Broome let his condition slide, and was grossly overweight when he went into training for an 1853 fight against Harry Orme, which took place at a remote spot in the East Anglian fenlands beyond Lakenheath. It was an epic struggle, by far the best advertisement for pugilism that had taken place for years. The straight-hitting, sharp and accurate Broome won in 31 rounds lasting two hours and 18 minutes, at the end of which he knocked Orme unconscious with little more than a gentle blow to the nose. *Bell's Life* analysed Broome's style:

'He is a good, straight hitter, clever at stopping, an excellent wrestler, and quick on his pins. He is, however, remarkably awkward in getting away when in difficulty – instead of jumping back, as we are accustomed to see others do, he turns his back and runs, leaving himself open to severe punishment from a cleverer tactician than Orme. Although he was much out of condition, and was hit very hard, both in the ribs and on the frontispiece, and several times was in great difficulties, he persevered most gamely throughout, and took his punishment like a thorough glutton. Should he make another match, he ought to commence training much earlier than he did on the present occasion, and reduce himself certainly to 11st 10lb, which is the outside weight at which he ought to fight. If he does this, we think, looking at the way in which he fought on Monday, he will prove himself a tough customer to all comers, and the man who wrests the laurels of the Championship from him will have reason to be proud of his achievement.'

The train back to London took three and a half hours, but was crammed with passengers, such had been the appeal of the fight. Broome's claim to the title faltered after his forfeit to Perry in 1855, a year in which he also twice pulled out of agreements to box Tom Paddock. Broome did not heed the advice of the *Bell's Life* chronicler and failed to keep a cap on his weight. When out of training, he blew up considerably, and then had to work it off as soon as a fight was arranged.

After the two false starts, he agreed to box Paddock on 19 May 1856 and worked hard to remove the excess pounds. By the day of the fight he looked in marvellous shape, but by now he was 30 years old and the good life had softened him. Paddock, from Redditch in Worcestershire, was a couple of years older. Public interest was high, even though the train tickets to the venue were costly – an intentional move by the Pugilistic Association, descendant of the Pugilistic and Daffy clubs and which was attempting to keep some kind of control over the sport, designed to put off the wilder members of the mob. Demand was so great that the rail owners quickly added seven extra carriages and filled them all. The train stopped unexpectedly near Ipswich – the police had been fed intelligence that it was to go on towards Diss in Norfolk and so were waiting further down the line – and around 500 people descended from the train to the selected field.

As soon as the fight began at six minutes past one, Broome looked nothing like his old self, and although Paddock began cautiously, he gradually took control. By the 25th round, Broome's face was disfigured – his mouth and eyes swollen and his nose bleeding. By round 29, it was reported that his face changed every round and was 'much out of shape'. He kept persevering in the unique way that prize-fighters did when all was quite plainly lost, but although he inflicted some facial damage on Paddock, did not have the ability or condition to turn it around.

By round 51, Broome was absolutely sold out, the left side of his head grotesquely swollen, his left eye shut tight, and his body plainly wracked with pain. He tottered on unsteady legs yet still attempted to throw punches.

Paddock finished the fight with a blow to the chest that left a visible bruise. Even then at the end of the rest time, Broome tried to get up before sinking back on to his second's knee. The sponge was thrown up, and Tom Paddock, at the age of 32, had regained his position in the major league of English pugilists.

The victory stunned the country's sporting men, but nobody outside his immediate circle could have foreseen the decline in Broome's abilities. He was given the respect he deserved for even when so obviously beaten he had stuck at the job for an hour and three minutes. He was ferried back to London by seven o'clock and put to bed, where in spite of his physical disfigurement most of his anguish appeared to be emotional and psychological. Paddock celebrated with a party at the pub of his friend Alec Keene, the Three Tuns in Moor Street, Soho. He had earned £400, and at the presentation the following Friday, began the collection for Broome with £10. The gathering increased that to £62 14s, and eventually with outside donations, it was even higher.

Broome announced his retirement, living at first in London, but later that year taking over as landlord of the Albion Tavern in Warblington Street, Portsmouth. He built this up into a sporting house and backed several promising fighters without producing a champion. He was involved in racing as well in some minor capacity, but he had piled on the weight and appears, from reading between the lines, to have been mentally affected by his career. There is no absolute evidence of that, but it would hardly be a surprise, given the nature of his battles. He died, aged only 39, on 2 November 1865.

His elder brother Johnny once rode his own horse, Eagle, to fourth place in the Grand National, and also won a fortune on the 1853 Derby, but was then involved in a case known as the Brighton Card Scandal, which cost him his friends as well as his money. His fortunes declined until he killed himself by cutting his own throat in a pub in Broad Court, off Drury Lane.

Tom Paddock

Tom Paddock's claim to the championship lay in the fact that he beat Broome. Nevertheless Broome's earlier forfeit to Perry, which was accepted as relevant at the time but which has sometimes not been acknowledged by historians, allows the matter to be in dispute.

Paddock was born on a farm near Redditch in 1824, and made his prize-fighting debut at nearby Mappleborough Green on the Warwick road in January 1844 when he defeated Fred Pearce of Cheltenham. At the end of the year he beat the 30-year-old veteran Black Countryman Elijah Parsons at Sutton Coldfield. By then he was described as the 'Redditch Needle-Grinder', which means presumably that he had given up the idea of farming for a living.

At Coleshill Castle on 27 January 1846, Paddock beat Nobby Clarke, who was seconded by the 'Tipton Slasher' but quit scandalously after 42 rounds. Perry was not amused by the lack of effort Clarke showed, called him a coward and had to be restrained from giving him another beating on the spot. Clarke wanted a chance to clear his name and fought Paddock again at Stony Stratford, Buckinghamshire, on 6 April 1847. This time Paddock knocked the fighting heart out of him in 35 rounds. At his peak, Tom was a rough, solid, almost rounded fighter who traded on durability and stamina.

A rush of blood cost Paddock his fight with Bendigo in June 1850, but then he was genuinely outclassed by Perry the following December. Having been put in his place by 'The Slasher', he lost more ground when he was surprisingly beaten by Harry Poulson in a gruelling fight spread over 71 rounds and 95 minutes at Sedgebrook, near Grantham, Lincolnshire, on 23 September 1851.

At Cross End, north of Derby, nine days before Christmas, 1851, he gained revenge by handing Poulson a savage beating in 86 rounds. The magistrates interrupted the proceedings, but the mob ignored them and when one Mr Jedidiah Strutt considered it his moral duty to push through the throng to enter the ring and literally read out the Riot Act, the policeman who attempted to clear the way for him was beaten unconscious. That unfortunate upholder of the law, whose name was Wragg, was carried to hospital in Belper where two surgeons saved his life. At the end of the fight Paddock and Poulson travelled to Derby where they were arrested. Both were jailed for ten months with hard labour.

Illness kept Paddock out for another year after his release in November 1852, but then he signed to fight Poulson a third time. This took place on Valentine's Day, 1854, at Mildenhall in Suffolk – and these two well-matched, tough men slogged it out for 102 rounds lasting two hours 32 minutes. It was reckoned to be the best of their three meetings in which both gave and took heavy punishment. Incredibly, Poulson's second, Jerry Noon, was heavily criticised for throwing up the sponge and retiring his man when he was still pleading to be allowed to fight on.

Paddock's constitution was remarkable. Within five months he was back, outlasting Aaron Jones in a ferocious, brutal scrap that went on for 121 rounds and left the loser with eyes cut and swollen to slits. Tom even had to beat Jones in a return before his defining victory over Broome.

Unfortunately, he was unable to capitalise on that victory. He formed a travelling booth with Broome for a while, but pulled out of a match with Perry when he surprisingly failed to find a backer. He also admitted when he explained his withdrawal that he had suffered serious losses on the racetrack. Soon afterwards he was stricken low by rheumatic fever and taken in a serious condition to Westminster Hospital. Tom Sayers began a fund to help him out financially, and then when Paddock eventually recovered, they set about making a match for the championship which the little Brighton genius had taken from Perry.

By now, however, Paddock was 34, ring-rusty, with his system weakened by his long spell of sickness. Paddock walked 50 miles a day early in his training, desperately attempting to shed the pounds and build up his strength, but he would probably never have been good enough to beat Sayers. They successfully avoided the police and fought at Canvey Island, about 30 miles east of London. Sayers, in spite of carrying a few surplus pounds, outclassed him from the start and eventually knocked him out in the 21st round.

Paddock could hardly see and was dazed as he came up for the scratch for the last time. He rushed blindly forward but, as pitiful as it sounds, in the wrong direction. When Sayers landed a heavy left hand to the cheek, he staggered and reached out with his arms, as if attempting to cling on to something. Sayers set himself to throw a right, but then pulled it, aware that Paddock was completely helpless. Instead, he grabbed his right hand, shook it and steered him back to his corner. Paddock's seconds signalled the official surrender by tossing up the sponge. It was some time before Paddock could understand that he had lost, and when the news finally sank in, he wept tears of despair and desolation. On the boat back to London, Sayers walked among the fans and collected £30 for the beaten man.

Paddock should not have boxed again, but in 1860, at the age of 36, he fought the 6ft 2in, 210lbs Sam Hurst and was knocked out in five rounds, which were crammed into less than ten minutes. He took part in a few exhibitions, but then his uncertain health finally got the better of him, and following a long illness he died on 30 June 1863. He was 39.

9

THE UNITED STATES OF AMERICA

There is no doubt that prize-fighting existed in America in the eighteenth century as a result of British migration, but as in Ireland, it had no discernible structure and remained uncommercialised. French traveller Moreau de St Mery, who roamed the USA between 1793 and 1798, described a bout in uncommon detail:

'Boxing has its rules and regulations. The two athletes settle on a site for the fight. They strip to their shirts, and roll up their sleeves to the elbows. Then at a given signal they run at each other and swing on chest, head, face and bellies, blows whose noise can only be realised by those who have been present at such spectacles ... At the end of the fight the boxers are bruised, disfigured, and covered with blood, which they spit out, vomit out, or drip from the nose. Teeth are broken, eyes are swollen and shut, and sometimes sight is completely obliterated. Boxing matches are always held in the later evening, by the light of the moon, unless the participants belong to the lowest orders, or are drunk, in which case they fight in broad daylight where any one can see.'

In 1798 a 'professor of fencing and pugilism' named G.L.Barrett advertised his services in the *Columbian Sentinel* and similar notices appeared throughout the next 15 years – enough to suggest that sparring in academies or houses of professors was a relatively common practice.

It is generally recorded that the first American championship fight was between Jacob Hyer and Tom Beasley in 1816, but this is stretching the truth. It was the first fight that commanded enough attention to be recorded, but it seems to have come out of a personal quarrel and, after a preliminary attempt to stick to the rules in force in Britain at the time, descended into an anything-goes kind of brawl. Hyer, who was a 6ft 2in, 182lb butcher born of Dutch parents on New York's West Side, broke his arm, but kept on fighting. Beasley, who was a seaman, was badly cut and bruised, but also stuck solidly at the job. Eventually, they were parted by friends and the match was called a draw.

Boxing continued in a haphazard way and in 1823 the *New York Evening Post* recorded a 40-minute fight near the Grand Street ferry between an 18-year-old butcher and a man described as 'the champion of Hickory Street'. The teenager won and collected the prize of $200. There were also two battles recorded between immigrants from the British Isles, Ned Hammond of Dublin and George Kensett of Liverpool, and slowly the tradition developed until by the 1830s, the more organised fights were given the benefit of round-by-round reporting in the more supportive newspapers, such as the *New York Herald*. Customs hardened into accepted rules and gradually prize-fighting became a sport that, while never formally welcomed was at least grudgingly accepted. By 1828, the *National Intelligencer*, published in Washington, was able to suggest pugilism as a safe, modern alternative to duelling. Mostly the purses were small, but every so often a bout would attract enough interest for the wages of the fighters to escalate, as when Pat O'Donnell and Jim O'Hagan boxed near Newark, New Jersey, for $100 a side in 1832.

Jem Burke, the extrovert English champion known as 'Deaf Un', was the first major prize-fighter to work in the USA. He sailed to the States following the death of Irish challenger Simon Byrne in 1833, impressed in sparring with his speed and accuracy, and eventually fought his main sparring partner Samuel O'Rourke in New Orleans in 1837. This was ruined by a mob invasion after only three rounds. Burke returned to New York and on 21 August 1837 fought a landmark battle with Tom O'Connell at Hart's Island, which is in Long Island Sound. Burke won a one-sided affair in ten rounds before a civilised crowd, which had arrived by steamboat from Catherine Street docks in the city. Burke then returned to England to re-establish his claim to his old championship.

Boxing in the gymnasium or at a teaching school increased in popularity in the cities, especially on the east coast. In Boston, a 'professor' named John Sheridan ran a thriving pugilistic club. One or two professional prize-fighters existed and moved around the country, but mostly the sport existed at an amateur level. There was substantial opposition from moralists who felt prize-fighting was hardly the way forward for a young nation intent on becoming the most decent society on earth. They had a point. While anybody could box, it did attract some of the more savage members of the community, if not as fighters as spectators. Riots occurred from time to time – and if its opponents could never put a stop to it, at least they succeeded in preventing it from rising to the level of a major sport during the bare-knuckle era. It was never popular enough to entice entrepeneurs into risking their cash to promote a major fight, and so remained fairly static on the fringes of sporting society.

Tom Hyer was not born until New Year's Day 1819, after his father Jacob had boxed, or more accurately brawled, Tom Beasley in the bout that was recorded for posterity and has since been given exaggerated status. Nevertheless, Tom inherited his father's interest in using his fists, and was of a similar build to the old man, standing 6ft 2½ in and weighing around 180lb. He fought twice in the prize-ring and is fairly remembered as the first genuine American champion. At Caldwell's Landing on the Hudson River on 9 September 1841, Hyer outlasted John McCleester, who was also known as Country McCloskey and George McCheester, in a marathon that lasted 101 rounds and five minutes short of three hours. Some wanted McCleester to be pulled out after the end of the 100th, but Hyer grumbled viciously: 'O, let him come on, let him come on. I'll kill him this time.'

Thankfully, he didn't quite do that, but he hit him relentlessly until McCheester, McCleester or McCloskey, was rescued by his second, Yankee Sullivan. The beaten man recovered, and eight years later repaid the compliment to Sullivan when he took on Hyer in a bout that is accepted as having championship status. It was a grudge match: Sullivan had been flattened by Hyer in a bar at the corner of Park Place and Broadway. Accordingly, the official fight drew unprecedented interest – and both men were guaranteed an incredible $10,000. They dodged a police boat which ran

Yankee Sullivan

aground, and fought before a few hundred of the most persistent fans on a snowy day at a barren beach named Still Pond Heights, Maryland, on 7 February 1849. Hyer, 30lb heavier and four inches taller, won a fast, brutal battle in only 18 minutes and 16 rounds. Hyer's eye was lanced to prevent it shutting, but he kept in control, finally driving the smaller man to the ropes and throwing him heavily. Hyer cemented his triumph by falling across the stricken body – a move that would have been illegal in England, but which was allowed in the USA. Sullivan, who had taken his beating without complaint, was hurt so badly that he was carried to Mount Sinai Hospital in Baltimore.

The fight result was transmitted by the newly installed telegraph lines to major newspaper offices around the north-east, outside which people gathered to hear the news, and the next day Hyer was carried home through Chestnut Street in Philadelphia, which was blocked by hundreds anxious just to get a glimpse of him. Hyer was arrested by the Philadelphia authorities, but the case had to be brought in Maryland and the police failed to do it. He was soon released from custody to continue the celebrations. A month later Massachusetts became the first state to ban prize-fighting, which had previously come under general, loosely applied headings like riot and disorderly conduct. However, although the law stated that by taking part in or organising a prize-fight a man could face a jail term of ten years and a $5,000 fine, punishment was rarely applied.

Hyer never boxed again. Attempts to match him with John Morrissey and the English champion William Perry, the Tipton Slasher, both came to nothing. There was also a bizarre incident in October 1854 when Hyer, by now 35, met Morrissey in New York, but instead of attempting to fight with his fists, offered his rival a revolver and suggested a duel! In 1855, Hyer was lucky to escape death when a man named Lew Baker shot him, but the bullet only grazed his neck. He was involved in other pub brawls and lived on the edge of the underworld, his attempts to run saloons and gambling houses failing miserably. He was a down-and-out, walking with the aid of crutches, by the age of 40. Hyer died of heart disease on 26 June 1864 in New York City. He was 45.

Yankee Sullivan was a strange one, a mysterious character whose identity has remained open to question for a century and a half. He was apparently an Irishman, from Bandon, south of Cork, and said to have been born on 12 April 1813. It seems likely his real name was James Ambrose, although he also used Francis or Frank Murray and Frank Martin from time to time. He lived the low life in London in the 1830s, mixing pugilism with a life of crime until, either for larceny or the accidental, drunken killing of his wife, he was transported to Botany Bay in 1837. Or so the story went anyway. He was a farm labourer in Australia, but eventually stowed away on a ship to New York and then returned to England as Yankee Sullivan, hoping that nobody would remember him as James Ambrose.

He issued a challenge to any 154lb man in the country, and was lucky to beat a good fighter named Hammer Lane, who broke his right arm in the third round. Lane still managed to give Sullivan a gruelling struggle, but eventually the sponge was tossed into the air by his seconds. Sullivan had antagonised the crowd by constantly punching Lane on the obviously broken arm. He then returned to America. He claimed to have beaten the best England could offer, and set himself up with a bar, the Sawdust House in the Bowery in New York.

He beat Vincent Hammond, an exiled Englishman, in 10 minutes near Philadelphia, and followed that by trouncing Tom Secor in an hour in front of

2,000 people on ground near the New York Narrows, the stretch of water that divides Staten Island and Brooklyn. Sullivan pulled faces and mocked Secor as he won easily.

He also beat William Bell, an Englishman who called himself Professor and ran some kind of boxing academy in Brooklyn, at Hart's Island on 29 August 1842. Bell was clever and dangerous, but had one glaring deficiency when it came to boxing Sullivan: he fought fairly! Sullivan was seriously hurt at one point, but conned the inexperienced Englishman into easing off by telling him he wanted to quit. When Bell, who had Sullivan in a stranglehold, released his grip, Sullivan clouted him in the ear and threw him heavily.

But when prize-fighting was growing into a sport of serious proportions, the first ring fatality in America cast it into the shadows. On 13 September 1842, an Englishman named Christopher Lilly fought Irishman Thomas McCoy near Hastings, New York, 25 miles up-river from the city. It was a terrible fight, even by the raw standards of pugilism. By the 70th round McCoy was in a shocking state: his lips were grotesquely swollen, his forehead was lumpy and blue with bruising, and blood coursed down his chest from the cuts on his face. His chest heaved as he attempted to fill his lungs, and even as he tried to fight, he vomited blood. His eyes swelled to slits and calls came up from the crowd for it to be stopped.

'For God's sake, save his life,'someone shouted with dreadful accuracy. Lilly's corner, which included Yankee Sullivan, asked for victory to be conceded, yet McCoy and his seconds would not give in. At the end of the 118th round McCoy was choking yet defiant, but in round 119, two hours and 41 minutes after walking cheerfully to the scratch mark, he fell down dead.

It caused outrage. Lilly fled the country, but 18 of those involved with the fight were arrested for their part in it. It was a test case – and the jury knew it. If they acquitted the accused, prize-fighting would be effectively accepted in law. Sullivan, and fellow boxers George Kensett and John McCleester were all found guilty of fourth degree manslaughter – and Sullivan received the maximum sentence of two years jail. McCleester was jailed for eight months with a $500 fine, and Kensett got four months and $200.

Sullivan didn't serve his time. For some reason he was pardoned a few months later and released, but the wave of revulsion against prize-fighting had hardened. Yards of purple prose were churned out – including a vivid piece of sensationalism from preacher-writer Horace 'Go West, Young Man' Greeley, who claimed the fans were a 'festival of fiends' and who apparently 'were in raptures as the well-aimed, deadly blows descended heavily upon the face and neck of the doomed victim, transforming the image of God into a livid and loathsome ruin'.

Decent, right-thinking, middle class America was deeply moved. And according to popular theory, prize-fighters and all those who associated with them were living evidence of the kind of society that would exist if there were not moral guardians to protect the nation and its children. Rubbish, of course, but popular rubbish. And it sold well. Boxing had a hard time for a while. Bad press became routine. Newspapermen couldn't admit it if they did enjoy watching or writing about a good fight. Who could afford the risk of publishing an article supporting pugilism when the majority of the readership opposed it? In short, boxing went to ground.

Gradually, however, after a decent wait, its ugly, mis-shapen head began to rise above the long grass again! The publication *The Spirit Of The Times*, which had actively supported prize-fighting before the Lilly-McCoy tragedy, began to show interest once more. As the pendulum of opinion swung, the Spirit editor was confident enough to run a special offer on the five Pierce Egan volumes of *Boxiana*. Modern collectors, who if they find a set are usually asked to pay a four-figure fee to purchase them, can only sit back and reflect that the readers of *The Spirit Of The Times* were asked to shell out the princely sum of $15 for theirs!

America was a rapidly changing nation, welcoming immigrants to its shores with promises which it was rarely able to deliver. In the late 1840s, poor, desperate, hopelessly optimistic Irish families arrived at the rate of 20,000 a year, only to find a nation already harbouring prejudices and reducing them to the ranks of an underclass. They were 'offered' houses for rent by supposedly friendly settlers, often from their own race, who turned out to be no more than exploiters and thieves eager to charge crippling rents for rooms in the attics or cellars of houses few others wanted. Slowly, their position improved, as other blocks of immigrants arrived with their dreams of a fresh start and undreamed-of freedom and wealth, but in the middle years of the century, it was the Irish who propped up the social framework. And, perhaps not unlinked to that fact, Irish prize-fighters stimulated tremendous interest among their own.

Tammany Hall, the most powerful and notoriously corrupt political club in New York City, had long wooed the Irish vote – and employed boxers as bouncers at its meetings and as ballot-box riggers.

Yankee Sullivan lost to Tom Hyer in February 1849, and almost five years later boxed the other celebrated Irish immigrant fighter of the day, John Morrissey, for $1,000 a side at Boston Corners on the border of New York and Massachusetts before a crowd of maybe 6,000 people. Morrissey was cut, battered and knocked down repeatedly and seemed bound to lose, but somehow rallied in round 37 and the under-pressure Sullivan went down in

John Morrissey: an unscrupulous fighter-politician.

confusing circumstances. Arguments raged as to whether or not he should be disqualified for falling without being hit, or whether or not Morrissey's supporters had cut the ropes, and then the words spilled over into a brawl which involved Sullivan himself and seconds from both sides. In the middle of the melee, the referee called time, but after two minutes and with Sullivan still showing no signs of returning to the official battle, Morrissey was given the verdict.

Two weeks later Sullivan was arrested in New York City and handed over to the Massachusetts authorities, who had finally decided to act over the breaking of the State laws. Morrissey was arrested later and eventually agreed to pay a $1,200 fine as an alternative to a 16-month jail term. Sullivan was bailed out with the help of his former conqueror Tom Hyer, and soon afterwards left in disgust for the 'new land' of California where he helped rig elections in return for a modest fee. Unfortunately, his larger-than-life personality attracted too much attention and when a 'Vigilance Committee' set to work to clean up San Francisco, he met a gruesome end. Several undesirables were thrown out of town, two people believed to have committed murders were hanged without proper trial, and Sullivan was picked up on 26 May 1856, convicted of a generalised crime of disturbing the peace, rigging elections and generally being a nuisance, and sentenced to deportation. Four days later, however, Sullivan was found dead in his cell. He had bled to death alone after being cut on his right arm, but while the vigilantes claimed he had committed suicide, others said he was murdered. He was 43 years old.

They called John Morrissey 'Old Smoke' after a saloon brawl with a man named John O'Rourke in which his hair and body were burned by coals from the fire. In spite of the pain from his singed flesh, he fought on until he won – and gradually over the ensuing months, he sought out each one of O'Rourke's gang of friends and gave them a hiding. Morrissey's parents had moved from Templemore, Tipperary, to Troy, New York, when he was three. The only son in a family of eight children, he might in other circumstances have turned out to be a hard-toiling family provider, adored by his sisters and the pride of his parents. Life is rarely so romantic. In truth, he was a ruthless, unruly youth who had little schooling, worked fitfully at a variety of jobs and was well known to the police because of his violent temper and scant regard for the law. However, Morrissey was probably saved from descending into a short and brutal life in the gutter by one crucial part of his character – his naked ambition.

He taught himself to read and write and by the age of 20 in 1851 was in San Francisco, where he learned how to run a gambling house. His journey to California was typical of his adventurous spirit. Twice discovered as a stowaway on ships travelling around Panama and Mexico, he was in danger of being stranded, but when he sorted out a rebellion among passengers over the lousy quality of the food they were expected to endure on board, the captain of the second steamer let him travel in relative comfort the rest of the way. Within a year, he had found himself a new set of friends, whose lawless, uncompromising ways brought him the so-called championship of California. He was awarded an 11th round foul against George Thompson when his friends whipped out their guns and threatened his opponent, who had been winning easily. Thompson got himself disqualified because he feared for his life. That travesty of a fight took place at Mare's Island for a $2,000 sidebet on 31 August 1852.

On the back of that, Morrissey returned to his old stamping grounds in New York. He wanted to fight Tom Hyer, but plans fell through, and instead he beat Yankee Sullivan in their controversial fight for $1,000 a side in Boston Corners. American boxing was in chaos. Sullivan was a rogue, but Morrissey and his supporters were positively frightening. Low life ruled the business, which had nothing whatsoever to offer the fair-minded or any sportsman interested in honest and open competition. Morrissey's reputation grew, based on his dubious performances against Thompson and Sullivan, but he remained what he was: an egotistical thug. By the mid-1850s he had friends influential enough to keep him out of jail when his violent excesses attracted the attention of the courts. In 1855 a street rival named William Poole got into a brawl with Morrissey in a bar in the Bowery, and the supposed prize-fighter was kicked unconscious by Poole's friends. Some hours later, a group of Morrissey's companions burst in and in the ensuing shoot-out, Poole was killed. The street word was that Morrissey had ordered the killing, but nothing could be proved and charges against him wouldn't stick.

On 20 October 1858 Morrissey fought the rising John Camel Heenan, a 23-year-old from his old home town of Troy, who had been in California at roughly the same time as Old Smoke but without coming into contact with him. Heenan worked as a labourer in the sweatshops of the Pacific Mail Steamship Company at Benicia, San Francisco. After that he was a miner, but then earned cash as an 'enforcer' in rigged elections and when the heat from the law began to increase, got out of town to return home. Interest in his fight with Morrissey was whipped up in the newspapers, and eventually they signed, apparently with mutual, simmering animosity, for $2,500 a side.

The public image was black and white, with Morrissey cast as the villainous representative of the underworld, and Heenan as the heroic son of decent working class parents. (His father toiled in the ordnance department of the Watervliet Arsenal for almost a quarter of a century.) To avoid the police, the fight was held at Long Point Island, a barren stretch of land on the Canadian side of Lake Erie, and fans were transported across from Buffalo in New York State in steamers. Some had travelled from as far away as New Orleans and the usual ragbag of humanity, from gamblers and murderers, to common crooks, genuine sporting men and adventurers found its way to the site. The *New York Tribune* huffed that the gathering, as it formed in Buffalo, was 'the most vicious congregation of roughs that was ever witnessed in a Christian city', a cautionary note designed to scandalise and intrigue its more impressionable readers. Boxing was back in business.

Heenan, whose final preparations had been disrupted by an agonising abcess on his leg which had confined him to bed for a week before the fight, tossed his hat into the ring just before twenty past one in the afternoon. News of Heenan's injury had been widely known and Morrisey's unruly, boorish supporters were in ebullient mood. The preparations dragged on, but eventually they cleared the ring and Heenan made a big effort to finish the fight as quickly as possible. Morrissey's limitations were exposed as 'The Benicia Boy' bloodied his nose and drove him into a corner, but Heenan's luck deserted him when he missed with a heavy blow and hurt his hand on the stake. Morrissey was outclassed but Heenan was still sick with fever and his stamina ran out. Both men were helped up for round 11, but while Morrissey swayed and stood, Heenan eventually swung a huge haymaker, missed and crashed on to his face, out for good. The whole thing had taken only 21 minutes. The boats returned to Buffalo around 12 hours later and the result was telegraphed back to New York where crowds milled around the newspaper offices to hear how it had gone.

> 'So much rowdyism, villainy, scoundrelism, and boiled-down viciousness, concentrated upon so small a space,' wrote the *Tribune's* correspondent. 'The talk of establishing the Prize Ring in America, under an orderly supervision, is simply nonsense ...'

But it was unstoppable. Whatever the moral minority thought about it, the movement towards a popular press was going to cater for popular tastes. And if that meant writing about boxing, then so be it. The number of column inches devoted to the gossip and activities of the ring increased. With the Morrissey-Heenan fight, boxing established itself in America.

Heenan wanted a rematch, but Old Smoke, with a lot of hard living packed into his 27 years, announced his retirement. Six months later Morrissey ran a benefit for the family of an old prize-fighter, William Harrington, who had vanished mysteriously, and established himself as a worthy citizen with considerable popular support. He was a gambler whose business expanded rapidly until by the time the Civil War broke out he was one of the pillars of New York society. He was playing the Wall Street stock market successfully by 1861 and three years later was well-connected enough to build the famous race track at Saratoga, with the help of William R. Travers and Leonard W. Jerome, who was Winston Churchill's grandfather. His old hell-raising friends of a decade earlier must have barely recognised the apparently sophisticated, immaculately turned-out businessman of substantial position whose influential associates helped him serve two terms on the US Congress and New York State Senate. Some did not forget, however, and on his death in his bed at home in Saratoga on 1 May 1878 at the age of 47, while still a senator, the *New York Tribune* sliced up his reputation bitterly:

> 'Prize-fighting would not do any longer; so he reformed himself into a gambler, and set up a first-class hell ... Having opened a gilded and

alluring pest house for the corruption of good society, he asked the applause of the virtuous on the ground that he no longer made it a business to exchange blows with a half naked ruffian for the amusement of the mob.'

On the retirement of Morrissey, Heenan assumed the American championship and earned money with a tour of exhibitions. And in 1859, with the help of his new wife, the allegedly glamorous, certainly notorious actress Adah Isaacs Menken, he began the plans that would take him to England to fight a little man from Brighton named Tom Sayers in the Fight of the Century, the story of which would fascinate and thrill millions of sports fans for generations to come.

10

FIGHT OF THE CENTURY

John Camel Heenan's arrival in England early in 1860 signalled a sudden excitement across the nation and unexpectedly, magnificently, for a few, fleeting months, the prize-ring recaptured its youth. In drawing rooms and drinking houses, in the workhouse and in Westminster, men chewed over the merits of Heenan and Tom Sayers, of the outcome of their forthcoming fight, day and night. Perhaps in some kind of massed relief, maybe a delayed response to the close of the Crimean War in 1856, or in a subconscious revolt against the new disciplines imposed by the Imperial spirit, a patriotic but more chaotic, less structured enthusiasm spread across the nation, on a scale unparalleled since the first battle between Tom Cribb and Tom Molineaux half a century before.

Heenan was followed by the American press wherever he went, which made the customary security arrangements for pugilistic participants more difficult to organise. When the need came to move him quickly and safely, he was an unwieldy subject. He did nothing to contravene the law of the land, of course. On the contrary, he was a model citizen: upright, civilised and respectful. Nevertheless, he was by profession a prize-fighter ... and his intentions, while unstated, were hardly a secret. Accordingly, he was arrested and bailed in Bedford as magistrates and moralists sought a method of quelling, containing or at least diverting the rising tide of interest. However, they could pin no crime against him, and nothing came of it. Finally, with the date of 17 April 1860 an open secret, but the identity of the location fiercely guarded, the do-gooders and law-upholders stood aside. Parliament was virtually emptied.

Word was passed among the Fancy that trains to the fight would leave Waterloo Station in south London before dawn. Crowds swarmed into the capital and swamped the platforms, the lucky ones clutching a three-guinea ticket stamped 'To Nowhere'. Finally, the steady procession clattered out of London into the Hampshire countryside on that calm, fresh spring morning, and came to a halt at the village of Farnborough, a few miles from Aldershot.

Tom Sayers

And so, what kind of a man was this who could inspire so many minds, and stir so many souls, who strode out to meet his destiny on that bright day all those years ago?

Tom Sayers was a cobbler's son, born on 15 May 1826 in a rented terraced house, No. 74 Pimlico, Brighton, which is now called Titchbourne Street. He was never schooled, and was therefore illiterate, as most of the great fighters of old had been. The youngest of his parents' five children, he spent his days on the stony beach, helping fishwives and fishermen, and learned to fight along with the rest of the boys, who wrapped worn-out socks and stockings around their fists for mufflers. And like the others, he grew up quickly.

At 13, he walked to London, where his sister Eliza had married a builder, Robert King. He was given labouring work, but wasn't disciplined enough to do it. Maybe it was his nature, or maybe he was just another stroppy teenager with the world at his feet, but after one row too many he stormed out and walked back to Brighton.

He was never lazy. Soon after returning, he was working as an apprentice bricklayer, and after work learning his other craft, that of a boxer, at the Druid's Head pub in Brighton, which was run by brothers Joe and Harry Phelps, whose own elder brother had been killed in a bout with the great lightweight champion Owen Swift at Royston in Hertfordshire in the 1830s.

Sayers' first fight was at Newmarket Hill outside Brighton, when he stepped out of the crowd to answer a challenge to box a local man named Haines. It was stopped by a magistrate after 17 rounds and called a draw. Small fights like that brought in only beer money, of course, and he returned for a second spell with his sister and once again her husband gave him work, this time as a bricklayer on the Hippodrome Race Course at Notting Hill. When the job was finished, he returned to Brighton and was one of the 3,500 men who built the magnificent Preston Viaduct. For a man of his ambition, however, the Sussex town was not enough. Back in London, he lived in the Agar's Town slum north of the City, working on the construction of both King's Cross and St Pancras railway stations, and when the day job was done, as a turnstile attendant at the Copenhagen Grounds athletics track where meetings were regularly held. He seems to have had no particular pugilistic ambition, although he was quite happy to accept the tradition of solving disputes with his fists. Men did this as a matter of course, often downing tools for an hour or two while 'an honest fight' settled an argument. In one such incident, while working for Robert King at Wandsworth, Sayers trounced a 6ft 3in Irish workmate named Con Parker so seriously on the local common that there were fears for the big man's life. The police looked for Tom for a while, but the teeming metropolis had many hiding places, and after lying low in Tooting, he was smuggled back to Camden when the heat had died down.

By 1849, he was living in a small house in Bayham Street, Camden, with his 17-year-old girlfriend, Sarah Henderson, who was expecting his child. And with the birth of their daughter, also called Sarah, the need for extra cash became more pressing. He decided to put his fighting talents to more lucrative use. He advertised in the prize-fighting paper, *Bell's Life*, stating his availability to take on all-comers, whatever their weight, even though he was no more than 5ft 8in and barely 140lbs. He attracted a backer named Viddler, who persuaded the old champion Peter Crawley, who ran a pub in Smithfield, to help with his training. On 19 March 1849, near Greenhithe on the Kent bank of the Thames, he knocked out Aby Couch in 13 minutes for a paltry £5.

Sayers' first serious opponent was Dan Collins, who worked as a waiter in Tom Spring's Holborn pub, on 22 October 1850 near the Kent village of Edenbridge. After nine rounds they were interrupted by a magistrate and moved on to Red Hill in Surrey, where they resumed at round ten! Sayers hurt his right hand seriously, but doubled up with the left. In the 37th he was badly winded but made it to the scratch, and fought back well. At sunset, in round 50, a draw was called. As Collins' skill was known from sparring sessions in Spring's pub, Sayers' own reputation was enhanced by his performance, and an attempt was made to match them six weeks later in a 'double header' alongside a fight between Young Sambo Welsh and Cross. Unfortunately, these two slugged it out for two and a half hours, and with daylight fading, it was decided there was no time for Sayers and Collins to put on a meaningful exhibition. Eventually, they did box again on 29 April 1851, and this time Sayers had improved so much that Collins, who was only four pounds heavier at 142lbs, took a one-sided boxing lesson, lasting 84 minutes.

After this it was not easy to match him. Too big for the lightweights (who scaled 126lbs in those days), his backers did not want to risk him against the top middleweights and heavyweights either. Yet none of the lesser fighters wanted much to do with him. Nevertheless, at the start of 1852, he attracted a wealthy patron, his old employer at the Copenhagen Grounds, John Garrett. Fairly quickly, a fight with the popular East End character Jack Grant was arranged. Grant, who was around Sayers' size and 26 years old, was a flamboyant rogue who wore a white top hat. He had taken part in one fight with Mike Madden in 1848 which had lasted 140 rounds and five and three-quarter hours, ending only when it became dark. He had also come through several other severe fights, and was widely respected. At Mildenhall in Suffolk,

Tom Sayers: fans attending his fight with John Heenan held train tickets stamped 'To Nowhere'.

Sayers defeated Grant in 64 rounds and two and a half hours. Grant was suffering from agonising cramp and his corner also feared his intestines had been ruptured, which prompted them to toss in the sponge. Grant's injuries were extremely painful but not as serious as feared, and he recovered at a local inn. After this victory, Sayers decided he would concentrate on making prize-fighting his career.

On a foggy morning at Long Reach in the Thames not far from Dartford and Gravesend in January 1853, Sayers defeated Jack Martin in 23 rounds of a match made at 147lbs. Although Sayers won well in 55 minutes, and was still strong on his legs when he applied the finishing punch, his face was cut and battered. Martin was unconscious for five minutes, but ferried back to town in the steamer which had brought them all to the site. Some of the Fancy who did not feel like the boat ride back walked across the marshes to Dartford and caught a train. At the station, the old champion Bendigo kept everyone amused by composing and reciting loudly a poem celebrating the day's events.

Although he had promise, however, Sayers was some way short of an overnight sensation. At 27, in October 1853 at Lakenheath in Suffolk, a three-hour train journey from Shoreditch, he lost to a man of his own size, Nat Langham of Hinckley, Leicestershire. While Langham, who claimed the middleweight championship, was in perfect shape, Sayers was fat after a series of training mishaps. He had a heavy cold, and then some kind of facial skin condition, and at 152lbs was about 5lbs overweight. By the sixth, he was grinning through the blood, and although he had his share of successes and worked well, especially to the body, the longer the fight went on, the more Langham seemed the more capable of winning. Langham was floored heavily by a left hand in the 20th, and by the 45th the Leicestershire man seemed sick and weak, but he stuck to his game plan, rallied to floor Sayers in round 48, opened cuts over both of his eyes, and survived all of Sayers' attempts to finish him. By the 56th Sayers' eyes were rapidly closing and by the 60th he could no longer see. In round 61, cries of 'Take him away' came out of the crowd, and Sayers' swings were hopeless, futile ragings against the weakness of his own flesh. Langham easily stepped around him and knocked him down. This time, Tom's trainer, Alec Keene, threw in the sponge as Tom sat and wept.

It was a bitter lesson. Langham retired to run a sporting pub which was to house the famous Rum Pum Pas club, and so frustrated Sayers' desire for a return, and instead Tom had to work his way back as best he could. When he beat a supposed professor of boxing, George Sims, in four rounds lasting five minutes at Long Reach in February 1854, he collected only £25. *Bell's Life* dismissed poor Sims, who when he regained consciousness asked to be thrown into the Thames, as 'a civil, well-behaved, courageous fellow, ridiculously over-estimated by his friends'. Sayers walked away without a scratch.

When he embarked on a sparring tour for several months, Sayers' relationship with Sarah Henderson ended. She took off with a local cab-driver, leaving him to arrange schooling for their daughter and a nursemaid for their son, Thomas. Depressed, he even toyed with the idea of emigrating to Australia.

It took until January 1856 for Sayers to be matched again, this time with the 38-year-old heavyweight Harry Poulson, who stood only 5ft 7½in tall but weighed more than 170lbs. Poulson had lost to Tom Paddock and had been working as a navvy before accepting this fight, but then drilled himself into fine condition and performed heroically to last 109 rounds in frosty conditions at Appledore in Kent. Sayers always boxed with his hands low, the right drawn across his belly to block body punches, the left ready to snake out into his opponent's face. Poulson, who was originally from Newark in Nottinghamshire, fought in the 'old style', with hands high around his face. It was a long, drawn-out struggle, with Sayers, in spite of having trained only lightly for three weeks, perhaps in the best form of his life. The night before the fight, Sayers stayed up to midnight carousing on the excuse that he was waiting for his fighting boots to be delivered. He eventually knocked Poulson unconscious with a right hand to the jaw after three hours and eight minutes. Poulson recovered quickly and repaired to a local pub, the Railway Hotel, where, although unable to see, found to his relish he was still able to eat and drink. Sayers complained of a sore head and body, but both men returned to London on the same train as their friends. Bendigo, who had trained Poulson, had gambled heavily on him.

As the Australian idea subsided, Sayers agreed to box the admirably stubborn Aaron Jones of Shropshire, who had twice fought gruelling struggles against both Harry Orme and Tom Paddock. They met for £100 a side on mud-flats near Canvey Island on 19 January 1857, a day described as 'piercingly cold', with the small number of spectators who had successfully tracked the steamer down the Thames all huddled inside greatcoats. Many others could not find the site, including one band whose boat left them on the wrong island, where they were forced to sleep out where they could. *Bell's Life* recorded that 'a perceptible shiver ran through the carcases of the combatants' when they stripped for action. Sayers was conceding something like a stone and a half in weight, and planned a long campaign. With cups of tea laced with brandy to combat the cold, they fought for 62 inconclusive rounds spread over three freezing hours, at which point both of them were exhausted. Jones moved to the scratch mark, but then retreated into his own corner, where Sayers did not want to fight him. Sayers, on the advice of his seconds, stayed in mid-ring, and when Jones repeated the strategy, a draw was called. Both had one eye closed, but Jones had also damaged his right hand, which made a quick continuation impossible.

The second fight, in the same spot on 10 February 1857, was accepted as a return match. Again, it was a long, terrible battle, which lasted two hours, with Jones, five years the younger man at 26, eventually going down in the 85th round. On the boat back to London, the tired but only slightly bruised Sayers took the hat around and raised the surprisingly small sum of £8 for the loser.

Next, at a dinner to celebrate his win over Jones, Sayers accepted a match of £200 a side with William Perry, the Tipton Slasher, for the heavyweight championship, which he won in ten rounds at the Isle of Grain in Kent on 16 June 1857. Sayers was suddenly the hero of his day, even though the man he had beaten was 38 years old and exceedingly rusty. In his fading years, a poor, sick man, Perry admitted he had never seen a fighter as good as Sayers, and reflected sadly: 'They should have left me alone.'

His pride had got the better of him, and had led to his ruin.

Tom Paddock, by now 33, wanted to fight Sayers next, but a bout of rheumatic fever hospitalised him. Sayers visited him and left £5 in his hand to help him manage until he was well enough to box again and then embarked on a sparring tour of the north. Meanwhile, Harry Broome said he had found 'an unknown' who could beat Sayers and backed his boast by putting up £200. Sayers matched it, and the mystery captured the imagination of the Fancy. They speculated on old Ben Caunt, Nat Langham, Bendigo and Broome himself, but were astonished – and disappointed – when it turned out to be a raw novice named William Bainge, who called himself Bill Benjamin. History has thrown these no-hopers into the pot from time to time, perhaps because prize-fighting is a world where everyone wants an angle or an edge, where gamblers suspect crosses around every corner, and where the unthinkable very occasionally, for no explicable reason, occurs. Dreamers, who do not realise the true nature of the art, want to believe they can be champions too ... and too often there are those who will, for the chance to make a quick financial kill, encourage them with an all-too-ready smile. So it was with poor Bill Benjamin, a farmer's son from Northleach, a village on the road from Oxford to Cheltenham. He looked the part at just short of 5ft 11in, and 168lbs, but appearances lied. As soon as they began to fight in foul weather on the Isle of Grain on 5 January 1858, Benjamin's inability was plain to see. He was very nervous, and although he had been taught how to stand and the very basic moves, he was in horribly deep. *Bell's Life* recorded the scene after the first knockdown:

> '... the Novice dropped. He was conveyed to his corner and the look of dismay upon his countenance as he glanced around was perfectly ludicrous. It was at once patent to all that he knew nothing of the business he had undertaken, and that the contest was virtually over ...'

It lasted three rounds and six and a half minutes, only because Sayers took his time and Broome shoved Benjamin up for the third when the beginner was obviously overawed. Eventually, Benjamin went down and stayed down, and later blamed his poor performance on a body shot he took in the opening moments of the fight. Sayers duly collected his money and had the champion's belt strapped around his waist in a ceremony at Owen Swift's pub, the Horse Shoe Tavern, in Tichborne Street, eight days later.

Tom Paddock then announced that he had recovered from his illness and made himself available to fight Sayers for £150 a side, the champion accepting the lowering from the norm of £200 because he knew the veteran from Redditch had no significant backer and little money of his own. He was also absolutely confident of victory, justifiably so, as it turned out. At Canvey Island on 16 June 1858, Paddock was cut down in 21 rounds.

Unbelievably, towards the end of 1858, Harry Broome once again brought up the name of Bill Benjamin, making every conceivable excuse for his man's appalling showing that January. Perhaps the most ridiculous was that Benjamin had literally been frozen by the weather, claiming that his system was shocked by the cold when he stripped and he was anxious to prove the charges of cowardice that had been lodged, unkindly, against him were unfair. Nat Langham helped him, and so did Bendigo, and he tried to learn his lessons, while Sayers, who probably treated the whole episode as a huge joke, barely bothered to train, contenting himself instead with benefit appearances around the country. During this time, his mother Maria died, and the mother of his children, Sarah Henderson, told him she was pregnant by her lover, James Aldridge. This affected him badly. He also took to riding after hounds and, since his ability as a rider was a match for Benjamin's as a fighter, he suffered regular falls. Somehow, he managed to avoid serious injury, but when he entered the ring for the return fight near Ashford in Kent on 5 April 1859, he had a pot belly and a fleshy torso. Benjamin had obviously learned since their first, farcical meeting, and was once again in excellent physical shape and fought well. However, even a woefully out of shape Sayers had too much for him, and in 11 rounds and 22 minutes, the Cotswolds farmer's son was pulled out by his seconds. To his credit, Benjamin wanted to go on, but he could hardly see, was near to exhaustion and had been heavily punished.

Before his epic struggle with John Camel Heenan, Sayers boxed only once more, when he defeated a fellow middleweight, Bob Brettle, at Ashford on 20 September 1859. Brettle was born in Edinburgh in January 1832, but had lived in the Black Country most of his life and was a glass-blower by trade. When he fought Sayers, he owned a pub in Digbeth, Birmingham, called the White Lion. Sayers trained at Newmarket – properly, this time – and Brettle at Ashbourne in Derbyshire. Unbelievably, a 36-carriage, doubled-engined train ferried 1,000 passengers out of London to witness the event. Brettle was a round-shouldered, fresh-faced character, who fought confidently out of a strange, crab-like stance, while Sayers' 33-year-old features were beginning to bear the signs of years of poor living, not to mention prize-fighting. He still had the style and the consummate ability, but the cracks were showing. Sayers won, drawing blood from Brettle's mouth in the opening exchanges and then landing a heavy blow to the shoulder, which dislocated it and forced a sudden

Sayers v Heenan: a 140-minute struggle that enthralled a nation.

finish in the seventh. A doctor put Brettle's shoulder back into place before he left the ring, and he recovered quickly enough to discuss the outcome with his friends. Sayers had been so sure of victory that he had gambled £200 on himself at odds of 1-10, in order to win £20.

And so, back to Farnborough on that April morning of 1860, when Sayers put England's fighting name on the line against Heenan, who had ironically been trained in America by Tom's old adversary Aaron Jones. Heenan and Sayers were smuggled separately to the field near the station, and by 7 a.m. were ready for battle. Heenan won the toss for corners and chose to have the sun on his back and to fight 'downhill'. At 7.29, they began.

Heenan's face marked up and cut in the first round before Sayers dropped lightly to the floor. The Englishman cheekily spent the entire interval standing in Heenan's corner watching the patching up of the wound. In the second Heenan began to use his weight and fell heavily on him to end the session, then in the third knocked him clean off his feet and a powerful blow to the jaw ended round four 'amidst the shouts of the Yankees'. Heenan landed a tremendous blow to Sayers' right arm in the sixth – some say it broke it – and from then on Sayers waged a defensive, one-handed battle, his arm swollen and dangling uselessly at his side. His left, though, thudded into Heenan's cheek and closed his right eye in a seventh round which lasted 13 minutes until Sayers slipped and fell. The eighth round went on 20 minutes, before Sayers touched down, but in the tenth Heenan threw the Englishman easily. By round 13 both looked tired, but four rounds later Sayers was still smiling happily. The 21st saw Sayers fall from a punch to the nose, but in the following round it was clear that Heenan's left hand was 'much puffed'.

Sayers had gone down at the end of all of the first 21 rounds, but knockdowns mattered little. Because of his size, Sayers needed to take rests to prevent the much more powerful Heenan wearing him down quickly. In the time he allowed himself, Sayers also landed persistently with left hooks to the face, but in the 23rd round it looked as if he might be nearing the end when Heenan fell heavily on top of him. By the 25th Sayers was weak but cheerful, and the English corner claimed in vain for a foul after the 27th when Heenan landed a punch when Tom was down. But Sayers came through his bad spell and by the 29th he seemed the fresher of the two. Heenan's left eye was closing – and betting was suddenly even. Heenan retired for advice after both men had fallen to end the 34th and two rounds later his face was a gruesome mess. Sayers, though, was weak enough now to be caught and dragged to the ropes. Heenan did just that and was throttling him there when, with the police ready to move in, Sayers wriggled free and fell. It happened again in the 37th and this time Sayers could not extricate himself, instead contenting himself with slamming blows on the inside into Heenan's face. Police closed in, the ring was rushed, and to most of the crowd the fighters were no longer visible.

Five more so-called rounds took place with the ring full of people and the referee unable to take control. At the end of the 42nd round the official finally regained his vantage point and ordered a halt. Heenan rushed off promptly, springing across the field with surprising agility, but within minutes was totally blind. And so it was all over – at 9.49 a.m. and after two hours 20 minutes.

BELL'S LIFE REPORT OF THE FIGHT:

ROUND ONE: Heenan at once threw himself into very fair position, his left well balanced ready for a shoot, and the right across the body. Tom's position was the same as ever, lightly but firmly planted on his pins. He smiled and nodded, and on Heenan trying to lead off his left, got well back. Heenan tried again, his reach being tremendous, but again did Tom get well away. Tom now essayed a draw, but 'The Boy' was awake. Each feinted and dodged to find out a weak point, but for a short time each fortress was too well guarded. At last Tom let go his left and right, but out of distance. Heenan shook his nob and grinned, then again tried a lead, but was short. They got gradually to Heenan's corner, who appeared disposed to fight on the defensive, and the sun being in Tom's eyes seemed to bother him not a little. At length they came together, and sharp left-handers were exchanged, Tom getting on 'The Boy's' nose, drawing first blood, and Heenan leaving his sign manual on Tom's frontispiece. heavy counter-hits followed, Tom again getting on the nose and receiving on the nob. More sparring ensued to a close, when Heenan seized Tom round the neck, but Tom pegged away at the back of his head until he made him leave that, and Tom fell laughing.

ROUND TWO: Heenan showed marks of Tom's handiwork on the back of his neck, and Tom's forehead was flushed. Heenan kept to his corner, whither Tom went to draw him out; when he thought Tom was near enough, 'The Boy' lunged out his left, but Tom stopped him and got back. Heenan tried again and just reached Tom's nose. After one or two feints, a pretty counter took place, Tom getting one on the nose and receiving a sharp one over the right eye. Heenan then closed, got well hold of him, and threw the Champion, falling heavily on him. Offers to take 2 to 1.

ROUND THREE: After a little lively fiddling, Tom got too near to the big 'un, who instantly slung out his left straight and full on the bridge of Tom's beak, knocking him clean off his pins. (First knockdown for Heenan).

ROUND FOUR: Tom, on coming up, looked rather astonished, and his eyes blinked in the sun like a dissipated owl. Heenan went at once to him at the scratch, dodged him, and once more planted a heavy spank with his left, this time on the jaw, and down went Tom again, amidst the shouts of the Yankees, who now offered 6 to 4 on Heenan. The Sayers party looked excessively blue.

ROUND FIVE: Tom's mug showed visible marks of 'the Boy's' powers of hitting. He was cautious, and kept away from his man; Jack followed, and letting go his left on the mouth was well countered by Tom on the proboscis. Heenan now bored in, and after dodging Tom, got again heavily on the sneezer, and Tom fell.

ROUND SIX: Tom's countenance, though not swelled, was much flushed, while the Boy was almost scatheless. He was somewhat wild, and tried both hands, but missed. Counter-hits ensued, in which Tom received the full weight of Heenan's ponderous fist on his right arm, which was driven back against his face. Tom reached Heenan's left cheek, leaving his mark. Heenan retaliated on the right brow, and Tom fell.

ROUND SEVEN: Tom's right peeper displayed marks of pepper, and it was perceptible that he had sustained severe injury to his right arm, which was beginning to swell, and which he now kept close to his body, as if to support it. Still he went to Heenan in his corner, and that hero delivered his left, but not effectively, on the chest. Tom danced away, and as he turned round napped a little one from the right on his back. He was quickly out of harm's way, and coming again, dodged his man until he let fly, when Tom countered him heavily on the right cheek, drawing the claret and raising a considerable bump. The blow staggered Heenan, who stood all of a heap for a moment.

Soon did he collect himself, and as Tom came again, lodged a little one on the nose, but was once more countered very heavily on the right cheek, the cut being increased and the bump enlarged. Slight exchanges followed, in which Tom received on the right eye and Heenan went to his corner for a sponge. He seemed in no hurry to come away, and Tom stood in the middle of the ring until Heenan went slowly to him, and tried his left, but it was no go. He tried again, but only just reached Tom's brow. Tom now feinted and got home on the right peeper, Heenan missing an uppercut. Tom danced away, came again on another tack, and bang went his left on the sore spot, a heavy spank, and he was instantly out of danger, laughing; Heenan rushed after him, but was well stopped, thrice in succession.

Again and again Tom went to him, and baulked his efforts to effect a lodgment, and then Heenan napped another slashing crack on the right cheek, which had the effect of at once closing his dexter goggle. He retreated for a wipe, and was followed by Tom, and some mutual cautious dodging and feinting took place. At last Heenan got on the top of Tom's smeller, but not heavily, and Tom then avoided another attempt. Once more did Heenan retire to Jack Macdonald for consolation and advice; Tom walking round and eying him in an inquisitive manner, as if admiring his handiwork.

Tom, after satisfying his curiosity, went close, and slight exchanges followed, without mischief. Heenan tried his left and was stopped. Both very cautious, and neither disposed to go within gunshot. Heenan now led off and got slightly on the mouth with his left, Tom retaliating on the closed peeper. Mutual taps and stops, and then Tom got his left heavily on the old spot another cracker, whereupon Heenan once more retired into the privacy of his corner, amidst cries of 2 to 1 on Sayers. Tom, after a few turns and a touch of the sponge, went to him, but Heenan shook his nob and seemed disinclined for work. Tom finding he could not draw him, retreated, whereupon 'The Boy' came out, and let go his left viciously, which was beautifully stopped. He then feinted, and got well on the bridge of Tom's snorer as he was retreating, and again knocked him off his pins. Tom rolled over, laughing, and was carried to his corner. This round lasted 13 minutes, and was a fine specimen of stratagem and skill, especially on the part of Tom. His right arm now was much swollen, and so painful that he could make little or no use of it.

ROUND EIGHT: Tom slowest to the call of time, but directly he was at the scratch, 'the Boy' retired to his corner, whither Tom had to follow him. Heenan at once let go his left, but Tom laughed and jumped back. A slight exchange followed, and Tom napped a straight one on the sniffer. Heenan now missed a couple of well-meant shots, and Tom jumped away from a third, and as he turned his back upon Heenan got a right-hander on the back of the neck. Heenan followed him up, but Tom grinned and jumped nimbly away. His activity on his pins was as remarkable as ever. Heenan pursued him, and at last lodged his left slightly on the nozzle, and once more turned on the tap. Tom, however, countered him on the damaged cheek, which caused 'The Boy' to retire for the kind offices of Jack Macdonald. On Tom's going to him he let go his left on the kisser, drawing the carmine, and this led to pretty exchanges at long shots on the cheek. Heenan at this time appeared weak, and the hopes of the Sayers party were greatly in the ascendant.

Heenan preferred his corner to the scratch, and Tom had some difficulty in persuading him to leave. This he at last accomplished, and some beautiful stops were made on both sides. Another break away ensued, after which they countered effectively, but Tom was heaviest on the right cheek, which was now swelled as big as two. Heenan's blow alighted on Tom's oration trap, and drew more of the ruby. On his trying to repeat this lodgment, Tom stopped him cleverly. Capital exchanges followed, in which Tom was again at home on the cheek very heavily. Heenan rushed at him, but Tom was away, and after once or twice being baulked, Heenan again retired to his corner.

After Tom had scrutinised him carefully, he rubbed his hands and went to him, whereupon Heenan let fly his left, but Tom got well away laughing; Heenan shook his head and also laughed good-humouredly. Tom now crept in, and pop went his left on the plague-spot, and off went the Champion laughing. More dodging and stopping on both sides, until Tom was once more on the cheek a slogger. Heenan retaliated sharply on the bridge of the snout, but was stopped in a second attempt, and Tom nailed him on the right cheek very heavily and got away. Heenan tried to take the lead, but Tom jumped back. 'The Boy', persevering, got well on the forehead, but was unsuccessful in a second essay. The first was sufficient to leave a bump on the gallant Tom. More sparring until a severe counter-exchange took place, in which Tom got a hot 'un on the whistler, which shook his ivories, and turned on a fresh tap. It was a staggerer, but Tom recovered and went to his man, when more severe counters were interchanged, Heenan getting another rum one on the cheek, and dropping his left with effect on Tom's sneezer.

Both now indulged in a wipe, and washed their mouths out. They came again, now like giants refreshed, and each in turn tried a lead, but each was well-stopped. Tom's right arm, from the continual stopping such a heavy cannonade as Heenan's, was now much discoloured and swollen, and utterly useless for all purposes of hitting, and he was thus deprived of his principal weapon. After a good deal of this, another heavy exchange followed, in which Tom was at home on the old spot, and Heenan on the jaw heavily, knocking Tom once more off his pins. This round lasted 20 minutes and was a splendid specimen of milling on both sides. Tom's nose and mouth were bleeding, but both his eyes were well open. His arm was his chief drawback. Heenan's right eye had been long closed, his cheek was fearfully swollen, and his mouth was also somewhat out of straight.

ROUND NINE: *Heenan came up as if he intended to force the fighting. He led off viciously, but Tom got well away. 'The Boy' followed him closely, and at last got on Tom's mouth, drawing more of the juice. He followed suit on the snuffer-tray with a like result, and counter-hits ensued, in which each did mischief. Heenan continued to bore in, and at last Tom, after getting a little one on the back, dropped laughing.*

ROUND TEN: *Tom was very slow to the call of time, and appeared to want nursing. It was evidently heavy work struggling against such superior mettle. He stood in the middle of the ring until Heenan went to him, when slight counter-hits were exchanged; after which they closed. Heenan lifted Tom from the ground and threw him heavily with the greatest ease.*

ROUND ELEVEN: *Tom again very much behindhand in coming to time, and the friends of Heenan did not appear in much hurry. When they did come up, Tom had to go into Heenan's corner. After a dodge or two Tom got his right on the good eye rather heavily, but it was not such a right hander of yore, and evidently gave him pain. Heenan returned on the chest, and Tom fell.*

ROUND TWELVE: *'Time, Time!' neither too ready. On Sayers at last facing his man, Heenan caught him, but not very heavily, on the jaw, and dropped him on the saving suit.*

ROUND THIRTEEN: *Heenan, first to leave his second's knee, now went to Tom, and after a dodge or two, popped the left very straight on Tom's nose, once more knocking him clean off his legs. He turned round on returning to his corner, and looking to Mr Falkland, his umpire, exclaimed, 'That's one for you, Fred!' Offers were now made to pay 5 to 4 on Heenan, but the takers seemed scarce.*

ROUND FOURTEEN: *Tom, very weak, came up cautiously and slowly, his nose being large enough for two. Heenan, seeing Tom's state, tried to force the fighting, but Tom got cleverly out of difficulty. Heenan followed him up, and popped a rattler on the throat, without a return. He paused, and then sent a little one on the scent-bottle, but Tom countered him well and straight on the nose, drawing the crimson in profusion. Heenan, nothing daunted, let go his left and was stopped. He then swung round his right heavily on the jaw. They got to close quarters and some heavy in-fighting took place, in which Tom was very busy. At length both were down heavily, Heenan under.*

ROUND FIFTEEN: *Neither seemed in a hurry to leave his second's knee, but Tom was slowest in answering the call. Heenan at once went to him, got the left well on the proboscis, and his right on the jaw, and down again fell the Champion in a heap.*

ROUND SIXTEEN: *Tom shook himself together, but was very cautious. He sparred as if requiring rest, until Heenan came in, when slight exchanges took place, Tom getting it on the nose, and Heenan on the whistler, but neither very heavily. Heenan then made a sudden dart, and planting heavily on Tom's mouth, once more knocked him off his legs. (Loud cheers for Heenan.)*

ROUND SEVENTEEN: *Tom did not display many marks from his repeated knockdown blows, but came up smiling, although somewhat tired. Heenan's mug was decidedly the most disfigured, being so much swelled. Heenan took the lead, but did not get heavily on. He tried again with his right, but the blow passed over Tom's nob. Counter hits followed on the nose, in which Tom's delivery was most effective, but Tom was down.*

ROUND EIGHTEEN: *Very slight exchanges, followed by a heavy counter, in which Heenan's mouth came in for pepper, and Tom got it slightly on the nose, and fell.*

ROUND NINETEEN: *Tom slow to time; Heenan not in a hurry. At last, on facing one another, Heenan went in to a close, and, throwing Tom, fell on him.*

ROUND TWENTY: *Heenan followed Sayers, who was on the retreat, and after one or two dodges, caught him on the jaw heavily with his right. He tried again, but Tom jumped back. Still he persevered, and heavy exchanges followed at close quarters, and both were in the end down at the ropes.*

ROUND TWENTY-ONE: *Sayers very slow, which Heenan seeing, dashed at him, slung out the left on the nose, and again floored the Champion.*

ROUND TWENTY-TWO: *Tom seemed none the worse for this floorer; it rather seemed to do him good, for he came fresher, which Heenan seeing, he retired to his corner. Tom followed and tried to deliver, but missed, and the Benicia Boy dropped him with another straight one on the jaw. Heenan's left hand was now much puffed, and did not seem to leave such impressions as formerly.*

ROUND TWENTY-THREE: *The time was very badly kept on both sides, and there were now complaints that the Benicia Boy was allowed a stool in the ring. An appeal was made to the referee, who at once ordered its removal, as contrary to the laws. Heenan rushed at Tom, who retreated and got one on the back. Tom then turned round and missed his right. They closed, and Tom pegged away merrily on the nose and left cheek, and in the end both down, Tom under. One hour and eleven minutes had now elapsed.*

ROUND TWENTY-FOUR: *The Benicia Boy, first up, tried his left by a sudden dart, but was stopped. An attempt with the right just landed on the side of Tom's nut, and he fell. (5 to 4 on Heenan still offered.)*

ROUND TWENTY-FIVE: *Tom, weak, came up slow, but cheerful. He waited the attack, which was not long in coming, and after getting a little one on the side of his head, Tom popped his left very heavily on the snout, drawing more home-brewed. Heenan, wild, rushed in and bored Tom down.*

ROUND TWENTY-SIX: *Tom, fresher, came up gaily, and tried to lead off with his left, but the Boy stopped him prettily. Another effort landed on Heenan's good eye. Heenan in return planted a rattler on Tom's jaw with his right, which staggered him, and was all but a knockdown. Tom soon shook himself together, whereupon Heenan let fly his left, but Tom was well away. Following up, 'the Boy', got on Tom's chest, but not heavily. Exchanges; Heenan on the 'tato-trap, and Tom on the nose, a smasher, each drawing the cork. Heavy counters followed with the left, and they broke away. Heenan came again, and got on Tom's snorer heavily with his left, once more staggering him. Twice after this did Tom stop Heenan's right and they closed. After some slight fibbing Tom fell, Heenan hitting him when down. An appeal of foul was overruled, the blow being obviously accidental.*

ROUND TWENTY-SEVEN: *'The Boy' came up determined and led off, but Tom was away. A second attempt was equally unsuccessful, and as Tom turned his back to dash away, 'The Boy' caught him on the neck, but not heavily. Sharp exchanges followed, Tom on the left cheek and nose, and 'The Boy' on the mouth. Heenan then went in and tried his left, but was short, whereupon he retired to his corner, had a wipe, and wetted his whistle, and then went to the middle of the ring. Tom joined issue at once, and some heavy exchanges took place, each on the nose, and Heenan now tried to close, reaching after Tom to catch him round the neck. Tom kept out of harm's way, but at length 'The Boy' bored him down at the ropes.*

ROUND TWENTY-EIGHT: *Both much fatigued, wanted all the time they could get. After some sparring, Heenan ran at Tom, who darted away. 'The Boy' rapidly pursued, and they got together, and in the fibbing Tom was busy on Heenan's good cheek, while he caught it on the mouth. In the end Tom was down.*

ROUND TWENTY-NINE: *Tom was still slow to time. 'The Boy' at once went to him, and got heavily on the top of his nut. Tom countered with effect with his right on the left cheek, and then popped his left on the proboscis. Heavy exchanges followed in Tom's favour, who met 'The Boy' very straight and effectively on the nozzle, opening a fresh bin. A break away, following by slight exchanges, led to a harmless close, and Tom slipped down.*

ROUND THIRTY: *Heenan's other eye was now quickly closing, and he had evidently no time to lose. He was strongest on his legs, but his punishment was far more visible than Tom's. He tried to lead off, but Tom met him neatly on the nose, turning on the red port. 'The Boy' rushed at Tom, and literally ran over and fell on him.*

ROUND THIRTY-ONE: *After standing some time in his corner, Heenan was fetched out by Tom, who had now recovered a little. A short spar was followed by another retreat, after which Tom went in and got a little 'un on the left cheek, but it lacked steam. More sparring, and Heenan again retired. Tom stood and examined him with the eye of a connoisseur until he came out, when good exchanges took place, Tom getting heavily on the mouth, and Heenan on the nose. A break away; more sparring for wind; Heenan again to his corner. On Tom going at him he slung out his left heavily on the nose, and prone once more fell the brave Champion.*

ROUND THIRTY-TWO: *Tom all alive, dodged, and caught 'The Boy' on the chin. He turned to retreat, and 'The Boy' nailed him on the body, but not heavily. Heenan then tried repeatedly to draw Tom, but the latter would not go into Heenan's corner. 'The Boy', therefore, had to go out, and some rapid hits and stops followed, without any apparent damage; each, however, got a small tap on the mouth. Heenan having taken another rest in his corner, came out, and got a hot one on the left cheek for his pains, which all but shut up the other eye. This brought on exchanges, each on the mazzard, and then Heenan reached Tom's nose. Heavy determined counter-deliveries on the nose ensued, after which Heenan floored Tom by a right-hander on the cheek. The betting was now even, Sayers for choice. It was obvious that, strong as Heenan was, unless he could make a decided change, he must in a very few minutes be blind.*

ROUND THIRTY-THREE: *The Benicia Boy, feeling he had no time to lose, rushed in, but only just reached Tom's chest. Both seemed fagged, and they stood a few seconds, and then went to close quarters, where Tom, as usual, was busy on 'The Boy's' frontispiece, until he let him slip through his arms on to the ground.*

ROUND THIRTY-FOUR: *Heenan again tried to force the fighting, but Tom got away. They then stood and sparred until Heenan let fly his left, which did not reach its destination. He retired for counsel, and then came at Tom and tried for his right at the body, but without success. Steady exchanges led to close and rapid in-fighting, and both fell, Tom under. Heenan's eye all but closed up.*

ROUND THIRTY-FIVE: *The Benicia Boy dashed viciously in, and caught Tom on the snout, but the blow was without powder. Tom retreated from the vigorous onslaught; Heenan followed and got home on the jaw with the right, still with no effect. Tom now turned and ran, Heenan after him, when, on turning round, Tom napped one on the nose. He, however, landed another little pop on the good eye. Sharp exchanges at close quarters ended in the downfall of Tom. Two hours had now elapsed.*

ROUND THIRTY-SIX: *The Benicia Boy's face was a spectacle to behold, while Tom was very weak. 'The Boy' rushed to a close, and caught Tom round the neck, dragging him to the ropes. At this time, the police, who had been gradually making their way to the ring, began a violent struggle to get close and put a stop to hostilities. 'The Boy' tried to hold Tom, but the latter slipped through his arms and fell.*

ROUND THIRTY-SEVEN: *Tom was first up, and seemed the better man; he made his left twice on Heenan's eye, and the latter at length caught him round the neck at the ropes and there held him. Tom's efforts to extricate himself were vain, but he administered severe punishment to Heenan's face. The police at this time got closer, there was a rush to the ropes from all sides, and we, in company with others, including the referee, were completely shut out from the view. We are informed that the round ended in both going to grass at the expiration of two hours and six minutes. We had hoped that the men would now have been withdrawn, as the referee had been forced from his post, and the police were close by. The battle, so far as it may be called a battle, was for the time over, and the men should have been taken away.*

However, although the referee sent orders for a cessation of hostilities, five more so-called rounds were fought, with pretty equal advantage. Heenan's right eye was fast closing, his left being in complete darkness. The ring was half full of people, however, and neither man had a fair chance. Much do we regret the unpleasant duty that now is imposed upon us, of finding fault with the Benicia Boy for conduct which was not only unmanly, but quite against the rules of the Ring, and had the Referee been present, would inevitably have lost him the battle. We can ourselves declare, as an impartial eye witness of the melee, that in the fourth of these supplementary rounds, while Sayers was on his second's knee, Heenan rushed at him in a very excited state, let fly left and right at Tom's seconds, floored them, and kicked at them when on the ground in desperate style, after which he closed with Sayers, and after a wild rally, they fell together.

The final round was merely a wild scramble, in which both fell. The referee by this time was able to get near again, and ordered the men to desist from fighting. Immediately after this Heenan rushed away from the ring, and ran some distance with the activity of a deer, proving that as far as strength was concerned, he was as fit as ever; but he had not been away from the ring many minutes before he was totally blind. Tom Sayers, although a little tired, and suffering from the arm and the desperate hug in the 37th round, was also strong on his pins, and could have fought some time longer. The blues being now in force, there was, of course, no chance of the men again meeting, and an adjournment was necessary. It was found that the authorities were up in arms in all directions, so that it would be a mere waste of time to go elsewhere. Backward home was therefore the word, and the men and their friends returned to the Metropolis shortly after three o'clock. The whole time occupied, up to the men's leaving the ring, was two hours and twenty minutes.

REMARKS: Up to the unfortunate departure of the referee, this was decidedly the very best Championship fight we ever witnessed. It was to the time aforesaid fought out with manliness, a fairness, and a determination on both sides worthy of the highest commendation. Without any attempt at shifting, each scorned to take a mean advantage, and loudly and repeatedly was each of them cheered. The game displayed on both sides was remarkable. The gluttony and bottom of Tom Sayers are too proverbial to need further comment at our hand; but as certain rumours had been flying about to the effect that Heenan was destitute of those qualities, we deem it right to express our belief that a gamer, more determined fellow, never pulled off a shirt. His punishment was terrible, and yet he took it round after round without flinching, and almost invariably with a smile on his face. We are bound to own that in this, as in his talent, he very agreeably disappointed us; and had we not known his career, we certainly should never have set him down as a novice. He has an excellent delivery with his left, which was as straight as a dart, and early in the fight was very heavy. It appears to us, however, that his hands are not strong, for before half the battle was got through his left hand was so much swelled as to be almost useless; and this, doubtless, was fortunate for Tom, who with his right arm gone, could have made but a poor stand against such a weapon had it retained its original hardness. Of his right Heenan makes but little use. Of his conduct at the conclusion of the battle we cannot speak in too strong terms. We trust it was occasioned by the state of excitement in which he was, owing to the ring having been broken, and by the fact that, being almost blind, he took the offending seconds of his opponent for some other persons.

The state of Heenan's eyesight was shown by the fact that he hit out with both hands at Jemmy Welsh, who wore a red and black striped woollen shirt, mistaking him for his antagonist. Of Tom Sayers we need not say more than that he fought the battle throughout with consummate tact and judgment, and, considering that his right arm (his principal weapon) was rendered almost useless from the commencement, too much praise cannot be awarded to him for his courage and coolness. We are of opinion, even without that arm, that he would eventually have pulled through, had the fight have been finished on the day. But it is useless speculating on possibilities or probabilities.

On the question of nationality, the only point that has been decided, and the only point in our opinion requiring decision, is that both England and America possess brave sons, and each country had reason to be proud of the Champion she had selected. Both were, doubtless, anxious to have it settled; but for ourselves, were we asked, we should say each is so good that he is deserving a belt, and we would call on our countrymen to subscribe for such a trophy as a reward for Heenan's enterprise and boldness in coming, as he had done, to face the British Champion on his own ground.

Sayers was helped away as Englishmen, with the safety in numbers that a home crowd enjoys, celebrated victory. Heenan had to be lifted into his compartment in the train to London, where he was plainly suffering from the battle. Sayers, by contrast, refused to go to bed, instead taking tea and complaining that the doctor had banned him from joining his drinking companions who were by now quaffing back champagne at the bar at The Swan in the Old Kent Road. Heenan was laid to bed at Osborne's Hotel in the Adelphi and spent 48 hours in a dark room, and was for a time considered to be in a critical condition.

Heenan returned to New York to a marvellous welcome, preceded by his wife Adah Menken, who on the back of his fame played to packed houses, and boxing, through this one fight, came to fresh life in the new world of the United States of America.

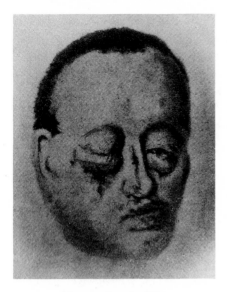

Heenan after the fight

Both men received silver commemorative belts and Sayers was given £3,000 by public subscription, on condition that he never box again.

The money was invested in a trust, and he received the interest to live on. To provide extra income and possibly for something to do, he drove a cab in London, but could not live moderately. He enjoyed a drink - and fairly soon was suffering the effects of his dissipation as well as, possibly, his long and gruelling fighting career. When the crowds lined the streets to await the Royal procession through the London streets, which followed the wedding of the Prince of Wales and 18-year-old Princess Alexandria at Windsor on 10 March 1863, Sayers, apparently oblivious to protocol, rode his horse-drawn cab along the route. The people were delighted and applauded him all the way.

When Heenan returned to England to fight Tom King at Wadhurst in Sussex on 10 December 1863, Sayers agreed to work in the American's corner, but by then was struggling to cope with the developing alcoholism and tuberculosis. Wrapped up against the cold in winter fur cap, yellow flannel jacket and heavy boots, he was also too drunk to be of much use to the man with whom he had shared the Fight of the Century only three and a half years earlier.

At the beginning of 1865 he became seriously ill and diabetes was pronounced in addition to his tuberculosis. He was cared for by his elder sister Eliza, whose husband had given him his first work in the capital when he was no more than a boy. He recovered and seemed well when he visited Brighton in April of that year, but at the races he was caught in a torrential downpour and soaked to the skin. He fought back the illness and drove himself on determinedly, insisting on being present at Epsom for the Derby in June. His sickness was plain for all to see. The same month he appeared at Clerkenwell Police Court where he accused a 17-year-old named George Powell of stealing a coat and telescope from his home. Powell had apparently lived at Sayers' house for 12 years, but the old champion denied he was a relative and also denied co-habiting with the young man's mother. Sayers came across badly when he gave his evidence, however, and Powell was discharged 'without a stain on his character'. Sayers was hissed and jeered as he left court.

He visited Tonbridge and Hastings, but was terribly sick and at the end of the summer he returned to London, where the final illness enveloped him. He died in a room above a factory belonging to a friend, John Mensley, a cobbler who had always made his fighting boots, in High Street, Camden Town, on 8 November 1865. He was 39. When he breathed his last, his father and his two children, Sarah and Thomas, were at his bedside. He was buried at Highgate Cemetery, north London, a week later. A crowd estimated at around 30,000 jostled to watch his body carried into the chapel and out to the grave.

Sayers lived on in the hearts of the English people, immortalised by that one bright spring morning when Parliament emptied itself into a Hampshire field and its scribes, among them Charles Dickens and William Makepeace Thackeray, followed to witness, not the dry business of the Commons, but the undimmed, ruthlessly exciting brutality of the prize ring.

Heenan parted from Adah Isaacs Menken, who went on to greater fame the following year as the 'Naked Lady' in a play called *Mazeppa* which toured the country. Her task in the scene which shocked America was to lie on her back tied to a horse wearing only a silk body stocking. It made her fortune – and she became one of the most scandalous figures of the age, with a succession of highly public affairs. Dickens, Rossetti, Swinburne and Dumas were all said to be her lovers. She died of breast cancer in Paris in 1868, aged only 33. For what it's worth, Adah Menken was her stage persona. Her real name was Adois Dolores McCord.

Heenan made that second attempt to become champion, for a prize of £2,000, against Tom King in 1863, but was already declining as an athlete and lost controversially in 24 rounds. He was never the same again, and although he challenged Mike McCoole to a fight in 1869 for £10,000, it never happened. He blew his money and was a poverty-stricken, saddened figure when he took off for Colorado in search of better air. He had reached Green River Station, Wyoming, in October 1873 when his lungs gave out and he died of a haemorrhage. He was only 38.

11

LAST OF THE BREED – THE SWAFFHAM 'GIPSY'

Never again would bare-knuckle prize-fighting grab the nation's senses and wring them dry. It was to take the advent of the rules ascribed to the Marquess of Queensberry, but in fact written by John Graham Chambers of the Amateur Athletic Club in 1865 and designed to cater for new 'civilised' values, to take it to new and greater prosperity.

Sam Hurst was a giant from Stalybridge in Lancashire, who stood 6ft 2½ in and weighed 210lbs. He was a decent wrestler and used his strength and size well without ever pretending to be much of an artist with the fists. When Sayers' retirement was accepted, Hurst laid claim to the championship, and cemented that by knocking out the faded Tom Paddock for £400 and the championship belt in five rounds lasting only ten minutes near Newbury on 5 November 1860. Hurst's original claim was based on a challenge to Heenan, which had been ignored. After the Sayers-Heenan fight, and the belated but nonetheless serious interest which the police took in it, relatively few were keen to watch Hurst and Paddock do battle. Hurst tossed his long, big arms around like the sails of a windmill and each of the first four rounds ended with the veteran on the floor. The fifth appeared to have ended with Paddock slipping down, but when Hurst turned and trudged back towards his corner, the Redditch man raced after him. Responding to the shouts of his cornermen, Hurst swung round and slammed a thudding right hand beneath Paddock's heart. He crumpled forward to the turf. The blow had broken two of his ribs and he was carried to the train.

In spite of his obvious power, Hurst's raw, novice-like approach attracted the interest of the brilliant Swaffham 'gipsy', Jem Mace. Born in Beeston, a Norfolk village, on 8 April 1831, Mace was a blacksmith's son who learned to box as a boy. In his memoirs, he recalled how much fighting was a part of his youth.

'Everybody learned to use his fists in those days; rich and poor, gentle and simple. Fighting was the one thing talked about. Every little village possessed its champion, and these used to meet one another, usually on Sunday, and fight to the finish with naked fists. I remember there was an old barn about a mile out of Beeston, to which the 'fancy men' of the surrounding villages used to come to settle who was best ... Another favourite place for fighting was the Ploughshare Inn, Beeston. One could always be sure of seeing a fight there on a Saturday night. Not a quarrelsome fight, you understand, but just a ding-dong battle to decide which was the better man ... the two combatants simply hammered each other till one cried 'enough' or fell insensible ... Some of the fiercest fights I have ever seen, outside the Prize Ring, were fought by young fellows of seventeen, or thereabouts, for the possession of the lasses ... the prettiest girls went to the hardest hitters.

'These 'love fights' used almost invariably to take place outside the Ploughshare, and this stood right opposite our cottage, so that I was able to get a good view of them from my bedroom window. The stocks, too, I remember, were close handy, and there was generally somebody in them on Saturday night. The prisoner also got a good view, for the crowd, always sympathetic and good-natured, used to keep a clear space for him to see the 'fun', besides supplying him with beer and "bacca."''

He was sent from home at 14 to become a cabinet-maker, walking to Wells with a handkerchief full of bacon and dumplings and his violin under his arm. In fact, he earned his living playing the fiddle in his employer's pub, at local fairs and gipsy weddings. And eventually he drifted into boxing when a fisherman smashed his precious violin outside a pub at Great Yarmouth.

'Fighters had to be fighters in those days. We fought for our lives, as it were. No drawing-room fighting. How can a man like Tommy Burns, for instance, who never fought a prize-fight in his life, and who would not be permitted by the authorities to fight one even if he wanted to ever so much, expect to vie with the men of the old school, who were at it with the raw 'uns as soon as they could walk almost?'

As an old man, Mace had little time for the new-fangled ways of fighting with gloves, for points in rounds of set duration, or for fighters who reached the top too soon.

Mace's first significant victory was in 1855 when he beat a boxer named Slack – a descendant of the old champion, perhaps? – at Mildenhall in nine rounds. His first after his arrival in London was on 17 February 1857 when he defeated Bill Thorpe in 18 rounds at a weight limit of 10st on Canvey Island.

Jem Mace

Bell's Life reported that Mace '... gave his antagonist the coup de grace in the most offhand and masterly manner ... he was one of the best boxers that we have seen for many a day. He is a quick and rapid fighter, and hits with judgment, precision and remarkable force.'

For a time, Mace ran a pub, The Swan Inn in Swan Lane, Norwich, but also challenged two of the best lighter fighters around, Bob Brettle and Mike Madden, for £100 a side. Brettle accepted, and on the banks of the Medway on 10 March 1858 knocked Mace out with a right hand to the temple in only two rounds, lasting only three minutes. He put his embarrassment behind him, and regained some credibility by beating Posh Price, whose arm he broke,

165

and Bob Travers, who was known as Langham's Black, on the fairly straightforward grounds that he was trained by Nat Langham and that he was, indeed, black. Mace showed how much he had improved by outclassing Brettle in September 1860. The fight was spread over two days, because the police intervened on the first.

Then he took on Sam Hurst for the Championship on Waterloo Day, 18 June 1861, on the mud-flats near Southend. Conceding about five inches in height and 70lbs in weight, few gave Mace a chance, even though his superiority of technique was not in doubt. Hurst was big, but also clumsy, too fleshy – and partially lame as a result of a broken leg. Mace knew it could not be a quick win, and so settled down to take Hurst as long as he could. He drew Hurst's strength from him gradually, until after eight rounds lasting 50 minutes, the big man was cut to pieces by Mace's jarring, unerringly accurate blows and finally knocked out flat on his back.

Even as Hurst lay there, Mace went round with the hat among the onlookers and persuaded them to part with a total of £35 for the beaten man. *Bell's Life*, while acknowledging Mace's flawless craftsmanship, sneeringly condemned Hurst for training in Turkish Baths. London was less interested in prize-fighting since the retirement of Sayers, and Mace's achievements were not widely celebrated. The leading entertainment act of the time was the amazing acrobat Blondin, who was appearing at Crystal Palace, in the wake of his incredible crossing of Niagara Falls on a tightrope with a man on his back! Who was the braver, Blondin or his anonymous passenger? Blondin's act at the Palace involved crossing a tightrope with an accomplice sitting in a wheelbarrow. Compared to dramatics such as this, which could be easily reached and watched from a comfortable seat, what was a prize-fight, which involved a lengthy, possibly perilous journey into an inhospitable wilderness with the risk that the contest would be one-sided, or even farcical?

Even before he had left the ring following his win over Hurst, Mace was publicly challenged by Tom King who, in the time-honoured way, threw his glove at his feet. They shook hands immediately and the match was agreed for 28 January 1862.

Tom King

King was born in Silver Street, Stepney in the east end of London, on 14 August 1835. It was a natural progression from London's docklands to a life on the open seas, and even as a boy he sailed in merchant ships to Africa. He worked in the docks while living in London Street off the Commercial Road, where he lodged with an elderly woman named Wingrove. After a day's work this reserved man would visit a German baker named Brabach, who would teach him the 'Three Rs' – reading, 'riting and 'rithmetic. He handed out a hiding to a local bully known as Brighton Bill in a dockside argument, and was then taught by the old champion Jem Ward, who at the time ran the George Tavern in Ratcliff Highway, St George's In The East.

King's first official fight was a win over a fellow novice, Tommy Truckle of Portsmouth, on the Kent bank of the Thames in November 1860. The 6ft 2in Londoner, who scaled around 180lbs, was already being talked of by Ward as a future champion, and was too good for Truckle. He won in the 49th round against a strong, determined opponent – and made a huge impression. The following Monday he was well enough to give an exhibition in a benefit for Tom Paddock at the Rotunda in Blackfriars Road. Talk of fights with John Heenan and Harry Poulson came to nothing, and he had to wait until October 1861 for his next bout, against William Evans, otherwise known as Young Broome, near the site of the Sayers-Heenan fight at Farnborough.

It was a tough, bloody fight, which King won in 43 rounds spread over 42 minutes, in two rings. The first attempt was interrupted in the 17th round by the police, and so the Fancy, as was their habit, moved swiftly across the county border from Hampshire to Surrey and continued after a break of only 20 minutes. When they restarted, Evans or Broome had a strap of plaster across a cut on his nose, swollen mouth and a black eye, while King had a swollen jaw and a cut left eye. Broome weakened first and repeatedly staggered up to the scratch only to be sent flying again. By the end it was a pathetic spectacle, and something of a relief when Evans went down on his face, out cold. When the poor man recovered consciousness, he could not see. He was ferried to the nearest safe house and put to bed, where for some time he shivered with cold and shock. Fortunately, by late afternoon he had recovered enough to return to London, where his friends treated him as if he had won. King spent a pleasant night celebrating coolly in the East End, apparently showing no ill-effects.

King then made his public challenge to Mace, and they set to training, the challenger at Hastings, the champion near Norwich. The day of the fight brought a desperate winter combination of drizzle, snow and sleet. The public were put off by rumours of a concerted police effort to stop the fight occurring in several counties surrounding London and warnings had been sent to railway bosses not to provide special trains for the Fancy. Religious zealots issued pamphlets warning against involvement in the activities of the Ring and one went so far as to call it 'a national sin'. Nevertheless, there were some who bought their tickets at Mace's pub in Shoreditch, or at Nat Langham's in St Martin's Lane, and those who wanted to see the fight assembled at London Bridge at 6 a.m.

In spite of the warnings by moralists, a train duly ferried them all out of the capital on a two-hour slog into the Surrey countryside to the village of

Mace v King

Godstone (which is now to be found on the edge of the infamous M25!) By round five Mace, outreached and outpunched, bled from the nose and mouth. The chilling rain made the ground slippery, and hampered Mace's attempts to use his speed and cunning. In round 27, King scored a heavy knockdown, but although he seemed the more tired of the two, Mace was having trouble with a damaged wrist. Nevertheless, the champion used his experience and wits to keep King out and gradually drew his strength. By the 43rd, Mace judged that his 26-year-old challenger was ready to be taken and stepped in with a tremendous blow to the throat. King gulped blood and stumbled, and Mace hurled himself on to him, sending him crashing beneath him. King was knocked unconscious by the fall and could not make it to the scratch.

Mace took to touring with Ginnett's Circus, meanwhile asking for the massive sum of £1,000 for his next defence. Bob Brettle claimed to have a mystery opponent to fight Mace, but King stepped in and he had issued his own challenge, which the champion accepted ... for only £200 a side. This time interest was high and curiosity as to the site widespread. Even the *Church Record* joined in the speculation, declaring solemnly that the fight would take place 'in the neighbourhood of Aldershot'. Mace had trained hard at the old training quarters of Tom Sayers at Newmarket, while King had also worked hard at The Baldfaced Stag near Woodford in Essex. The champion weighed 158lbs, the challenger around 20lbs more.

On the day of the fight, 26 November 1862, the crowd were thronging around Fenchurch Street station from 4 a.m., and the usual 'security' arrangements of the Fancy were broken down by mobs of thieves. Many lost their tickets, or all of their money, and others were simply so intimidated that they turned for home without attempting to make the journey. This was another severe blow for the game. In the end around 300 diehards took the train and steamer out to the banks of the Medway near Thames Haven – and were on hand to witness one of the most dramatic turnarounds in ring history. King boxed well ... but Mace boxed beautifully, and gradually took control.

Even though King was still strong and competitive, Mace's brilliance was such that by the 18th round Tom Sayers' old friend Johnny Gideon offered £30 to win £5 on the champion – and there were no takers. In round 19, Mace moved in to finish it, but in weaving into distance and coming up with a right hand, left himself open – and King chopped a devastating right of his own on to Mace's left cheek. The blow seemed to go right through him, and the champion staggered and reeled around the ring, before falling in a heap. His seconds, Bob Brettle and Bill Travers, worked furiously to get him out for round 20, and he staggered up, only to be knocked down by the first blow King threw, a solid shot to the nose. Mace was unable to shake off the effects, but refused to quit and came up weakly for the 21st, the left side of his face swelling alarmingly almost by the second. King only needed a little more than a push to put him down again, and this time the sponge was thrown up. It had taken 38 minutes.

King announced his retirement, but when John Camel Heenan arrived, reclaiming the championship, he changed his mind and agreed to a fight for £1,000 a side on 8 December 1863 'within 100 miles of London'. In fact, it turned out to be in the village of Wadhurst in Kent. A 30-carriage train ferrying participants and fans pulled out of London Bridge station before daybreak on a beautiful, mild winter's morning. It rolled through the misty countryside, past a posse of policemen at Reigate in Surrey, and on beyond Tunbridge Wells, easing gently to a halt outside the village.

The site – a field farmed by a tenant, John Wallis – was eventually selected a mile and a half's walk away from the train. The fight began at 10 a.m., Heenan considerably heavier at 198lbs, although both were the same height. They got straight down to business and after even one round, both men's faces were reddened from the pummelling they had taken. Heenan, who had the strangely muffled, sadly declining Tom Sayers in his corner as well as the man who did all the work, Jack Macdonald, was cut on the lip in the second round. The crowd did not approve of his 'hugging' style – rather than stand up and fight, he seemed intent on crushing the strength out of King by wrestling. However, the eighth round ended with King demonstrating his superiority in mauling as well as boxing by throwing the American heavily on to his back. But round 14 saw Heenan throw King with a venomous cross-buttock, and he ended the 15th by flooring the champion with a vicious right hand for the first serious knockdown. King held his boxing together, however, and closed one of Heenan's eyes. The American did throw King to end round 17, but from then on his effort petered out. With the crowd breaking through the outer ring, it seemed possible that the fight would have to be abandoned, but fortunately they behaved long enough for King to drive on to victory. It came after the 24th round when King threw him heavily and, with Heenan sprawled on the turf vomiting, the match was conceded. There had been much harder prize fights than this, but Heenan suffered terrible after-effects. He was still exhausted several hours afterwards and although he seemed to recover, three days later he passed out, and had to be nursed carefully back to health.

Although the tenant farmer, Wallis, appears to have been satisfied at the compensation he received for the damage to his field, the fight provoked the ire of the squire of Whiligh, George Courthope, who had been arrogant, bold, or daft enough to travel to the site in a bid to prevent it. Heenan's supporters somehow persuaded him to keep out of the way, but this tiresome man brought charges against King, Heenan, and their seconds as well as Jem Mace and Bob Travers at Lewes Crown Court. Mace's crime was to pass round the hat for Heenan, while Travers' offence was unclear. The magistrates persuaded Courthope to drop charges against Mace and Travers, and the others all pleaded guilty to taking part in a prize fight. King announced his retirement in court, no doubt hoping this would help his case, but he was treated no differently to the others: they were all bound over in the sum of £100 each.

A strange story appeared in New York, which claimed that Heenan had been drugged or poisoned, but that cut little ice in England, where a letter to the *Illustrated Sporting News* described it as 'all bosh', which it almost certainly was.

King made good money gambling on horse-racing, and also continued his old sporting pastime of sculling. He was also a passionate gardener who specialised in cultivating roses. When he died at the age of 55 in Stockbridge, Hampshire, in October 1888, he left a fortune of between £30,000 and £40,000.

Upon King's second retirement, Mace took over again. He was a technician, an innovator, who would box at his own pace, teaching himself as he went, until like every other athlete who stays too long, he couldn't make his body do what his brain had discovered was the right thing. Accordingly in his later days he became one of the master-teachers.

After his battles with King, at the age of 32 on 1 September 1863, and three months before the King-Heenan fight, Mace trounced Joe Goss of Northampton in 19 rounds spread over one hour 55 minutes near Wootton Basset, Wiltshire, five miles beyond 'the great engine works' at Swindon. It was another wonderful exhibition from Mace, who took his time – and then took out his brave, but overmatched challenger with one devastating right hand. After that, he took over as owner of an athletics track known as the Strawberry Recreation Grounds in Liverpool. Strawberry Fields Forever?

The rematch with Goss at Farningham in Kent on 24 May 1866 was ruled a draw because neither man was trying. Only two blows – one each – landed in half an hour! In his autobiography, Mace explained that he was lame with a damaged instep, and could not take the initiative. Unfortunately for the public, Goss also insisted on counter-punching and so they cancelled each other out. Mace remembered: 'No wonder the crowd abused us roundly. From their point of view, we most certainly deserved it. And all the while I was wondering why on earth Joe didn't sail in and make mincemeat of me. Every moment I expected that he would.'

Then Mace revealed that after it was all over, and they were returning to the city in considerable disgrace, he showed Goss his inflamed and swollen foot … only to be astonished himself when Goss rubbed away pink paint from his wrist to reveal ugly and painful bruises. Both of them were crocked to the point where they were afraid to lead for fear of taking a quick beating!

When they met again to restore their reputations, Mace won in 21 rounds on 6 August 1866. Mace's preparations were interrupted by a 14-day spell in jail after he had agreed to act as a second in a minor fight near Walsall.

Nat Langham, anxious to keep away the thugs who had made it a habit to gather at fights of importance, put a price of three guineas on the tickets and therefore it attracted only a steamer full of fans, who enjoyed a relaxed journey down the Thames to the Kent bank where the fight took place beyond the eyes of the law. In a fore-runner of tactics of a century later, Mace demanded and got a ring that measured only 16ft square instead of the usual 24ft. He wanted to fight Goss at close range. Mace took control when he cut Goss severely. There was – and is – no room for sympathy or unnecessary sensitivity when a fight is to be won and lost. Mace remembered it well:

'I cut his right eyebrow to the bone, the blood spurting from a gash extending halfway across his forehead. The sight of this decided my tactics. I visited it again and again, whenever I got the opportunity, bruising the exposed bone, and enlarging the wound each time, till I had him nearly mad with the pain and fury of it.'

By round 20, amid cries of 'Take him away', Mace was appealing to Goss's cornermen to surrender. Joe was staggering around, his gloves up, but unable to control his legs. Mace refused to hit him any more, and eventually Goss fell over and did not have the strength to get up. The champion returned to Liverpool the same day, where he was greeted by massive crowds all intent on a serious party. To his immense delight, the champagne flowed long into the night.

Mace expressed deep regret that he was unable to visit Adah Menken on her deathbed in Paris, revealing that they were 'old pals, although it was my cousin Pooley Mace that she chiefly favoured'.

Prize-fighting was dying out, however, ruined by its own crookedness, by the constant, intimidating presence of thugs who made it difficult for ordinary, honest sporting men to attend without taking ridiculous risks with their pockets and personal safety, by the ever-increasing outrage of the moralists and, by no means least, by the growing competence of the English police force. Effectively, it came to an end in the summer of 1868 – the year after the savage Anti-Popery riots in Birmingham – when an Act of Parliament made it an offence to allow a train to discharge passengers between stations when a breach of the peace was likely to be committed.

In frustration at the state of the business in England, Mace tied up his affairs in Liverpool and sailed for New York towards the end of 1869. With his departure, the prize ring in England virtually died out.

Tom Allen of Birmingham had gone to the States some time before, and settled in Pittsburgh, and no sooner had Mace arrived than Allen challenged him to a championship fight, which was arranged for Kennerville, Louisiana, on 10 May 1870. By then 39 years old, Mace saw no reason to apply himself to the grind of training perpetually and spent some time enjoying the New York nightlife before leaving to prepare with his cousin Pooley in the middle of a pine forest in Alabama. The fight itself attracted remarkable interest, and years later provided one of the most vivid memories of Mace's long life:

'Never in all my experience had I seen or imagined so picturesque and motley an assemblage. Men of all nationalities, seemingly, were there, and of all colours certainly. Creole dandies, glossy-coated and patent-leather booted, jostled bronzed backwoodsmen in homespun. Broad-hatted planters, in suits of white nankeen, were cheek by jowl with smartly togged 'sports' from New York and St Louis. The Chicago baseball club were there to a man, in their white and crimson playing colours. Meanwhile the Louisiana Jockey Club, which had its headquarters in New Orleans, had turned out in its full strength, each member clad in correct morning costume – frock coat, light trousers and top-hat.'

Allen was unbeaten, acknowledged as the champion of America and 13 years Mace's junior – a very real threat. But Mace was too good for him, and won a horribly one-sided encounter in ten rounds and 44 minutes. While Mace remained unmarked, Allen's face was swollen and grotesquely distorted. He finished in unimaginable agony, with a dislocated jaw, and dislocated shoulder, and was carried away in a horse blanket.

In 1871, Mace's main rival was the Irish-born American Joe Coburn. They should have fought at Port Dover, Canada, on 11 May but when they arrived at the site, they found hundreds of policemen already sitting at ringside. They knew if they put on a proper contest, the likelihood was that they would be arrested and jailed – and so they sparred gently for what must have been an incredibly tedious hour and 17 minutes, before the crowd were put out of their misery by the inevitable police intervention. No charges resulted. When they fought again in Bay St Louis, Mississippi on 30 November, a draw was ruled after 12 rounds with Mace on the brink of victory. As he waited for his train north, disgusted and frustrated by the decision which had cost him the prize money, Mace was twice shot at. Both times the bullets missed. In a town named Virginia City, Nevada, he beat a local favourite, Bill Davis, in front of a crowd of around 10,000 people, and then repeated the verdict near San Francisco.

When work dried up, he moved to Australia and New Zealand, travelling with his own booth and passing on his knowledge to another great trainer, Larry Foley, who taught the legendary Peter Jackson and future triple world champion Bob Fitzsimmons. Back in Britain Mace unwisely accepted a fight with young Charlie Mitchell of Birmingham in 1890 when he was 58. Even though it was restricted to two-minute rounds, Mitchell won in the third.

Mace maintained his interest in boxing to his last days, although in spite of the fact that he was once said to be worth an astonishing £100,000, he was sadly reduced to 'touching' the great heavyweight champion James J. Jeffries for a handout when the American came to London. In May 1909 he was honoured with a benefit night at a former music hall in Villiers Street, off Charing Cross. He was with a travelling fair which was set up at a place called Pit Heath in Jarrow, County Durham, when he was taken ill and carried to a house about a quarter of a mile away at 6 Princess Street, where he died in 1910. He was 79. The death certificate recorded the cause of death as pneumonia and senile decay. He is buried in Anfield Cemetery, Liverpool, and a cross was also erected out of respect in the churchyard of his birthplace, Beeston in Norfolk.

12

LOOKING FOR AMERICA

Buoyed by the firm belief that John Camel Heenan had been robbed against Tom Sayers, the American prize-ring found a unity it had never previously enjoyed. No case can be made to suggest the sport was organised, but Heenan's perceived heroics in the Farnborough field in April 1860 appealed to a wider sporting audience than boxing had ever touched before. People were also inclined to warm to Heenan more than they had unscrupulous characters like Yankee Sullivan, Tom Hyer and 'Old Smoke' Morrissey. If it was true that he liked a drink, then at least he had no definite links with organised crime, and apart from rumours of a role as a heavy in California at election time, had not so far used his muscle to unsocial use. He seemed a decent guy. America was also a land with a growing sense of national identity and pride, and Heenan's fight with Sayers, coupled with the alleged injustice of the decision, fitted the mood admirably.

Yet no sooner had it begun to develop, this feeling was buried beneath the swirling ocean of emotion which took the fledgling nation into civil war. The hanging of John Brown in Charleston, Virginia, in December 1859, provided a focal point for those who saw the slavery issue as a major stumbling block in the unifying of the country. Attitudes hardened, social divides between a perceived 'north' and 'south' were quickly polarised, and resentments bubbled over into a deep pool of righteousness. In these circumstances, throughout history, no matter who turns out to be right or wrong, if any can be determined fully, the tidal sense of a mass of humanity takes those who are locked into that peculiar time and place in a particular direction. When this phenomenon occurs, the result is a ferocious, emotional, collective confidence which in turn produces war. And for the time it takes for the tide to wane, those who oppose it, who attempt to change direction, are murdered as traitors.

John Brown was hanged after being convicted of treason, murder and conspiring with slaves to create an insurrection at Harper's Ferry, Virginia. In June 1860, most of the delegates from the southern states at the Democratic Party convention walked out because of disagreements over slavery, and Abraham Lincoln's nomination as the Republican candidate in the presidential elections brought angry statements of intent in the south. For example, Southern Carolina made it plain that if Lincoln became president, they would be in favour of a southern confederacy. On 6 November 1860 Lincoln, who had also advocated the right of labourers to strike, was duly elected ... and the following month the nation divided. In May 1861 at Montgomery, Alabama, the Confederacy Congress declared war on the Union.

For four years, Americans fought among themselves for that elusive chameleon of a principle, freedom. Lincoln's inspirational, incredible Gettysburg address was a symbol of the new world beyond war, but the truth for the vast majority, as it usually is, was a life made miserable by grief, injury and abject poverty. In these times, most ordinary people eked out their existences as best they could, their fortunes and energies exhausted. The war subsided, and then effectively ended with, first the surrender of General Lee at Appomattox, and then with the assassination of Lincoln by John Wilkes Booth at Ford's Theatre in Washington DC on 15 April 1865.

Sporting events never stop completely in times of war, but their importance and effect is usually trivialised. Sometimes they actually become incorporated into the war effort, as warlords consider them useful social diversions during lulls in the action. Boxing, in the wake of the Heenan-Sayers fight, appears to have been in widespread use for this purpose. Heenan received some criticism for travelling to England to fight Tom King instead of joining the Union forces, but his deeds were now largely irrelevant. The fact that he had fought Sayers at such a time and with such a controversial result was enough. He had become an inspirational symbol to a generation of ordinary men, who were now thrown by the war effort into male companionship and given an increased awareness of their need to be able to fight on one level or another. Because of a combination of these circumstances, boxing had become an acceptable activity to a multitude of American men, enhanced rather than diminished by war.

Or so it was in the more 'civilised' parts of the country. Elsewhere, in the vast Western stretches of cattle land, in the frontier and gold-boom towns, fist-fighting developed at its own pace. One major prize-fight was on 2 January 1865 in the Leviathan Hall in the raw, gold-mining town of Virginia City, Montana Territory, where Con Orem and Hugh O'Neil fought – in unpadded buckskin gloves, but under London Prize Ring Rules – for the supposed middleweight championship of America. After 185 rounds, lasting three hours and five minutes, they agreed on a draw under insistent pressure from

Joe Coburn

the referee, and were paid an equal share of the gate receipts of $425 each. The middleweight title was also disputed two years later by Tommy Chandler and Dooney Harris at Point Isabel, California. Chandler won.

Mike McCoole and Joe Coburn fought for $1,000 each and the American heavyweight championship in an open field outside Charlestown, Maryland, on 5 May 1863. Coburn, who was originally from Middletown, County Armagh in the north of Ireland, won in 67 rounds and 70 minutes, establishing himself as champion, but retired after travelling to Ireland and failing to obtain a fight with the English champion, Jem Mace.

Coburn later changed his mind, but by then things had become confusing. A Californian named Bill Davis claimed the title, but lost a 43 round fight with Jim Dunn in Pike County, Pennsylvania, in May 1865. Dunn, who was from Kildare, lost interest in boxing and went on to become a prominent politician in Brooklyn. Davis once again boasted that he was champion. McCoole disputed that, and proved his point by defeating Davis in 34 rounds, averaging a minute a round, at Rhodes Point, Missouri, in September 1866. McCoole beat the Englishman Aaron Jones at Busenbark Station, Ohio, in August 1867, but then Coburn came out of retirement and challenged him nine months later at Cold Spring Station, Indiana. The fight was thwarted by the police and both were jailed for 40 days. Similarly, when an Englishman, Joe Wormwald, and a big Irishman named Ned O'Baldwin, were matched at Lynnfield, Massachusetts, in October 1868, they were arrested only ten minutes into the contest.

Life in America was just as precarious as in the teeming cities of England. Wormwald died in Canada of chronic alcoholism at the age of 31, and Jones was 37 when he was found dead, poisoned, in Leavenworth, Indiana, by a woman he had jilted, on 16 February 1869. O'Baldwin was shot by a business partner, Michael Finnell, in a saloon in West St., New York, in September 1875, and died after lingering for two days. He was 35. These were ugly days, when the gentile sophistication of life in the well-to-do New England towns was starkly contrasted by the slums of the major cities, and especially New York, which was the first point of call for immigrants from Europe, and the vast frontiers further West. Names that are now legend to us carried out the deeds that have been passed down, often romanticised by film. George Armstrong Custer, Sitting Bull, Buffalo Bill Cody, Jesse James, Cochise and Wild Bill Hickock all lived in the decade or so after the end of the Civil War.

Another prominent fighter was Jimmy Elliott, who was born in County Athlone in Ireland in 1838 and raised in New York. After he lost on a foul to Jim Dunn at Bull's Ferry, New Jersey, in 1863 he was jailed for two years. He issued challenges when he was released in 1865, but although he handed out a battering to Bill Davis and claimed the championship, his ring appearances were haphazard. He beat Charley Gallagher at Peach Island near Detroit, and lost to John Dwyer at Long Point, Canada. He also fought a brief gloved contest with John L. Sullivan in 1882 and lost in seven minutes. He was shot dead by a gambler, Jere Dunn, in the Tivoli Restaurant in Chicago on 1 March 1883, and buried in Calvary Cemetery, New York. Dunn served two years eight months in Sing-Sing for manslaughter. Years later Dunn refereed a fight between Paddy Slavin and Jake Kilrain at Hoboken, New Jersey.

Mostly, fights were long and arduous, but the shortest on record was at Leavenworth, Kansas, on 4 January 1868. Tom Dow knocked out Ned Kiely in seven seconds.

Birmingham-born Tom Allen entered the championship argument when he defeated Bill Davis, and then beat McCoole's face into a horrible mess before losing on a disqualification in June 1869. Allen was born in April 1840, stood 5ft 11ins and weighed 175lbs. Before he left for America he had a solid grounding in England, where he won several fights and drew with Joe Goss. Allen became an American citizen after losing that horribly one-sided affair with Jem Mace, but claimed the title when Mace was accepted to have retired. On the face of it, this was an outrageous move because he had beaten no-one of note.

McCoole disputed Allen's right to the title and they met again near St Louis in September 1873. This time, however, 33-year-old Allen won easily in seven rounds and 20 minutes.

He went on to beat Ben Hogan, a German-born adventurer, in 1872. Hogan was a storybook figure: a spy for both sides in the American Civil War, a gambling house owner, oil magnate and a producer of plays, he could also box. Hogan claimed Allen had fouled him out of the fight near Council Bluffs, Nebraska, but no-one took any notice. He also lost a gloved contest on Broadway with the celebrated lightweight champion Billy Edwards. While living in New York, he became a committed Christian, and spent his time preaching on the streets.

Charley Gallagher was a giant Canadian, who lost to both Bill Davis and Jimmy Elliott, but then pulled off an amazing upset by defeating Allen in a mere three minutes. When they fought again, Allen outclassed him, but a free-for-all broke out at the end and the referee, disgusted by the anarchy, ruled a draw and washed his hands of the whole thing. Gallagher died of consumption in 1871.

Mike McCoole

John Dwyer was a Canadian who lived in Brooklyn. He retired after his 1879 win over Jimmy Elliott, which he felt had entitled him to be regarded as champion, and eventually became the chief clerk in Brooklyn County Court.

Mike McCoole was born in Ireland, but raised on the banks of the Mississippi, where he earned a living as a boatman. A little over 6ft tall, he weighed around 200lbs, and fought between 1858 and 1873. By then a drunk, he was arrested in St Louis in October 1873 for shooting dead another pugilist, Patsy Mavery. Although a coroner found him guilty of wilful murder, nothing came of it, and he left to live in New Orleans, where he died in 1886.

These were maverick times, with nobody possessing the kind of authority that was necessary for boxing in the United States to operate as a sport. Allen continued to claim the title, until he lost it controversially to his old rival from England, Joe Goss, in Kentucky in September 1876. Both were well past their best – Allen was 36 and Goss 37. The fight took place in two rings – in Kenton and then Boone counties – because they were moved on by law officers. Allen was well on top, but then he knocked Goss down and hit him again in the face as he knelt on the floor. Disqualification was the obvious result. Allen quit the ring to run a saloon in St Louis and died there in April 1904, around the time of his 64th birthday.

Joe Goss stood only 5ft 8½ ins and scaled around 150lbs. Born in Northampton on 5 November 1838, he was two months short of his 38th birthday when he beat Allen, but in 1880 he boxed an exhibition with the bigger, heavier, younger, infinitely better John L. Sullivan, who badly exposed him even over three rounds. Sullivan knocked him down in the second and eased off to allow the spar to run its course. Goss, an extrovert, gregarious man, had been fighting for more than 20 years – and one fight in England, against Bodger Crutchley, had lasted 120 rounds.

And then there was Paddy Ryan, born in Thurles, between Kilkenny and Tipperary deep in the south of Ireland on 15 March 1853, the youngest of 11 children. Ryan emigrated to Troy, New York, and had his first major fight against Goss for the title at Collier Station, West Virginia, on 30 May 1880. Ryan was inexperienced, but Goss was too old and worn anyway and probably any half-decent, 27-year-old who stood 5ft 11ins and weighed in the region of 200lbs, would have accounted for the 41-year-old champion. The fact that Ryan needed to go into the 86th round before he knocked Goss out with a right hand counter probably said enough about Ryan's limits. Goss's long career had eaten away his physical resources and inside five years he died of Bright's Disease, which afflicts the liver and kidneys, in Boston in March 1885.

Ryan was called the Trojan Giant, which made good newspaper copy, but the fact remained that the prize-fighting 'champion of the world' was a near-novice who had been lucky enough to beat a man old enough to have known better than to have moved away from the fireside. Pugilism was in a mess and probably seemed to have little in the way of a future.

In England fight people had nothing left to celebrate. They were faced with looking back at their heritage or across to the 'New World', and it must have seemed that the days when there were believable champions, of Mendoza and Jackson, of Belcher and Pearce, of Cribb and Spring, had gone forever. The old values were exhausted, the old ideas dimming, the old excitements mimicked by a succession of magicless men. The Marquess of Queensberry's rules were steering the sport into a new age, but the fighting world had become a confused, uncertain place, filled with doubt and perpetually undermined by rumours of fixes. Men must have wondered if and how it would survive.

Its champions, for pity's sake, were even wearing gloves!

13

JOHN L. SULLIVAN

And so on to the edge of the gloveless Dark Ages came John L., the unbeatable son of a mother who wanted a priest for a son, and who got only, gloriously, John L., a bully, an idol, a big-mouthed drunk, a braggart who believed his own boast that he could lick any son-of-a-bitch in the house, and who, in the ten long years of his sublime and ridiculous prime, probably could.

Sullivan's parents, Michael and Catherine, emigrated separately from Ireland after the catastrophic potato famines of the 1840s. They married in Boston in November 1856, settled in the Roxbury district and on 12 October 1858, Catherine gave birth to their first son, who was to become the greatest, most revered and most hated fighter of his day.

He probably left school at around 15 – he did not, as he liked to put about, attend Boston College and was not coached for the priesthood by Jesuits – and certainly worked as an apprentice plumber, tinsmith and mason. He qualified at none. He earned spare cash in semi-professional baseball and by 1859 had drifted into boxing. Officially, it was banned in Massachusetts, but that didn't stop 'exhibitions' happening in supposedly select clubs. His talent was extraordinary. After only a handful of bouts, he enjoyed sparring sessions with the great 'professor', Mike Donovan, and the champion himself, Joe Goss. Donovan was then a 33-year-old veteran outweighed by 40lbs but with still-majestic skills. However, the novice heavyweight gave him all he could handle for the required four rounds in which Mike hurt his right hand so badly on Sullivan's solid skull that he was unable to box again for eight months.

Donovan, who had been boxing since 1866, was widely acknowledged as a ring genius whose size had been the only barrier between his skills and the open championship of America. In his first bare-knuckle bout at St Louis in July 1866, he lost on a foul after three hours and 15 minutes against Billy Crowley, after which he was coached in the finer points of the art by an accomplished fighter named Patsy Kenrick. He had several wins, then took three years out from 1869 until 1872 to work as a ship-caulker but returned to boxing and moved to New York. After winning several gloved fights quickly, Donovan figured in a bare-knuckle bout with Jim Murray in Philadelphia, but the fight was curtailed by the police after an hour and five minutes.

In 1878, after three evenly split bouts – one win each and a draw – with William C. McClellan in California he issued a challenge to any middleweight (meaning around 150lbs) in 'America or the world'. Nobody took him up on it, and his admirers and fans presented him with a belt offering their recognition of him as the middleweight champion of America. Donovan fought, with gloves and bare fists, anyone he could, even if it meant conceding as much as 50lbs. After he retired in 1891, he became the instructor at the New York Athletic Club for many years and his textbook *The Science Of Boxing*, published in 1893, demonstrated his ability as a teacher. (His son, Arthur, became the leading referee of the 1930s.) Donovan was mightily impressed with Sullivan. The image bequeathed us of the older John L. is of a heavy, ponderous slugger with a big punch but not much skill. In fact, in his youth he had the speed to match his power, even if his aggression was still somewhat raw and untutored. In 1880 Donovan was convinced he had just boxed the next heavyweight champion.

After an exhibition in New York – his first appearance there – against a local boxer, Jerry Murphy, in April 1880, Sullivan sparred with Joe Goss at a benefit for the ageing champion at Boston Music Hall. Goss had a defence lined up for the end of May against Paddy Ryan, but pulled on the gloves for a three-round spar with Sullivan in front of a crowd of 1,800. He must have wished he hadn't. Sullivan was too quick and powerful for him and knocked him down heavily in the second round. The ring announcer had to help him up, but then Goss staggered drunkenly around. Sullivan eased up in round three, but Goss was groggy and dazed and only just made it to the end. The supposed exhibition made Sullivan's name in his home city.

When Goss lost the title to Paddy Ryan in a long battle, the scene was set for Sullivan to fight Ryan. However, the big man from Troy saw no point in rushing into that, and the 'Boston Strong Boy' or 'Highland Boy' as he was then known, was forced to wait more than 18 months for his chance. In the long term, it did him no harm. He stopped George Rooke in a Boston spar and twice defeated the highly rated 'Professor' John Donaldson in Cincinnati before the end of 1880, the last time in a clandestine fight in front of only 30 people in a crumbling beer hall known as Pacific Garden. It wasn't strictly a boxing match, even though they wore gloves, for they had no ring and Sullivan supposedly even resorted to kicking Donaldson at one point.

He boxed another three-round exhibition with Mike Donovan at the

Boston Music Hall in March 1881, in which the 'Professor', knowing more of what to expect, boxed beautifully and made Sullivan look a novice. The *Boston Globe* painted the picture:

'(Sullivan is) the strongest man in the profession. A well-directed blow from him has seemingly force enough to lay low a full-grown Texan steer, and when he gets upon the stage he considers that it is the proper caper for him to immediately throw all the brutal force in him into his arm and launch it forth at his opponent.

'In this manner he opened the bout with the Chicagoan; the latter, who is really a scientific man, coolly dodged out of the way, and all through three intense and exciting rounds, the great burly Highlander was unable to plant one well-directed blow on the face of his opponent.

'The latter, however, was more successful, getting in some telling face blows.

'The affair was not at all satisfactory, the conduct of Sullivan being of such a brutal description as to invoke the hearty disapproval of the spectators, who gave vent to their displeasure by prolonged hissing.'

Two months later Sullivan enhanced his reputation in New York by hammering John Flood, a local roughneck known as 'The Bull's Head Terror' in eight rounds on a barge in the Hudson River, anchored near Yonkers. Fight fans, who had paid $10 each to go aboard, saw Sullivan smash Flood to the deck (literally) in the eighth round. Thoroughly beaten, he had blood pouring from an ear, and a horribly swollen face.

Sullivan also fought in Philadelphia and Chicago before the year was out, and again created a big impression, but a spar in New York with Steve Taylor, a former Jersey City coroner, was a listless affair and the crowd jeered and complained.

Paddy Ryan finally fought Sullivan in Mississippi City on 7 February 1882. Ryan had milked his status as champion while he could, and prolonged his reign by opting to keep away from the ring as long as possible. Before agreeing to box John L., he had established his own saloon in Albany, New York. At one time he said he would never fight again, then complained that he was out of shape, but eventually was pressed into getting himself in condition. He took off 30lbs while training in Rockaway Beach, but Sullivan had no such preliminary matters to take care of. Already close to his fighting weight, he went straight to work.

Interest across America was huge, with the moralists out in force. Some authorities demonstrated their disgust that a prize-fight could excite so much feeling, and feared the mass movement of social flotsam and jetsam in search of the site would cause serious problems. The fight was announced as to take

Sullivan v Ryan: the day the fabled 'Boston Strong Boy' burst on to the scene.

place within 100 miles of New Orleans, which upset the good administrators of Louisiana, but they need not have been so concerned. Although reporters claimed to have spotted outlaws Frank and Jesse James among the throng, as well as the bank-robber Red O'Leary, there was no serious trouble. Fans paid $10 a head for tickets on the 12-carriage train out of New Orleans north to Mississippi City, a journey of around five hours. The town sheriff was solemnly informed that the fight would be held in Biloxi, and took off with his marshalls to ride the 20 miles to make sure it didn't happen. In fact, once the law-upholders were out of the way, a ring was set up on lawns in front of the Barnes Hotel and by fight time – midday – a large crowd had gathered, including ladies who sat on the verandah of the hotel.

The first photograph of a championship fight is of this scene as the boxers, their blurred shapes having been retouched, battle before a dense, standing throng, some of whom had come from as far as San Francisco and

183

Cincinnati. Sullivan was made to wait 15 minutes in the ring, before Ryan emerged from the hotel, won the toss for corners and put the challenger facing the sun. Sullivan landed a stinging left hand, and after a brief spell of in-fighting, stepped back and dropped the champion like a fallen redwood with a pulverising right hand. The first round had taken only 30 seconds, and already the fight was as good as done. By the third round Ryan was battered almost into exhaustion. He tried to wrestle to buy time, but Sullivan whacked away at his head with remorseless, relentless intent. Ryan did land one right hand to the neck in the eighth, when both were wrestled down, but in the next he fell unconscious from a succession of right hands. It was all over in nine rounds and slightly less than 11 minutes.

Sullivan vaulted the ropes, went to the hotel to change and boarded the train. Everyone had left the scene by 2 p.m., and the law enforcers returned to find the crime perpetrated and the criminals vanished! Ryan later came out with the immortal description of Sullivan's power. He said the first punch felt as if 'a telegraph pole had been shoved against me endways'. Ryan also complained about the effects of an old hernia problem, but admitted his plans to wrestle through the early stages had been destroyed once Sullivan landed his punches.

Betting had been huge – more than $200,000 had been gambled in New York alone – and with that one fight it became plain that prize-fighting, be it bare knuckle or with gloves, was here to stay, whatever the authorities thought of it. Newspapers filled their columns with descriptions of the epic battle, and one even quoted Ryan's dismayed mother as declaring: 'I could lick that man Sullivan myself.'

Not only did Ryan lose his title, his expected payday of around $600 turned out to be a paltry $85. He went home to lick his wounds, and got down to the business of earning a living again. He moved from the saloon in Albany to another in Chicago, but was already yesterday's man.

Sullivan's ten-year party began, with his $4,500 winnings being put to immediate use. Wherever he went, he was mobbed. Whatever he did was celebrated by his admirers or slammed by his critics. Whatever he said was quoted. The backslappers began their work, and Sullivan enjoyed every minute of it. He was 23. The world must have seemed a fine place.

Nevertheless, he was uncertain about which course his career should take. The bare-knuckle championship was considered the only one of genuine status, and the interest his fight with Ryan drew was extremely beneficial to him, but the intentions of the law-keepers were plain. Prize-fighting without gloves was to be driven out, and Sullivan's own profile was already so high that it was difficult for him to move discreetly enough for a major fight to be held without interference from those who would intervene and throw him in jail. Sullivan's attitude towards gloved fighting seems to have been pragmatic. If they had to be worn in order for money to be earned, then so be it. He released a public statement of intent the month after his victory over Ryan:

'I am willing to fight any man in this country, in four weeks from signing articles, for five thousand dollars a side; or, any man... for the same amount at two months from signing articles; – I to use gloves, and he, if he pleases, to fight with the bare knuckles. I will not fight again with the bare knuckles, as I do not wish to put myself in a position amenable to the law.'

He went on to challenge fighters who had already been making noises about wanting to fight him for the championship to 'put up or shut up'.

One of his wins in alleged exhibitions in 1882 was a three round knockout of the ageing Jimmy Elliott in gloves before 5,000 people in Washington Park, Brooklyn. Sullivan offered Elliott $500 if he could stay four rounds, and extended that to $200 to all-comers. After the second round, Elliott's trainer Johnny Roche is said to have sucked the blood from his damaged nose and spat it on to the wooden boards. Elliott was flattened by a blow to the neck in the next round. The only man to last the allotted four rounds with Sullivan was an Englishman named Joe 'Tug' Wilson from Leicester, who went down nine times in the opening session, eight times in the second, four times in round three and several more in the last. On most of these he came in close, grabbed hold of an angry champion and then slid down out of harm's

John L. Sullivan

way. At the end of four he was still standing and picked up his prize money. Sullivan was angry, frustrated and embarrassed.

His most significant exhibitions in 1883 were against Charlie Mitchell of Birmingham and the New Zealand Maori, Herbert Slade. Mitchell was a carefree, reckless character who had been boxing with knuckles and gloves since 1878, when he was a boy of 16. He had made his name in England by winning a heavyweight competition in December 1882 and three months later arrived in New York on the 'Republic' with the intention of fighting Sullivan. Still only 22, he was small and light – and extremely clever.

Sullivan suffered a spell of ill-health – he coughed up blood, a sign not of tuberculosis but of the extreme nature of his late night drinking habits. Nevertheless, he agreed to 'spar' with Mitchell in soft gloves in Madison Square Garden, New York City, on 14 May 1883. The 24-year-old champion chased the Englishman for all he was worth, bundled him down several times, but was then floored for the first time in his life by a surprise punch. The shock waves reverberated around the great arena as almost 10,000 people rose to get a better look. But Sullivan was not hurt and got up to slam away until the security men, headed by one Clubber Williams and backed up by a 90-strong squad of policemen, intervened to stop the fight after the Englishman had been thrown heavily to the boards. Mitchell, who finished with a damaged back, had showed up Sullivan for what he was: A still raw, rapidly improving, all-action slugger who did not know nor apparently need to know the finer points of ringcraft. At one point as Mitchell dodged and ducked, he laughed openly in the champion's face. It might be said that they did not grow to like each other as a result of this brief encounter!

In contrast to the sly, nippy Mitchell, Slade was a big, hard-hitting novice who had been discovered by the great Jem Mace in New Zealand. He was 6ft 2½ in tall, scaled around 196lbs and was 27 years old. They fought in Madison Square Garden in August 1883, drawing a 10,000 crowd, which seems incredible now in view of the fact that it was officially a four three-minute round 'exhibition' under the new-fangled Marquess of Queensberry Rules. Sadly, as soon as they moved from their corners, the mismatch was obvious.

Sullivan, a 2-5 betting favourite, looked every inch the real fighter, while Slade was tentative, uncertain and clumsy. At one point the poor man actually turned his back and fled around the ring with Sullivan charging after him, roaring like a bull. By the third Slade was too dazed to fight after shipping a left hand to the ear and crumpling on to the ring floor. Amazingly, Sullivan's cut of the purse was around $7,000. In 1883 alone, Sullivan made around $40,000 in the ring, and more followed in 1884, when nobody was found who could even extend him, and yet the paying customers could not get enough of him.

By now he was married and, true to prize-fighting tradition, had his own saloon. The drinking continued unabated and by 1885, when one of his opponents was his old adversary Paddy Ryan, the exhibitions had become pretty much of a circus. Ryan was as near broke as makes no difference and struggling to support his family, which included his elderly mother. He was also fat and in no condition to box, but for the money it was worth the embarrassment: before 5,000 people in the Garden, they fought for a mere 30 seconds before the police stopped the fight because they were deemed to be slugging, not sparring. With the benefit of hindsight and given the nature of the times, it seems incredible that the paying customers did not tear the place down.

By 1885, the popularity Sullivan had enjoyed was now more uneven. Yes, he had his drinking companions and his gregarious nature appealed to ordinary men whose lives seemed hum-drum by comparison, but there were also emerging signs of a darker nature. In 1885, his wife Annie petitioned for divorce because of his drunkenness, cruelty and abuse. John L. contested it bitterly, blamed their differences on his wife's family, denied striking her, being cruel to her or that his drinking had been a problem, and the result was a sensational few days in court, after which the judge found in favour of the world heavyweight champion. From then on they lived mostly apart, but the marriage remained legal for almost a quarter of a century more.

In August 1885, Sullivan beat Dominic McCaffrey in a gloved fight that some considered for the championship under the Marquess of Queensberry Rules. Sullivan had to remove 30lbs to get himself in some kind of fighting shape at a little below 210lbs and in fact finished the fight with a by now illegal wrestling throw. His roller coaster took a terrible plunge in 1886 when his two year old son John, who lived with Annie in Rhode Island, died of diphtheria. He grieved privately, and continued touring where he could. The most notable 'exhibition' was in San Francisco when he knocked out Paddy Ryan in three rounds and then tended him in the corner, alongside Ryan's seconds. He was given a terrific ovation for that, and newspaper reports of this incident and his generosity in giving handouts to the needy actually increased his popularity.

Poor Ryan, by contrast, turned down a chance to stay with Sullivan as a sparring partner on tour, and did odd jobs, living from hand to mouth for the rest of his life, which ended after a brief illness in Green Island, New York, on 14 December 1900. He was 47.

John L. had not defended his championship in a genuinely accepted match since he won it, and in 1887 left on a European tour that would, at last, put an end to that. He drew large crowds in Birmingham and London, and also took in Ireland. Finally, in dire need of funds, he responded to a challenge from Charlie Mitchell and defended his title against the only man to put him down, in a rain-soaked, muddy field on the horse-training grounds of the unwitting Baron Alphonse Rothschild at Apremont, near Chantilly, north of Paris.

Prize-fighting produced some bizarre fights in some odd locations during its strange and uneven history, and few more so than this. Rothschild, one of the wealthiest men in Europe, was a philanthropist and collector of art. He had played a significant part in the manner of the French survival following the defeat of Napoleon III by the Prussian Army at Sedan in September 1870, firstly by guaranteeing the French compensation to Prussia and then by supplying food to the starving people of Paris when the Commune was savagely repressed by the national assembly of Adolphe Thiers. And on to

Rothschild's lands on the chilly, wet morning of Saturday, 10 March 1888 strolled a motley band of fight followers, along with Sullivan and Mitchell, leading contender Jake Kilrain, Mitchell's father-in-law 'Pony' Moore, referee Bernard Angle and Sullivan's fiancee, Anne Livingston, who dressed as a man to circumvent the quaint 'no ladies' rule.

By now, Sullivan's reputation by far outweighed his skills. Bad living had worn him down and the speed of his youth had gone. He was 29, too bulky and slow, but with his punch and inordinate strength intact. Mitchell was too light to do him much harm, but was also good enough to avoid Sullivan's predictable rushes. He sniped away, refusing to meet Sullivan head on, and moving constantly. More than once, the frustrated champion would boom: 'Is this a fight or a running match? Why don't you stand and fight?'

Even Mitchell's chief second, Jack Baldock, tried to get him to trade punches, but the fighter knew better than his advisor and had planned a long, cunning campaign. The ground churned into mud, and each time he went down from a moderate blow, the Englishman would taunt Sullivan. Generally, however, the fight was not ill-tempered. Twice, Sullivan rebuked Mitchell for spiking him and each time Charlie apologised.

From round four, Sullivan's right arm was damaged – he missed Mitchell with the fist and connected with the wrist and forearm, causing a sprain – and the injury lessened his effectiveness even more. This was also his first fight since he broke his left arm in a supposed exhibition with Patsy Cardiff in Minneapolis in January 1887. Sullivan grew weary and stiff in the freezing cold, and when the rain set in fully in the 15th round, he suffered terribly. Conditions were appalling, even though the ring had been positioned close to a large wall which provided shelter from the prying eyes of the police and from the wind. Sullivan refused brandy, but by the 31st round his teeth were chattering. In the mud, it was difficult to plant the feet for a seriously heavy blow, and Mitchell slipped and slithered around contentedly. At one point, it seemed the gendarmes had arrived, but the distant figures turned out to be gamekeepers, who stood and watched the spectacle which probably leant considerable weight to the traditional French argument that the English were part-stupid, part-insane!

By the 39th round, after three hours and 11 minutes, neither man was prepared to commit himself to throwing a punch. Mitchell was fresh, walking around comfortably, while Sullivan stood like a tired, snorting mammoth, out of his time and as if staring into a huge, unwelcoming future. This was how it was going to be: Men would no longer play into his hands by standing still and slugging to the finish; rather, they would box on the move, knowing how to beat him but uncertain whether or not they could carry it off. Eventually, Mitchell offered Sullivan a draw, and the champion accepted.

Afterwards, as they left the estate, some in carriages, the police arrested almost everybody who had either taken part or borne witness to the bout. Jake Kilrain and Bernard Angle were among the few who eluded capture. Later that day, in prison in Senlis, Sullivan's right arm was so badly swollen that a doctor was called to lance it. The following morning they were released on 6,000 francs' bail and repaired to the comfort of a local hotel. On the Monday, they had lunch together before parting company. Sullivan was sentenced to three days' jail in his absence, and fined 2,000 francs, but as he had already left the country it was academic. There are conflicting reports as to whether or not Mitchell stayed to sit out his nights in a cold cell. I suspect that although his inclination was to avoid it, as he was bailed for 3,000 francs of his friends' money, he may well have done so. Within a month, Sullivan returned to Boston.

To his intense annoyance, the champion was pilloried at home, where the fight was well documented, because he had been unable to finish off a man who was both smaller and lighter. He took the criticism badly and for years did not appreciate attempts to discuss either the event, or Mitchell, although they eventually became firm friends and in middle age even tried more than once to set up exhibitions.

Mitchell was a good fighter under both bare-knuckle and gloved codes, who went on to challenge James J. Corbett in Jacksonville, Florida, for the championship and a $20,000 purse in 1894. He lost in three rounds after, in his own estimation, making the young champion too fired up. He remained a boxing devotee to the end of his life, particularly admiring the skills of little men like Pedlar Palmer and Jimmy Wilde, and died in Brighton on 3 April 1918.

In spite of adverse comments by journalists, Sullivan remained popular among his own. He returned with grand stories of his European tour, with a sizeable profit from his combined fees of $25,000, and used both to entertain anyone who was prepared to listen. Not surprisingly, he was soon short of funds again and needed the proceeds of a testimonial benefit in Boston which drew 3,000 people. Most of the cash was claimed by his latest manager, Harry Phillips, to whom he owed a substantial sum. They parted company after the debt was settled. Another benefit in New York drew only 300 people, and provided nothing but embarrassment.

Although he was champion, he was a fat, slow, sad, blustering athlete whose body was that of a man considerably older than his 30 years. He didn't really want to fight any more, but he needed ready money, and nothing paid as well as fighting. Then he fell ill, with an intestinal complaint linked to his ferocious drinking, and almost died. The experience frightened him, and temporarily at least jolted him into a spell of clean living. He regained his strength and resolved to mend his ways. His new zeal also enabled him to show interest in boxing ... and, taunted by the opposition of newspaperman Richard

Kyle Fox, he agreed to fight Jake Kilrain. Fox had long been championing Kilrain's cause, but it was Sullivan who lodged the advertisement which launched the fight, in the *New York Illustrated News* in December 1888. The champion demanded six months to get ready, and put a price of $10,000 a head on the bout. Kilrain and Fox agreed.

The last bare-knuckle championship match in history was made for 8 July 1889 within 200 miles of New Orleans. With the inspired help of champion wrestler and fitness philosopher William Muldoon, Sullivan worked himself into shape, complaining miserably at first and then growing accustomed to the regime to the point where, if he could never be said to be enjoying the hard work, at least he was encouraged by the results. Muldoon was a single-minded character who believed mental strength was the basis for physical fitness. 'Mind is the man; the body is merely the house. It is possible to keep the house in order if you have the mind to do so,' he said.

Kilrain was John Joseph Killion, born at Green Point, Long Island, New York, on 9 February 1859. Like Sullivan, his ancestry was Irish, and he grew up in Boston, but there the similarities ended. Kilrain was a solid, upstanding citizen who fought to provide for his family, after first earning a living as a mill-worker and enjoying some success in rowing. His first fight was in 1880 when he was 21, and his last a one round knockout by Frank Slavin in Baltimore in 1896, when he was 37. He fought Charlie Mitchell and George Godfrey, and drew an epic, which lasted 106 rounds, with Englishman Jem Smith near Paris in December 1887. Kilrain was also wise with his money, opening bank accounts for his two children and taking out life insurance for his fights. He worked hard to keep his wife, her sister, and his own parents as well as his children, in the family home in Baltimore. Most felt he had a huge chance of ending Sullivan's long reign. The *New York World*, for example, declared boldly: 'According to all such drunkards as he, his legs ought to fail him after 20 minutes of fighting.'

However, they had reckoned without the work of 44-year-old Muldoon, who took Sullivan out of his enfeebled state and made him, for the last time, a boxer of formidable powers. Muldoon offered to do the job for nothing if John L. failed to win, even though it meant four months of effort, drilling the big man into shape. He took Sullivan to his farmhouse in Belfast, New York State, and set to work on him. Sullivan was so ill from drink when he arrived that for a week he could do no more than lie on his back. He could not sleep properly and his stomach could keep down only oatmeal and warm milk. It was several weeks before he could absorb solid food or meat.

Sullivan knew how ill he had been and knew why. He also knew that he had to box Kilrain and that Muldoon was his only chance of winning. It says volumes for his determination that in four months he lapsed into his old ways on only one night. Even then, Muldoon followed him into the two available bars and paid the owner to close them for the night. Sullivan was furious but returned to camp. Muldoon ate with the champ – and even took to sleeping in the same room. He was so fanatical that he slept for only a few hours each night and was up an hour before Sullivan, at 6 a.m., to oversee the preparation of breakfast. Muldoon had him work the dumb-bell weights before breakfast, then morning roadwork – eight miles in the week, 20 miles on Saturdays, a gym session in the afternoon and then wrestling as well as bag-work and skipping. The finale was a bath of cold water and rock salt in which he not only had to sit, but had to bathe his face to harden the skin.

Out of all this, Sullivan hated the roadwork more than the rest put together, but the humourless Muldoon set the pace and he trudged along eight or ten yards behind, accompanied by his sparring partner, Mike Cleary, and two English mastiffs. In this way, Muldoon at first nursed the heavyweight champion of the world back to health and then removed 40 pounds of blubber from his rapidly ageing body. Any of the champion's old cronies who found their way to Muldoon's farm were sent packing and were not even permitted, such was the great trainer's influence, to take rooms at the local hotel.

Towards the end of his stay, Sullivan was no longer speaking to Muldoon, but at least continued to listen to his orders, and four days before the fight they set off together for New Orleans. It was typical of Muldoon that he took drinking water bottled from a well on his farm for Sullivan's use until after the fight as well as all the food they required.

Prize-fighting remained illegal in what was then the 38-state nation and staying ahead of the law was a part of the excitement. For days newspapers carried items about the fight, none more than the *Daily Picayune* in New Orleans, which carried as well as detailed news of the contestants, the declared intentions of the law officers to prevent its occurrence. The governors of Texas, Louisiana, Mississippi and Alabama warned its officers to be vigilant, but what more could they do? The Louisiana governor, Francis T. Nicholls, who had as a Confederate colonel lost an arm and a leg in the Civil War, went so far as to remind railroad owners of their obligation to ferry state troops to the scene of any potential disorder.

William E. Harding, who wrote as 'Referee' in the widely respected *Police Gazette*, urged that Sullivan and Kilrain box in New Orleans itself, arguing that the more public the match, the better chance of fair play there would be. Newspapers carried the betting odds and lists of supposed big wagers. They covered the arrival of Kilrain and Sullivan, who stayed in a house at No.29 North Rampart Street as a guest of the Young Men's Gymnastic Club. Kilrain was housed at the Southern Athletic Club, which nearly 100 years later was still the home of a boxing gym. Far from being hidden away, on his first night in town Jake was introduced to a 1,200-strong crowd at an amateur boxing night at the St Charles Theater.

The *Daily Picayune* declared: 'The city is fighting mad. Everybody has the fever and is talking Sullivan and Kilrain. Ladies discussed it in street-cars, men talked and argued about it in places which had never heard pugilism mentioned before.'

Everybody knew the great fight would happen, but when the 'Big Fight Special' rolled out of the Queen and Crescent railyards in New Orleans just after midnight, only a handful of the 2,122 paying customers were certain of its destination. They crowded on to the seats, stood in corridors, hung on to roofs and rode even on the cow-catchers to keep an eye out for obstructions or breaks in the line, or even the presence of the state troopers. At the border with Mississippi, the local infantry had laid stacks of bayonets on the track, but the train driver didn't so much as slow the engine. The train sent the weapons showering into the air and steamed on.

And it was almost dawn when the intrepid band arrived at Richburg, a village in Marion County, which was in effect a lumber camp on a 30,000-acre pine estate belonging to 'Colonel' Charles W. Rich. The day before, Rich had put labourers from his sawmill to work at creating a rough and ready ring and proper enclosures for Press and backers, and enthusiastically lent his name to sporting history. Incredibly, the writers of the *Daily Picayune* had published a hunch that Richburg would be the site. When the Richburg sheriff, whose name was Cowart, made a token attempt to wire for help, the message was accepted 'subject to delay'. His request for volunteers to aid his attempt to uphold the law pricked the conscience of only one man in the village, and accepting that the efforts of one professional and one amateur were unlikely to achieve anything other than putting their own safety at risk, Sheriff Cowart issued a statement of protest and an order that peace be maintained, and then accepted a place at ringside! Tickets for places close to the ring – including the train fare – cost $15, with those further back priced at $10. The total gate was $24,830.

Kilrain, who had travelled on the same train as Sullivan with their respective parties the previous day, made his way through the crowd, accompanied by cornermen Charlie Mitchell and Mike Donovan, just after 10 a.m. He tossed his hat into the ring in the accepted manner and then climbed through the ropes, carrying an American flag as well as his green and white colours. Sullivan followed almost on his heels, with Muldoon and Cleary close behind. Both men appointed timekeepers – Tom Costello of Cleveland for Sullivan, and W. 'Bat' Masterson, the legendary gunman who had cleaned up Dodge City along with his friend Wyatt Earp, for Kilrain. The referee was John Fitzpatrick of New Orleans. Muldoon had done his work magnificently. Now, according to eye-witness reports, all that showed of his old ways was what was described as 'a small

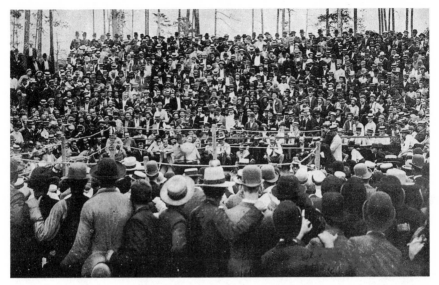

Sullivan v Kilrain: the last of the bare-knuckle championship fights. It lasted 75 rounds.

protuberance in the lower belly', which we take to be the remnants of his beer gut.

Donovan later said Kilrain beat himself, losing his nerve in those vital last moments when it became obvious that the champion had somehow got himself into shape. Maybe, maybe not. Certainly, the challenger began positively enough, grabbing Sullivan by the shoulders and throwing him over his hip after only 15 seconds. Kilrain, like Mitchell before him, planned a long fight, mixing up hitting, holding and wrestling with evasive tactics. As he had done with the truculent little Englishman, at one point Sullivan stood back and yelled: 'Why don't you fight, you son of a bitch?'

Kilrain laughed. From the corner Mitchell kept up a torrent of abuse, which served only to enrage the champion further. Then in round seven Kilrain, who had been dazed badly by a heavy right hand which ended round six, slung over a roundhouse right which tore open Sullivan's ear. The blood trickled down in a steady stream.

Slowly, the heat rose to a terrible 104 degress, and each man descended into his own personal hell, slogging on for round after round. After round 12, with about 40 minutes gone, Sullivan was confident enough to tell Muldoon he could 'fight till daybreak', and Kilrain seemed to be ready for the taking. But the clinging, choking heat drained them both of everything but their spirits. Kilrain raised an ugly lump below Sullivan's eye and worked on it, but as the rounds moved into the 30s he was shoved up for each session, Sullivan laughed and sneered: 'You're a champion? Of what?'

But by round 44 Sullivan was suffering most. He began to vomit with great, violent shudders, in mid-ring. Kilrain stood back and offered a draw, but the champion snorted contempt and, still retching, began to fight again. Kilrain's seconds tipped whisky down his throat between rounds to numb the exhaustion and pain, and shoved him out again, adding dehydration resulting from alcohol consumption to the list of potential dangers. Sullivan refused all refreshment. From round 70 onwards, it was no longer a contest of any description, merely a witness to the depths of resolve which can prop up the human spirit. Kilrain was broken, beaten, utterly spent, and yet would not concede. By the 75th round his head rolled on his shoulders as if his neck were broken, his back was blistered and he could not control his legs. A doctor warned them that if he came up for round 76, he would die, and the sponge was tossed up at the end of a struggle which had run its course in two hours 16 minutes and 23 seconds.

After the fighters had left, Sullivan still exchanging insults with Mitchell, the crowd tore down the ring and ripped up what they could for souvenirs, including squares of turf. In their delinquency, they were aware, perhaps dimly but nevertheless aware, that they had just witnessed the dying of an era. Never again would two men battle with bare fists under London Prize Ring Rules for the championship of the world.

On the train away from the pine forests of Richburg, Kilrain sat in despair, still in his fighting gear, his wounds barely even patched up. He considered the humiliation worse than the pain and apologised for letting his people down. The next day he left New Orleans for New York, parted company with Mitchell, and went into hiding in Virginia before returning to the family home.

By contrast, Sullivan enjoyed his journey hugely, even though his hands were painfully swollen, and after a deep mustard bath he repaired to the Young Men's Gymnastic Club where he drank his fill and tossed dollar bills from the windows to the crowds below. Unfortunately, the police were gathering the will to make a point, and although they somehow missed him in New Orleans, he was arrested on the train at Nashville. After a night in jail, he was released and returned to Chicago and then New York, where the celebrations continued unabated.

However, the law-keepers were nothing if not stubborn. In a double swoop, within days of each other Sullivan was arrested in New York and Kilrain at home in Baltimore. And in Purvis, Mississippi, on 16 August 1889, Sullivan was found guilty of taking part in a prize fight, but innocent of assault and battery. For some reason, Kilrain's trial was delayed until December, and in a laughable solution, he was found not guilty of prize-fighting but guilty of assault and battery. Kilrain was jailed for two months and fined $200. He lost an appeal and was released to serve his sentence by working ... for none other than Charles Rich! He was happy to confine himself to life in Richburg for the necessary time, and then departed a free man.

Sullivan's appeal meandered on amid the quagmire of Mississippi law and his one year jail sentence was eventually dumped in favour of a $500 fine. A warrant was still out for Sullivan's backer, Charlie Johnson, by the time of the Sullivan-James J.Corbett fight three years later.

Kilrain, the sober, kindly family man, deserved to keep his money, but he lost it when his Baltimore saloon was burned to the ground. He fought on, losing a six round decision to James J. Corbett and in 1891 knocking out George Godfrey in 44 rounds. Long after he retired from the ring in 1896 he continued to work in a string of menial jobs, the last of them as a night watchman. He was 78 when he died of old age – officially diabetes – at Quincy, Massachusetts, in December 1937.

The costly diversions of the law notwithstanding, Sullivan knew the end of his career was approaching. For one, he acknowledged he could not stand another training camp with Muldoon. He could have fought anybody, but prize-fighting with bare knuckles was becoming a risky business. He ignored a challenge from the Englishman Jem Smith, and dismissed the great black heavyweight Peter Jackson, who would almost certainly have beaten him. Like so many of his generation, he did not consider those with black skin worthy of his time or attention. (He had complained that his overnight stay in Nashville jail had been spent in a cell which housed black as well as white prisoners.)

Peter Jackson

Jackson was a magnificent fighter, born one of eight children of a minister in St Croix in the Leeward Islands in July 1861. At 18, he found a job on a ship and sailed to Sydney where he took up boxing, eventually learning under the first of the great Australian teachers, Larry Foley. He won the Australian heavyweight title in 1886 with a 30 round win over Tom Leeds and two years later made his American debut by knocking out George Godfrey in 10 rounds in San Francisco. Before Sullivan fought Kilrain, Jackson had also beaten the giant Joe McAuliffe, Sullivan's 'exhibition' adversary Patsy Cardiff and one Shorty Kincaid. His ability was plain to see.

Four months after the Sullivan-Kilrain battle, Jackson was in London, defeating the English champion Jem Smith on a foul in only three rounds. In Dublin he demolished Irishman Peter Maher in two and then returned to America, having made a wonderful impression. Sullivan, however, wanted nothing to do with him. In May 1891, Jackson fought a 61-round draw with James J. Corbett in San Francisco, in a methodical, 'thinking man's fight', which some say was one of the finest demonstrations of the technical side of boxing ever staged. Basically, they cancelled each other out and the result was a stalemate. In his autobiography, *Roar of the Crowd*, Corbett claimed he was robbed of the decision, but acknowledged:

'That night I thought Peter Jackson was a great fighter. Six months later, still being tired from that fight, I thought him a great one. And today, after 33 years, as I sit on the 15th floor of a New York skyscraper writing this, I still maintain that he was the greatest fighter I have ever seen.'

But Sullivan continued to bluff and brag behind his self-imposed colour bar. In 1892, Jackson returned to London and at the National Sporting Club knocked out both Jem Smith and Frank Slavin. It was obvious, by then, however, that he would not be given a world title chance. He spent his time on the stage, and ran a coaching academy in London. Eventually at the age of 36, he was persuaded back to test the young James J. Jeffries in San Francisco in March 1898. He was knocked out in three rounds. He eventually returned to Australia and fought for the last time in Melbourne in December 1899, aged 38, when in spite of his age and the onset of tuberculosis he was able to draw over 25 rounds with Billy Warren. He died in Roma, Queensland, in July 1901, at the age of 40, and buried in Toowong Cemetery, Brisbane, under a stone which read: 'This Was A Man'.

Sullivan recovered from the Kilrain fight and took to the stage in a play named *Honest Hearts And Willing Hands*, which served him well until the summer of 1892. He drank and ate as he pleased, and he was a bloated relic of the great athlete he had been just those few short years before. But the world wanted to know whether or not he would fight again. Was he the champion, or not? He didn't want to fight again, but didn't want to be called the former champion either. In March 1892, he issued a challenge, designed to satisfy his critics. It was a typical combination of bombast and bigotry.

'I hereby challenge any and all of the bluffers who have been trying to make capital at my expense to fight me either the last week in August this year or the first week in September this year at the Olympic Club, New Orleans, Louisiana, for a purse of $25,000 and an outside bet of $10,000, the winner of the fight to take the entire purse ... I give precedence in this challenge to Frank P. Slavin, of Australia, he and his backers having done the greatest amount of bluffing. My second preference is that bombastic sprinter, Charles Mitchell, of England, whom I would rather whip than any man in the world. My third preference is James Corbett, of California, who has achieved his share of bombast. But in this challenge I include all fighters – first come, first served – who are white. I will not fight a negro. I never have and I never shall.'

And the challenge ended with the news, dreadful to all advocates of bare-knuckle fighting, with the promise: 'The Marquis [sic] of Queensberry Rules must govern this contest, as I want fighting, not foot racing, and I intend to keep the championship of the world where it belongs, in the land of the free and the home of the brave.'

With that statement, pugilism changed forever. And on 7 September 1892, at the Olympic Club in New Orleans, wearing gloves, James J. Corbett toyed with the bloated, 33-year-old, Muldoon-free Sullivan before knocking him unconscious in the 21st round.

It was time for the moralists to have their day, none more so than the leader writer of the *Daily Chronicle*.

'Surely everybody will be heartily thankful that John L. Sullivan has met his match at last, and not only that, but has also got what schoolboys would call a jolly good hiding. A less attractive prize-fighter never lived. He is a bully of the worst kind. A dozen times at least he has been before the magistrates for abusing his wife and for years his chief amusement seemed to consist of punching people less bull-necked than himself – policemen, cabmen and anybody who did not bend the knee before him.'

None of this would have worried Sullivan overmuch. By then he had grown used to what men thought of him. He knew that for every one who detested him, there were a dozen who would gladly pass the time of day with him over a drink or three. He also knew his time had come and gone. In his 1892 autobiography – which is monumentally unreliable as a biographical source, but nevertheless entertaining reading – he actually advocated the use of gloves.

Noticeably, the official reaction to boxing had been changed by something as simple as the covering of the knuckles. The New Orleans police force entailed 17 sergeants, 13 corporals and 121 patrolmen to deal with the throng who milled around the wooden arena which was specially extended for the event. Significantly, they were present to control the crowd and not to prevent the fight.

After his defeat Sullivan played the stage, giving his own monologues, and loving the limelight, but gradually his health deteriorated, as his drinking hardened. He once fell off a moving train after standing on the backboard to urinate, and spent several weeks in hospital. From time to time he was commissioned to 'write' newspaper articles on major fights, for example the 1910 epic at Reno, Nevada, between Jack Johnson and James J. Jeffries. By then he had long been declared bankrupt, and although he later gave up alcohol his body had been weakened by its effects. He took to lecturing on the evils of drink, for a price naturally, but nothing could halt his decline. He did remain incredibly popular, for whatever his faults, and there were many, he had always remained essentially a hero to the common man. After the death of his second and much-loved wife, Kate, he went downhill and died of heart failure in Abingdon, Massachusetts, on 2 February 1918. Under his pillow was all the money he possessed in the world – $15. When they buried him, the ground was frozen solid and his grave had to be blasted out by dynamite.

He, and all those stubborn old ghosts of the prize ring, would have enjoyed that.

William Muldoon lived into his eighties, worked for the New York State Athletic Commission, and was ringside when Gene Tunney ended Jack Dempsey's reign as heavyweight champion in Philadelphia in 1926. He also outlived the first of the great promoters, Tex Rickard.

'We are sentenced to death as soon as we are born,' Muldoon said once. 'And then we are given a reprieve which will be extended only by the grace of God, and as we live properly.'

14

A LINGERING SHADOW

Bare-knuckle boxing drifted on, of course, but was never again prized as a way of life worth the mention in sporting society as a whole. However, it never quite died out, its shadow lingering almost unnoticed in the background. It took time for it to be replaced entirely by gloved boxing, and its participants were harrassed by the enforcers of the law whenever they could be apprehended.

In the Coventry Standard of 13 July 1889, a sober court report recorded that at Solihull,

> 'William Shingleton of Dudley and Charles Regan of Tipton, pugilists, were summoned for creating a breach of the peace at Hall Green on the 12th of June by engaging in a prize fight. Regan was also summoned for assaulting Pc Hinman, who found them at Hall Green Racecourse.
>
> 'Several persons were on the field and around the gateway there were several hansom cabs. There was a ring formed in the field and in the centre were the two defendants dressed in fighting costume.'

Regan's assault charge arose from his having 'shook his fist' in the Pc's face. Both were bound over for £10 to keep the peace and Regan was fined £1 plus costs for the assault.

Mostly, of course, fist fighting went on well away from the prying eyes of the police and even further away from those who would write about it, from whatever standpoint. The memoirs of the great Welsh heavyweight, Tommy Farr, were discovered after his death and published in 1989. Farr was from the mining communities of the Welsh valleys and learned to box on the travelling booths of men like Joe Gess and Jack Scarrott. He did most of his fighting with gloves and, of course, went on to take the great Joe Louis 15 rounds for the world heavyweight title in New York in 1937. As a boy, however, he remembered his father, an Irishman from Cork, as,

> *'a miner with a passion and a relish for knuckle-fighting, in which, since it was the law of the mountains, there was no softness in him. He allowed none in others.'*

The Queensberry Rules and the case for gloves

The single major factor in the replacement of bare-knuckling with gloved boxing was the introduction of the Marquess of Queensberry Rules, which were published in 1867. Originally intended for use in amateur boxing, they were soon seen as a potential lifeline by those involved in the professional business. The Marquess didn't write them, of course, merely lending his name to the ideas of John Graham Chambers to give them social clout.

The most radical change the Chambers-Queensberry rules implement was the use of gloves, but there were other important formative items, principally the introduction of the ten count in the event of a knockdown to replace the old half-minute's grace to make it to the scratch line and the stipulation that rounds should be three minutes in duration and followed by a one-minute interval.

The standardisation of rings had been an idea since the days when Bill Gibbons made them for the Pugilistic Club, but Chambers and the Marquess actually turned principle into rule for the first time. They advocated that a boxing ring be 24-feet square, or as near that size as it is practical for it to be. Gloves were nothing like the 8oz. and 10oz. 'pillows' in use today, obviously. They were simply designed to protect the hands and, if the drawings of the 18th and 19th centuries are even roughly accurate, were far smaller than the old-fashioned mufflers used to protect British aristocrats in their sparring houses in establishments like Gentleman Jackson's and, further back, Broughton's Academy. Some carried no more padding than a driving glove, others were as heavy as 2 oz.

Did gloves make boxing safer? Safety in sport can be measured in many ways, but fatalities have happened in boxing from its earliest times. The punches of Jack Broughton killed George Stevenson in 1741 and led to the first set of rules. The Prince Regent, later George IV, backed off from the sport after the death of a boxer named Earl in 1788. Simon Byrne died three days after boxing James 'Deaf' Burke in 1833, after which Burke left for the United States. There were others.

Medical assessment of former boxers was haphazard, but even in the days when life was a brutal, chaotic and generally risky business, it was acknowledged that some men suffered physical impairment as a result of their ring careers. Gloves were intended to soften blows to the head, obviously. But the converse side of that was that they lessened damage to the hand. Boxers in bare-knuckle days would spar for openings and out of the necessity to protect their hands tended to let fly with a solid blow to the head less frequently, and probably only when they were fairly sure of it landing cleanly.

Although these old-timers certainly hit hard enough to hurt and cut, and what must have been seemingly interminable battles were waged until one or the other was barely able to stand, the successful boxers knew how important it was to look after their hands. Gloves altered that, and although we have no films of the great bare-knuckle fights, almost certainly allowed boxers to fight with greater speed, afforded them less worry about landing clean blows, and enabled them to absorb more punishment.

The argument is still going on. Even today there are those who press for heavier gloves than the 8oz. and 10oz. generally on offer. However, these 'pillows' allow boxers to throw more punches – and take more, thereby in the views of some, risking the possibility of blows to the head being absorbed by men who are perhaps close to exhaustion and dehydrated towards the end of a fast, hard and long fight. The effect of punches on tired men is often more dramatic and extreme than similar blows on men who are warmed-up but still relatively fresh.

They may also allow boxers to compete more often. Most bare-knuckle champions had relatively few contests, perhaps between a dozen and 20. As with anything there were exceptions, of course, but nobody in those days approached the numbers chalked up by champions of the 1920s like Johnny Dundee, Benny Bass and the wonderful middleweight, Harry Greb. Dundee, who held the world featherweight and junior-lightweight titles, had 337 fights, according to the *Ring Record Book*, between 1910 and 1932. Bass, featherweight champ in the 1920s, had around 240 fights, while the latest count for Greb is 301. There were many others with similar records.

And at the turn of the 21st century in Britain there were several boxers with more than 100 bouts. Seamus Casey of Derbyshire and Dean Bramhald from Doncaster clocked up more than 160 each, while at the time of writing the still-active Peter Buckley of Birmingham was rapidly approaching 150. In bare-knuckle days this was unheard-of. Take a boxer who has 100 fights. That's probably around 600 rounds of competitive action, let alone sparring sessions in the gym. If on average that man takes even 20 punches a round, that means he has absorbed something like 12,000 blows in his career. I would contend that this just could not have happened in bare-knuckle boxing.

While the introduction of gloves was generally applauded, the sport in Britain had to come through a crisis sparked by a spate of ring deaths at the turn of the century. Astonishingly, all the fatalities happened at the National

Sporting Club in London. In his splendid 1956 history of the influential NSC, Guy Deghy recounted the crisis in detail. Jimmy Barry of Chicago and Walter Croot from Leytonstone in north-east London boxed for the world bantamweight championship at the club on 17 November 1897. Barry knocked out Croot in the 20th and final round.

'The final blow did not strike the spectators as a particularly hard one, but Croot had to be carried out of the ring, and since he showed no signs of recovering, he was taken to Charing Cross Hospital. There, a few days later, he died of brain injuries.'

On 7 November 1898, a regular boxer at the club, Tom Turner from Holborn, was knocked out by a Paddington rival, Nat Smith. The next day's newspaper report ignored the fact that Turner had been badly hurt, simply reflecting that 'a better night's sport could not be wished for'. The NSC hierarchy reacted sniffily to journalists' questions when word of Turner's condition in Charing Cross began to circulate. Someone issued a statement declaring that Turner felt better and simply needed time for full health to be restored. However, Turner died – and it was revealed that he had never regained consciousness after being knocked out.

Arthur 'Peggy' Bettinson, the influential and archly pompous secretary of the NSC, offered the platitude that accidents happened. Charges were brought against Nat Smith and several of those involved in the staging of the contest – not Bettinson, incidentally – but came to nothing.

The NSC really does seem to have had little interest in the health of those who boxed within its supposedly hallowed walls. On 29 January 1900, a Scottish flyweight, Mike Riley, died after a bout with Matt Precious. Bettinson wrote later that the Riley-Precious fight was 'the *piece de resistance* of this moving evening' and that Precious, from Birmingham, won easily. He omits to say that Riley died. This time as well as the victorious boxer, Bettinson and referee Bernard Angle were among those charged at Bow Street police station. The inquest ruled that the death was an accident, and that the NSC had made reasonable provision to prevent such an accident, but manslaughter charges were tossed out by a jury.

Amazingly, on 24 April 1901, a boxer known as Billy Smith, whose real name was Murray Livingstone, was killed in a bout with Jack Roberts at the NSC. It was the fourth ring fatality in the same building in three and a half years. This time ten of those involved were charged with Livingstone's 'felonious killing and slaying'. These included Roberts, Bettinson, referee Eugene Corri and house second Arthur Gutteridge, grandfather of journalist and ITV boxing commentator Reg Gutteridge. In a landmark case, they were all acquitted – the jury was out for two whole minutes! – and boxing, with gloves at least, was given unofficial approval as a legitimate sport. But anyone around at that time could well have come to the conclusion that boxing with gloves was a far more dangerous activity than bare-knuckling had ever been.

Boxing took off as a major international sport in the 20th century and so it is unfair to compare directly the number of ring deaths with those of the bare-fist era. There were so many more contests in which something could go wrong. However, deaths in the ring were frequent. *Ring* magazine tried to keep track of the numbers and each year in its annual and record book would list the number of deaths. Usually up to the end of World War Two these were in single figures.

However, the boom that accompanied peace brought with it, if the *Ring's* counts were anything like accurate, a significant increase in the number of fatalities. In 19 years from 1946-64, ring deaths were in single figures only three times. The worst year was 1953 when there were 22 recorded deaths. Perhaps because of a general increase in medical care and provision, from the second half of the 1960s until the end of the century the totals each year dropped back to single figures again.

So much for safety.

Bare knuckles in a gloved world

According to the most recent research, there were British professional gloved champions at middleweight and heavyweight by the 1870s and at bantam and featherweight in the 1880s. The first lightweight champion, Dick Burge, came along in 1891, and from then on boxing with gloves progressed at a terrific pace, and bare-knuckle fighting declined with equal speed.

By this time boxing had spread across the British Empire: in Melbourne, Australia, on 1 November 1855, a bare-knuckle battle between James Kelly and Jonathan Smith lasted six and a quarter hours. Much later, in South Africa in 1890, Barney Malone and Jan Silberbauer battled away for five and a half hours and 212 rounds. However, there too, gloves caught on quickly and by the early years of the century was popular enough to provide world title challengers and, in the case of Australia, house the world heavyweight championship.

Bare fist boxing did not die out altogether, however.

A rare record of a specific bare-knuckle fight comes from the memoirs of Billy Shinfield, a lifelong boxing man from Alfreton in Derbyshire who wrote an invaluable document of the way things were. From its battered notebook, Shinfield's deliberate long-hand almost screams from the page as he describes a bare-knuckle battle between his father, Nehemiah, and a local rival, Sammy Tutt of Normanton in what must have been around 1915. They agreed the fight in the Angel Hotel in Alfreton with a cap full of gold sovereigns the prize, held by a local magistrate, Tom Spencer. The fight was set for late at night on an allotment after the pubs had turned out. Tutt, being a hard-drinking man, arrived with a belly full of ale, while Nehemiah Shinfield had rested in bed.

'He would have killed Father if he'd had no beer because he was two or three stones heavier. He punched low, swung punches from all angles and tried to strangle and butt the old boy. But he could not nail him. Dad slipped and swayed away from him.

'After 24 minutes by the timekeeper Sam tired. Dad went to work. Where he got his energy from, I don't know. Sam went down on his knees for a rest. Dad stood back, but Sam did not say 'enough'. He got up after a minute or so. Dad had dipped his head in a water bucket. Then Sam squared up again. Dad hit him in the stomach and a cracker to the chin. He was flat out.

'His pals took him home on a flat cart. The horse was frightened by people screaming and yelling and tried to bolt. The street and gardens were packed. There were no admission charges. The local copper looked on. I was only ten years old and I am not ashamed to say I cried for most of the fight, which lasted 38 minutes. I was terrified.

'Dad could not put his bowler hat on for weeks because of the lumps on his head, but Sam was in hospital for some time. Dad visited him. I have met many old friends of theirs who saw the fight and they have said poor old Sammy was never the same after it. He died when he was 49.'

I am sure there were many other battles like that which were fought the length and breadth of the country, although officially the sport had altered forever. Gradually, people lost interest in it as other entertainments became available. There were easier and more organised ways to settle disputes and gloved boxing provided plenty of opportunity for those who saw it either as a sport or a business.

Bob Fitzsimmons, the Cornishman who held the world heavyweight title from 1897 until 1899, wrote near the end of his life to the first great boxing writer of the 20th century, the American Nat Fleischer:

'The cave-men of the ring are extinct. Champions such as we had when I was in my prime are gone, never again to return. The champions of the future will be as children compared to the rough and ready battlers of twenty or more years ago. Fighting, like all other sports, is reaching out along lines of improvement ... You'll find as the years pass that fighting will become more and more scientific and championships will change hands on points and not on knockouts.'

Bob Fitzsimmons: one of the great champions of the pioneering 'gloved' days.

How prophetic that was. It took time – especially in America, where gloved fights continued to be held under the old 'fight to a finish' rules. For example, at the Olympic Club in New Orleans on 6 April 1893, just over six months after the Sullivan-Corbett fight closed the bare-knuckle era, local lightweight Andy Bowen and Jack Burke of Galveston, Texas, boxed a draw over 110 rounds and four and three-quarter hours. (A year later Bowen, incidentally, was killed in a fight with George Lavigne, who was cleared of manslaughter on the grounds that Bowen's death was a result of his head striking the unpadded floor of the ring.)

Gradually, boxing became more and more governed by rules and, some would still say, bogged down by them. By the 1920s, the world heavyweight championship, once the most prized jewel in the whole of sport, was changing hands in ten round contests.

Gypsies and travellers

One area of British society where bare-knuckle boxing did not die out was among gypsies and travellers. It is now accepted as strictly illegal and therefore is conducted mostly in private. It is not generally written about and appears to have no specific structure. It has good fighters, but no apparent sense of a championship that is handed down from generation to generation as was the case in the great days of the 'Championship of England'. While boxing prowess can be admired and celebrated, it holds no meaning beyond its own art. Its champions are unable to be acknowledged in a wider world because what they excel at is a criminal activity.

Idyllic times when it was permitted and openly conducted are still remembered in stories and songs, in which sometimes it is as likely that the subject of the song will lose as win. One poem, 'A True Story' by Eli Frankham, describes a fight between a gypsy and a non-gypsy. The gypsy loses... and the story has a neat twist in the tail: the winner had an even harder schooling than the gypsy – he went to Eton!

The essential feature of being a traditional traveller – and this title excludes the so-called 'new age travellers' – does not actually depend on being nomadic. Many traditional travellers do move about for part of the time, but about 60 per cent are settled on official sites and leave only for perhaps a fortnight a year. What makes a person into a Romany or an Irish Traveller is the following:

Relationship – ideally blood rather than marriage – with another Traveller;
a shared language, albeit one now heavily influenced by English;
a shared history and culture;
shared experiences, often including persecution and prejudice.

It is because of the shared culture and experience that bare fist fighting has survived and might be said to have flourished, so that almost every extended traveller family in Britain has at least one champion in its midst. Fights still happen. The best fights are for purses which can be, for a group of people for whom the bread-line is real enough at times, colossal.

Bob Dawson, whose information and words created this area of the book, said as this was being written that he heard of a fight on a traveller site in London with a purse of £20,000 – cash, naturally – plus side bets. That level of interest inevitably means challenges are thrown down between families and at any one time there are probably several such fights planned. Outsiders, however, are unwelcome. The contests resemble old-style boxing matches, but pay little regard to either the old London Prize Ring rules or those attributed to the Marquess of Queensberry. They do not occur in a ring; there is no professional medical help available, and rarely much attempt to stick to the idea of a round. Fights may be held in a field, a car park, in the centre of an official site or in a pub yard. Above all, the fights are very rarely witnessed by anyone except other travellers, even when outsiders are innocently curious. Writers, too, are treated with understandable suspicion which leaves much of the information second-hand. However Dawson, who has devoted a great deal of his own writing to recording gypsy and traveller history, has been an invaluable ally.

It is difficult to estimate how many fighters are active at any one time. Dawson said: 'I asked two friends and they named me almost 50 in a matter of minutes. The true figure must be far higher.'

As in the old bare-knuckle days, some fights happen virtually by chance and others are arranged with meticulous preparation. Dawson recalled one of the latter, which happened in 1991 between two Irish travellers at a car park in Crossmaglen, the town close to the border between Northern Ireland and Eire. One boxer, according to Dawson, was a Rooney, one of nine brothers, all of whom had deserved reputations as fighting men. His opponent was a McGinley, and among travellers the fight was billed as for 'the championship of Ireland'. Several hundred travellers suddenly descended on the town and, no doubt to the amazement of the local people and the police, within half an hour a huge ring of people had been made on the car park. Relatives of the fighters acted as stewards, linking arms to hold back the onlookers and to prevent them being caught up in the fight. The two competitors were bundled from vans, paths were made for them through the crowd and to cheers they entered the space which had become the ring. Both men stripped to the waist and the fight began.

Because there was no formal ring, the fight moved across the car park as the men swayed and veered around, taking or evading blows. The crowd was pushed back or allowed to come forward as the pugilists, both large and very fit men, hammered each other. At one point a steward was too slow to move himself in time, and he took a full blow to the chin which knocked him out and caused the crowd to move rapidly away. Eventually, after more than 40 minutes of hard slogging, McGinley accepted defeat and, bloody and battered, withdrew. The crowd drifted away to spend their winnings in local pubs or to take some disconsolate 'losing' drinks.

There is a great deal of fear of Irish travellers among English and Welsh gypsies because of their 'one-for-all and all-for-one' code. Offend one Irish traveller and you offend an army! There was, therefore, huge traveller interest in the fight between Rooney and McGinley and most of the English and Welsh gypsies were said to have been pleased by the outcome as Rooney was highly thought of in both communities. Often billed as his greatest fight, it is regarded as one of the classics of the century. Video tapes of it exist.

Dawson's stories reveal the extent to which bare fist fighting has survived:

'I have witnessed, or have been told of, numerous examples of spur-of-the-moment battles, but few as savage as one in 1994,' he says. 'During 1993 and 1994 several bands of Irish Travellers headed into northern England. They moved in huge convoys – anything from 20 to 150 trailers

– and often created mayhem in their wake. One extended family in particular caused masses of damage in the areas where they stopped and did much to smash what goodwill there was from house-dwellers to travellers.

'The group then decided to go into Scotland, with the intention of dominating the Scottish travelling people. On the way, they gave several highly respectable English gypsy families a very hard time, using threats, kidnapping and violence to take their homes and other belongings from them. I have verified this from several of the victims and the oral claims are extensive and consistent.

'Some of the English gypsies appealed for aid from Scottish relatives from an extended family called MacPhee, who seemed to regard these Irish as no wilder than pussy cats. A group of MacPhees headed south and met the Irish. A challenge was given and each side produced a champion, on the result of which the 'invasion' would, or would not, occur. The fight happened there and then. It was long and bloody, but the MacPhee was on the verge of winning when some of the Irish joined in to help their compatriot.

'The situation could have turned nasty, but the offenders were pulled away and the fight went on. Unfortunately, it had a cruel and bloody ending. Annoyed by the cheating of the Irishman's family, the MacPhee bit off the Irishman's nose and, so the story goes, ate it.'

Move over Mike Tyson, all is forgiven!

Dawson goes on: 'This was not the end of the story. Aggrieved at the outcome, a few weeks later, the Irish (with reinforcements) staged an invasion and were met by a large contingent of MacPhees. Fortunately, the Irish withdrew before a major battle could occur but were harried by the MacPhees all the way south back into England. Fortunately, such large-group confrontations are rare, and it is far commoner for disputes to be settled between two fighting men.'

Because only 60 per cent of travellers can be on sites, and therefore living legally, at any one time, due to the shortage of places, the rights of 'somewhere to stop' are fiercely guarded. Without a settled address, it is difficult to obtain health care or education, let alone water or the other norms of a modern society.

When Nero, a gypsy man of 50, left his pitch on a site in Yorkshire, he paid the rental and community charges in advance to cover his absence, so he could return. When he came back, he discovered his pitch had been taken by an Irish family. Again, the story was related by Dawson.

As politely as he could, Nero explained to the Irishman: 'This is my place.

It's been my place for ten years and I needs to pull back on. I wants to be fair to you, so I'll give you till next week to shift off, and meantime we'll pull our trailer next to a relative's.'

The next week they were still there.

'Now we can settle this any way you wants,' said Nero. 'We can do it the American way ...'

'American way?'

'Yes. High noon. Guns in the street. That way. Or we can do it the gypsy way and fight for it.'

'We'll fight. I'll rip your head off.'

Nero gave a wry smile and a few moments later the Irishman was lying unconscious on the ground. And Nero was rubbing his broken wrist.

But still the Irish did not move off. Instead, a couple of days later a truckload arrived at Nero's trailer. Five left the truck, led by a large, very broad man.

'You wanted to fight,' he said. 'Well, I'm here.'

'Now, let's do this like gentlemen,' said Nero. 'I'm not as young as I was. I'm 50 and you're all youngsters. I'll take you one at a time, but not all at once.'

He knew he would not have the stamina to take even one of them for more than a few minutes.

'You can take me first,' said the big man.

A few seconds later he was lying unconscious with Nero looking him over and holding the glowing knuckles on his one good hand. The rest decided not to take him on and left quietly, carrying the limp form of their relative with them.

The next day they were back. This time, their champion was a Goliath at least six inches taller than Nero, who is no midget himself, and as broad as a tank. Nero remembered looking up into the giant's face and wondering if he would even be able to reach his chin. And so he switched tactics, punching him as hard as he could in the belly and, as he fell, cracked him in the face. Fortunately, he soon recovered enough consciousness to be helped back into the truck.

'They couldn't 'a' lifted him otherwise,' said Nero later, with suitable modesty as he showed Dawson his badly mauled hands. No doubt he enjoyed telling the story and claimed he told the remaining members of the family: 'Now brothers, I'll fight as many of you as you want, forever. But I must insist you get off my pitch. I'll be pulling on tomorrow. Then come back and I'll fight you all an' a hundred more asides. Only just give me a day or two, 'cos I'm not as young as I once was and I'm a bit out of condition.'

Nero moved back on to his pitch and his 'squatters' did not return.

As in the old days, fighting on despite injuries is common. In one epic battle of about 1925, one man broke his wrist after two hours of hard sparring. He continued to fight for another 35 minutes and won.

I found another flavour of what fighting was like in the unregulated 1920s in the shape of the aforementioned memoirs of Billy Shinfield of Alfreton. Shinfield was not a gypsy, but estimated he had hundreds of bouts, unofficial and official, and went on to run a successful business, managing and promoting fighters and building and supplying rings. Shinfield remembered boxing a gypsy named Clay near Sutton-in-Ashfield. He was still a teenager when he was asked to box Clay for £1 by a scrap dealer, Joe Wooley. He cycled there with a friend and on the way attracted the interest of the local policeman who, when he found out what was going on, insisted on accompanying them ... to ensure fair play! Shinfield arrived to find a gypsy encampment settled in the field. The ring was erected, but it took time to find Clay, whom it transpired had been asleep in a cart.

'He was a little, thin man with a cauliflower ear. He knew nothing of the fight, but looked at me and said he would fight when Joe said he would pay him. He knew how to fight all right. He gave me all the trouble I needed for three rounds. By the fourth he had shot his bolt and I was on top. He grabbed me and said 'Easy, son'. I did ease off and he could not come up for the fifth round. He was exhausted.

'The sergeant held the money and gave me my pound. Clay, it appeared, was on the road and starving. I gave him five shillings ...'

Shinfield says he boxed Clay some time later in a booth and they became friends until the gypsy left the district.

'I did not see him for many years, until one day he drove into Raglan Street, Alfreton, with a lovely caravan, a wife and three grand little girls.'

Clay was travelling to see as many of his old friends as he could – he was dying of cancer.

Fighting never occurs between members of the same gypsy or travelling family, but each family has a champion who can be used if the need arises. A travelling life is notoriously hard, full of danger and threat, and a frightened and confused people view the need to have someone on their side as essential.

But it is far more than this. Fighting is such a part of the culture that it is a norm, and conversations about fighting, whether previous matches or boxing techniques, occur daily. Televised boxing is watched avidly, especially when someone from the community has put on the gloves and gone to the ring. Several of the most famous glove fighters are of gypsy stock. In the old days few liked to admit it, but now travellers and gypsies are more confident and proud in admitting their heritage. 'Gipsy' Johnny Frankham of Reading was British light-heavyweight champion in the 1970s, Hampshire light-middleweight Gary Cooper was British champ in the following decade, while Henry Wharton of York won British, Commonwealth and European titles in the 1990s and also boxed three times for world championships. Mark Baker of Kent, who fought for the British and Commonwealth super-middleweight titles in the '90s, once acknowledged that his first bout was a gypsy fight when he was a boy of 15 and his opponent was a grown man. 'Gipsy' Johnny Fury was a heavyweight contender for a while, and his brother Hugh also fought professionally. At the time of writing, Terrace Gaskin of Yorkshire was the Central Area flyweight champion.

Within their communities bare fist men regarded as clean, skilful fighters are respected far more than the rough, tough brawlers who ignore the finer points of the old art.

Arrangements are often made for a fight at a particular gathering. For instance, at a Saturday Christening a few years ago involving an exceptionally distinguished boxer, whom Dawson will refer to only as Dick, who was challenged to a fight there and then. It was our intention here to give a true flavour of the life and culture of bare-knuckle boxing, not to incriminate anybody. Therefore, we have refrained from naming the living except with their express agreement. However, the oral tradition among travelling people is, of course, highly developed. Their stories paint pictures. Dawson recalled the story of the fight arranged at that Saturday Christening and won by Dick on the following Monday:

> 'Those who do not know Dick – mainly travelling people from the south of England – tend to have the wrong idea about him. Although he is tall and clearly strong, he does not give the appearance of a fighter. Even his stance is unusual. He often stands in an unlikely pose with his knuckles uppermost and his wrists twisted inwards, and contenders who do not know him think he is 'easy'. It is, in fact, a technique he has taught himself. He is a southpaw with a very strong arm and an almost snake-like right handed jab.'

Families have fine fighters still. Even if I knew them, I could not prove who they were in a court of law – and as they would be incriminating themselves, they would be unlikely to admit anything either on tape or in print. For the same reason, they would not invite a 'non-gypsy' to witness, let alone write about a fight.

Some travellers still run boxing booths at fairgrounds. This old pastime has all but died out, however, because of the problem of insuring participants against accident. Boxing booths, where house professionals would take on all-comers in gloved contests, were extremely popular in the second half of the 19th century and the first half of the 20th. Many of Britain's world class boxers learned their trade travelling with the booths.

Joe Gess and Jack Scarrott, who ran two of the busiest, were based in Wales for many years. Jimmy Wilde, one of the greatest flyweights in history, worked for Scarrott regularly and said that when he was the English 112lb champion in 1916, he returned to the booth as a favour – and ended up boxing all-comers for FOUR hours! His purse? Forty pounds. Another British world champion, the Bournemouth light-heavyweight Freddie Mills, learned his trade as a teenage fighter on Jack Turner's south coast booth. In his first booth battle he fought the Welshman, Gypsy Daniels, and ended the evening with a headache and being sick behind the marquee. Today, he would have been taken to hospital. In those days he would have been back at work the next day. Daniels, who in the 1920s knocked out future world heavyweight champ Max Schmeling in a round in Germany, was an old fighter by then, but gave Mills his 'trademark' cauliflower ear. Daniels, incidentally, was not a gypsy. From Llanelli in south Wales, he was given the 'Gypsy' tag by an American promoter when boxing there and kept it. Mickey Duff, who in his time was boxer, matchmaker, manager and promoter, spent some of his teenaged years working the booths.

'Wherever we travelled I was always Billy Jones,' he said. 'If we were in Bournemouth, I was Billy Jones of Bournemouth. If we were in Brighton, I was Billy Jones of Brighton ... I once fought 13 times on a booth in Norwich – on Boxing Day!'

Among those from the travelling community who are no longer alive but who had fine reputations in their time were Bartley Gormon, brothers Opey and Hughie Burton, Fighting Tommy Lee, 'Nighty' Scamp, 'Little Wry Necked' Robin Winter and Tommy Winter of Leicester, a former regimental champion in the Army. In fact, there were several Bartley Gormons, all very able fighters, but probably the best was active in the 1920s and 1930s. Dawson also includes Bombardier Billy Wells, the best British heavyweight of the time surrounding the First World War, but this was new to me. Certainly, Wells was from Stepney in the East End of London, the grandson of a Thames waterman and son of a professional musician who taught a fife and drum band.

Again, I am indebted to Dawson's knowledge of the ways of the travellers' lives for the following analysis of the codes which govern fighting. There are unwritten rules about who will fight who in the gypsy community; because relationships within the community are so important and the level of community spirit so high, there has to be some kind of control. Impromptu fights between unmatched men are frowned upon, unless as a result of some undue amount of bragging, in which case it is considered fair. Simple disputes are settled by the two people concerned fighting. If it is a group matter, larger parties might become involved, but many gypsies regard these outbreaks of violence as contemptible. If women are in dispute, men will not become involved, and usually vice versa. Non-feuders will remain friends. For example, when men fight, women from both sides will sit together and chat and drink tea. And when women fight, men will sit peacefully together. This becomes more complex when opposite sexes become involved. For instance, if a woman does intervene if her husband is getting the worst of it, everyone else might pitch in. Such interventions are generally considered shocking, however. Fights between women are rare, but not unheard of, and can be vicious.

The worst story of women's fighting passed down through the generations took place around 1919 between one Eliza Boswell and her sister, Matilda Booth, on a common near Bakewell in Derbyshire. The oral tradition does not say what caused the fight but Matilda arrived out of the blue and ordered her sister out to settle their differences, even though Eliza was heavily pregnant. It took the form of a traditional bare fist match, and although those who knew her said that if she had not been pregnant she would have won, Eliza took a terrible beating. She retired to her bed in her horse-drawn wagon and was still there two days later when there was a catastrophe. The main pipes of a pump house on land above where the wagons stood burst. Water poured down the hillside, flooded the wagons and soaked everybody in its way. Eliza caught pneumonia and died within 48 hours. She was buried at the edge of the common, yards from where the fight had taken place, along with her still-born baby. The location of her grave is still known today.

Most fights are not particularly shocking, of course, but even now are declining. Dawson says the old art is threatened, not by the law, but by religion. In recent years Born-Again Christianity has swept through the community and, according to Dawson, more than half of gypsy people have been converted to a different way of conducting life and to settling disputes. They see, as directly referring to them, verses 22 and 23 of the 14th chapter of the Gospel According to Saint Luke: 'Go out on to the highways and along the hedgerows and make them come in. I want my house to be full.'

Dawson, who has done so much work towards the understanding of gypsy and travellers' way of life, is now near the end of his own. He is adamant that this new upsurge in Christianity is a serious change that will have far-reaching effects:

'People who have almost every hand against them have suddenly found themselves accepted by a God who forgives them their sins, real or imagined, and promises them a better life here on earth and eternal life to boot. Countless gypsies have testified to its veracity.

'The violent have overnight become fluffy kittens, drunkards teetotal, and thieves turned into saints. Those who had never prayed before – big, powerful men with reputations as pugilists – place their massive hands together like children and weep for forgiveness. The wild are tamed. There is no need to fight now, and the Born-Agains will not, despite being sorely taunted.

'So with that taming, huge gaps have been left among the fighting men. There are many who scorn the pugilists who have 'gone over' and there are still fine gypsy fighting men left. But every year sees fewer and fewer.

'By the end of the 21st century, will any be still involved in the sport that is above all others one of courage, fortitude and skill – or will the only bashers be of Bibles?'

In September 1999, the *Independent On Sunday* revealed that a 50-minute video on gypsy boxing had been refused a certificate by the British Board of Film Classification. David Monaghan, who directed the video, accused the BBFC of discriminating against gypsies. Monaghan's point was plainly put:

'The BBFC has passed films glorifying serial killers and finds the violence in films like *Reservoir Dogs* acceptable, but dismisses a documentary featuring gypsy men and their sport.'

However, the BBFC defended its decision on the grounds that the film was dangerously irresponsible and included 'instructional' material on how to use a fist bandage laced with broken glass.

A far cry indeed from the days of 'Gentleman' Jackson, Hen. Pearce and John Gully.

15

HARD MEN

As the 1990s drew to a close, the Brad Pitt movie *Fight Club* drew fresh attention to what now amounts to the bare-knuckle fad. It apparently spawned a number of 'underground' clubs for Americans to act out their fantasies of being professionally trained fighting machines, after which they probably returned to their day jobs as if nothing had happened. It also led to unsubstantiated claims that it was a sub-culture supported by the wealthy and socially privileged, just as pugilism was 200 years earlier. This, should we believe gossip, applied to England as well as the United States.

In the *Independent On Sunday* article, by Yvonne Ridley and Sophie Goodchild, that revealed the banning of the gypsy boxing documentary, claims were made that fights were happening 'once a week'. This is unlikely to be accurate and their unquoted source has also provided a vision that smacks of an excess of dramatic invention.

'Entrance is by word of mouth. The location of the bout is only revealed a few hours earlier with a furtive telephone call from the organisers. Punters also have to place a minimum bet of £100 for the dubious privilege of watching two men inflict savage and often fatal injuries with their teeth and bare fists. There is plenty of blood. It will be pouring from a fighter's ears and probably from his groin where he has been bitten by his opponent. He will have soaked his hands in vinegar but his fists will end up shredded to ribbons ... There are no official rounds; instead, the loser is the one whose injuries are so bad he can no longer stand up ...'

Ridley and Goodchild quoted one Roy York, who has allegedly refereed bare-knuckle fights for 12 years and who has therefore incriminated himself by the admission. York claimed: 'It's like watching gladiators in the arena. The women love it.'

The writers had relied on others supposedly involved in this world for their evidence. Whether or not the 'world' they revealed actually exists remains a matter for debate. Certainly, it's subject to a huge amount of self-glorification.

For example, while attempting to find a genuine bare-knuckle champion who would be prepared to talk to me, I was told of a man who was 'the business' and who would be happy to speak of his accomplishments. I was interested until I discovered this man's claims included a victory over Muhammad Ali in a hotel room 'war'.

As more evidence of the latter we can take the autobiographies of Roy Shaw and Lenny McLean, the big names in British unlicensed fighting in the 1970s, and the story of the supposed bare-knuckle king of the 90s, Joe Savage. Shaw and McLean enjoyed notoriety as boxers, with or without gloves, on a circuit that existed beyond the boundaries of the British Boxing Board of Control.

Taking them in reverse order: Savage, who is either shaven-headed or bald, looks like a print of a Broughton or a Figg. There the comparison ends. Like most of these supposed 'wild men' he was both humoured and exposed by full-time professionals.

His social profile was increased in December 1993 when he decided to enter a bizarre heavyweight competition at the enigmatically named Casino Magic in Bay St Louis, Mississippi. The event was one of those ideas that attract attention but which you always suspect will fall short of what it promises to be. The plan of Canadian promoters Donald Arnott and Trevor Walldon was financially ambitious: each fighter to enter would earn $20,000, and for each three-round bout they won, they would earn another $20,000. On top of that, the final would be worth $940,000 to the winner and $100,000 to the loser. The whole thing would be financed by live Pay-Per-View television, by sponsors, including the casino, the management of which hoped to attract high-rolling (which translates as big-losing) gamblers, and by the live gate.

It did draw a capacity crowd of 5,283, but the rest of the financial deal came apart and the lofty purses were drastically reduced. Nevertheless, while some fighters pulled out and were replaced by unproven no-hopers, there remained some ageing but tough old professionals: Tony Tubbs, James 'Bonecrusher' Smith, 'Smokin' Bert Cooper and Tyrell Biggs. Tubbs and Smith had held the World Boxing Association heavyweight title in the 1980s, Cooper had performed well in a world title bid against Evander Holyfield in 1991 and Biggs, an Olympic gold medallist in the Los Angeles Olympics, had lost his world title challenge against a peak Mike Tyson in 1987. Tubbs, Cooper and Biggs had come through serious out of the ring problems – mostly down to drugs and alcohol – while Smith was 40 years old.

However, in some kind of moment of madness, Joe Savage decided to add his name to the list of entrants. He turned up, too, and attracted publicity as a friendly eccentric. He billed himself as the British bare-knuckle heavyweight champion with 41 consecutive wins in an unbeaten career. The venerable British trade paper *Boxing News* had a man there, who reported:

'The bald, podgy, tattooed brawler who scaled 17st 7lbs was only supposed to be 30, but looked old enough to have fought Jack Broughton or Jim Figg. He'd come all the way from England, but never had a legitimate boxing match.'

Savage told the press:

'I fight for as long as it takes to put a man away. We don't use gloves. It's just go out there, hit them as hard as you can and put them out. There are no rounds, no refs, no gumshields. It's the last man who can stand up.'

This was all very well, but as the fighters prepared in the gym, Tubbs and Smith let themselves loose with a sparring war. Savage, we are told, watched it – and was suddenly confronted by the full, nasty reality of what he was about to let himself in for. Some even suggested he fainted, but that seems too extreme to be likely. Smith reportedly told him as he left the ring: 'Joe, this is what we do for a living. This ain't no street crap.'

Just before the tournament began, Savage withdrew. His hand was injured, he said.

He did fight one legitimate boxing contest in the town of Nanaimo, British Columbia, Canada on 22 April 1994. Maybe he saw a jaded, troubled 'Smokin' Bert Cooper lose a decision to a moderate Australian, Craig Petersen, in the first round of the Mississippi event, and believed on that evidence he had nothing to worry about. Or maybe he just didn't realise that against properly schooled professional boxers he was out of his depth. As soon as the bell rang, Cooper walked out and went to work. Poor Savage didn't know what to do.

The fight made a solitary paragraph in the American trade paper *Professional Boxing Update*, which recorded solemnly: 'Smokin' Bert Cooper exposed British bare-knuckle fighter Joe Savage with a devastating KO in 65 seconds. Savage, who claimed a 42-0 record in bare-knuckle contests, was down twice.'

Savage never boxed again, with gloves or knuckles, but years later and reportedly working as a bodyguard, he was still talking a good fight.

'You live off the adoration and the fact everyone has come to see you. It's only afterwards you feel the pain.'

Hard men of the street have always loitered on the edge of boxing. They combine a respect for boxers with an unspoken arrogance that, given the right circumstances, a fair shake, a nod in this direction or a wink in that, they could be better than any man on the planet. This is very easy to do – any of us are potential could-have-beens – and is also complete nonsense. There is a huge gulf between a fit man trained in the craft of the professional ring and a street thug. This is not to say that in a back alley somewhere the thug might prevail. Anything can happen in those circumstances. However, 'hard men' like to cultivate the legend that they will always prevail, both in a ring and out, which is not based on fact.

For all the self-aggrandisement of the best selling autobiographies by McLean, Shaw and even the old 1950s heavyweight Nosher Powell, the sad truth is that none of them were very good boxers. And in my view the McLean and Shaw books had a basic malfunction: they confused the respective heroes' cock-eyed views of right and wrong with human decency.

I saw a film of McLean fighting in the 1970s. It was a brawl that included the man who is now portrayed as 'The Guv'nor' stamping on an opponent's head. In that there was a referee, a ring, seconds and a bucket full of water ready to be tossed over an unconscious man's head, should the need arise, then it offered some faint echoes of the old sport. But the two activities should never be confused. McLean was a tough man, it's said almost impervious to punishment and pain, but had little ability beyond a rage borne out of personal misery and a confused standard of human ethics. He could not box. After his death, the excellent movie *Lock, Stock and Two Smoking Barrels* gave him

McLean v Shaw: action from one of their unlicensed brawls of the 1970s.

Nosher Powell: a genuine 1950s heavyweight who fought on major shows and sparred with Joe Louis.

cult status because he acted in it – and very well, too. The marketing of McLean's book was undeniably successful because it produced a bestseller. However the startling claim of the first sentence of the fly-sheet – 'Lenny McLean is the deadliest bare-knuckle fighter Britain has ever seen' – is laughably wide of the mark.

Powell would not claim to be a bare-knuckler, and certainly knew how to box, but the marketing of his book *Nosher* by the same publishing company that produced McLean and Shaw's books allied him to them. The sub-title on the front page was enough to show that through Powell they were continuing to cash in on a fad, a fake cult. 'When I hit you, you stay hit' was the message delivered by Powell. In the 1950s he was a sparring partner for champions, but never more than a decent London heavyweight. McLean described him as a famous movie stunt-man.

Shaw's book, *Pretty Boy*, perpetrated the myth further. The front cover declaration was like something from a Clint Eastwood movie script: 'If I come after you, beware 'cos hell's coming with me.'

Shaw boxed professionally – briefly, until he fell foul of the law – as Roy West because he was on the run from Borstal. He said he was managed by Mickey Duff, trained at the famous Thomas A Becket gym on the Old Kent

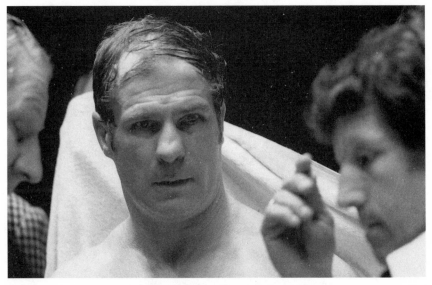

Roy Shaw: did box under a Board of Control licence,
but his legend was born on the unlicensed circuit.

Road and rubbed shoulders with champions like Terry Downes, the world middleweight champion, Henry Cooper and Terry Spinks, who won a gold medal at the 1956 Olympic Games when a teenager. He said Duff took him to ten professional wins, six by knockout, by the end of 1956, and years later said Duff had been quoted in London magazine *Time Out*, describing him as one of the most promising prospects he'd had at that time. When he came out of jail and attempted to renew his licence, he was turned down. He served time in Broadmoor, then fought on the unlicensed circuit.

I checked out Shaw's professional boxing status in 1956. I found the fight he acknowledges in his book as his debut against Denis Wingrove of Dagenham. It was indeed at Wembley Town Hall, was a six round points win and did draw nobbins – cash tossed in by the crowd in appreciation of a good battle. However, it was on 29 November 1956. *Boxing News* describes it as the debut of 'West', from Stepney.

'Fortunes fluctuated,' wrote their reporter. 'First Wingrove appeared wobbly, then West. But they kept punching away, round after round, and the surprising thing was that neither went down. West produced a useful left jab that frequently found its mark, and his cleaner punching earned him the verdict. A promising start by the Stepney boy.'

However, Shaw's claim that the arena was packed to the rafters with people wanting to see him and Wingrove is not borne out by the trade newspaper, who led their account of the seven-fight bill with a detailed account of a lightweight match between Arthur Murphy of Camden Town and Pat Price from Newry, Northern Ireland. The preview of the show does not mention Roy at all. Wingrove is listed among the 'other fights' against Tommy Leroy of Redhill. Leroy must have pulled out and 'West' replaced him as a substitute. The matches were made, not by Duff but by Eddie Derfield, a small-time operator who promoted regularly at Wembley, Paddington and West Ham.

And Shaw's insistence that he had ten wins in as many weeks just does not hold water. By his own admission he was arrested after a dance at the Ilford Palais on Christmas Eve, 1956. This was only 25 days after his professional debut. *Boxing News* does not record his having competed again after the Wingrove bout. There were four promotions in the London area that December: at Harringay Arena, Epsom Baths and the National Sporting Club. 'West' was on none of them. It is possible that he fought on shows that went unreported by the trade newspaper – maybe even in a novice competition where he was allowed to have several bouts on the same day.

When I asked Duff about the details Shaw had given in his book, the by then veteran fight promoter and manager was insistent: 'I didn't manage Roy Shaw. I might have thought about it, but I didn't.'

The truth seems to be that Shaw had one professional fight under an assumed name, after which he was jailed and never again boxed under a Board of Control licence.

The respective versions of the first fight between Shaw and McLean provide interesting comparisons of the truth. Shaw said the winner-take-all fight at a Croydon night club, in aid of the Freddie Mills Boys Club for Handicapped Children, was one-sided and ended in round three with the supposedly ferocious, unbeatable McLean quitting: 'I swung a wide left and a right that wobbled him. He hung on to the ropes and through gritted teeth, hissed "I've had enough".'

McLean said fighting in gloves ruined his chances. Gloves, he said, were 'for fairies'. He also said the end came halfway through the fourth round and claimed his own lack of fitness contributed to his poor performance.

'I don't want to make excuses and I don't want to take anything away from Roy. He gave me some punishment that would've flattened anybody else. But he couldn't hurt me and couldn't put me down. I've got to hold my hand up – I wasn't fit. I was used to the damage I could inflict with bare knuckles inside the first minute.'

Shaw also said McLean was beaten by former professional heavyweight Cliff Field from Dunstable and twice knocked out by a young South London amateur, Johnny Waldron, who was later the Southern Area professional light-heavyweight champion. I remember hearing this in the 1970s when I worked at *Boxing News*. Neither are mentioned in McLean's book.

A brief look at the ring achievements of Field is perhaps the best yardstick for McLean's true level.

Field won his first nine professional fights up to November 1970, when a Newcastle journeyman pro, Brian Jewett, beat him in three rounds. Jewett had won four of his nine starts. In 1971, Field was twice stopped by Billy Aird, who eventually boxed for the British, Commonwealth and European titles, and also beaten inside the distance by Richard Dunn, the Yorkshire southpaw who went on to fight Muhammad Ali for the world title in 1976. (It was a dreadful match: Ali won as he pleased in round five.) That four rounds defeat by Dunn marked the end of Field's professional career: of 15 fights, he won 11 and lost four.

To be fair to McLean, he did acknowledge the difference between what he did and what was required of professional boxers:

'I'll put you in the picture about the fighting game,' he said through his ghost-writer, Peter Gerrard. 'There's boxing proper. It's all licensed and strictly regulated by the British Board of Boxing Control. [Sic]. Everything's legit and above board, well, in the ring anyway. Behind the scenes it's as shitty as any business, no matter what they tell you. Boxers are vetted for health and background. So if you've got a metal plate in your head or a criminal record for violence, forget the licence. Once they climb in the ring, boxers have to stick to the Queensberry Rules. On the other hand unlicensed boxing is what it says. Unlicensed. It's still legal as long as it's in a ring, supervised and both boxers wear gloves. Though quite often, when tempers flare up, the rules go out the window.

'Bare-knuckle fighting is in a class of its own and definitely illegal. There are only two rules and that gets sorted before the off. One is the straightener – that's a stand-up fistfight and as near to a boxing match as street-fighting could ever get. The other is an all-in, where anything goes – kicking, gouging eyes and, if you're that way inclined, biting your opponent's nuts off. Bones are broken, ribs caved in, some fighters are blinded, and every now and then somebody dies. But everyone involved thinks it's worth it.'

McLean was no doubt lovable and loyal to his own, but what he achieved as a bare-knuckle fighter has to be measured against history. And the fact is, it just doesn't match.

Shaw's story seemed to carry a greater sense of perspective as far as boxing was concerned, possibly because he knew more of the licensed professional ring and had worked in the company of quality boxers at the Thomas A Becket as a young man. After the first fight with McLean, he did beat one-time world heavyweight title challenger Ron Stander from Omaha, Nebraska. Stander, thrown in over his head and butchered in four rounds by Joe Frazier in 1972,

Ultimate fighting is a poor imitation of the great art practised 200 years ago.

apparently fought Shaw in an unlicensed fight at Alexandra Palace in north London. The American had cracked ribs and didn't bother to train. Shaw's account was that Stander took everything he could throw at him, but eventually blows to the already damaged ribs brought 'Pretty Boy' victory. Shaw had great respect for Stander: 'I'm sensible enough to know that if he hadn't hurt his ribs before the fight, he would have mullered me – no question about it.'

McLean and Shaw fought each other three times, it seems. McLean won two and Shaw one. But did it matter? What were they fighting for? The role of 'The Guv'nor', according to McLean. While that had status in their world, it was just about as far from the notion and reality of the old Championship of England as disputed by the great names of pugilism as it's possible to get.

Unlicensed fighting, with gloves, still goes on regularly in London. Competitors are tough guys from the street and ex-professionals – I heard of one still taking part whom I know for sure failed a brain scan ordered by the British Board of Control and so lost his licence. He was a six round journeyman when he was licensed by the Board, but no doubt in his early 30s still liked a tear-up – even if that did involve risking serious brain damage for a few paydays. It's sad.

Like any other sport, physical damage is a part of boxing and most people accept that. The Board of Control does its utmost to protect the safety of its competitors and in the 1990s huge progress was made in provisions made for the care of boxers who might suffer acute brain injuries in contests. However, brain injury is the extreme. More often than not, injuries are superficial. Hardened fight-watchers know that blood flying around does not signify a serious injury. Cuts around the face and in particular around the eyes mostly happen because of clashes of heads, although punches can also inflict them, not to mention a stray elbow. Usually, these can be contained by the employment of an expert cut-man in a corner, who uses the only solution allowed by the Board of Control, one part adrenalin to 1,000 part water. This acts as a coagulant, of course. Still sometimes boxers do daft things that frustrate those who would see injuries controlled.

In April 2000, for example, I saw an exceedingly bloody contest at York Hall, Bethnal Green, which was eventually stopped when blood was pouring from the nose and mouth of a man who was being outboxed but not otherwise badly hurt. It seemed that his nose might have been badly broken, but post-fight concerns of medical officers led to the truth emerging: the boxer had suffered a slight headache on the day of the fight and took an aspirin, the effect of which, of course, is to thin the blood. A large part of the Board of Control's job remains the education of its licence-holders.

When even the efforts of the Board are dispensed with, then boxing can become very bloody and boxers will go on for as long as their nature allows. This is perhaps closer to the philosophy of the old bare-knuckle practitioners who regarded 'bottom', that is courage, above everything else. The spectacle of unlicensed, and even more so bare-fist fighting is more gory than licensed fighting. Fights will not be stopped simply because blood is pouring from a boxer's ear, for example, while Board doctors watch particularly carefully for that. As McLean said some all-in brawls include biting (which would not have been countenanced in Broughton's day) and attacking the groin. Blood splashing around is a part of the spectacle, part of the excitement. And in bare-

Ultimate Fighting: a fad that draws huge television ratings.

fist fighting boxers' hands must inevitably take a pounding. Shredded and swollen knuckles will be commonplace, broken fingers and dislocated thumbs ordinary hazards.

The logical extension of this unlicensed brawling is the 'Ultimate Fighting' craze that has swept America and caused the lawmakers to rethink their attitude to combat sports. This is a combination of all codes and of none of them: a hotch-potch of skills brought from a variety of martial arts allied to a basic aggressive instinct that takes us back 300 years before the days of James Figg. Boxing with bare-knuckles developed as an art form in the 18th century from one firm principle: that it was the 'Science of Self Defence'. Most Oriental martial arts have the same base – that it should not be misused, and should adhere to clear principles of discipline. Nothing is pure – and gloved boxing in particular has had more than its share of fat, unathletic heavyweights in the last few years to whom discipline is an alien concept. However, 'Ultimate Fighting' has demolished all of the traditional codes. Competitors go into the 'cage' rather than a ring – intentionally symbolic, surely – to batter each other into either submission or unconsciousness in the most violent way possible. The general feeling is that boxing has made itself too boring by its safety procedures – bigger gloves, headguards for amateurs and a tendency to stop fights sooner rather than later. In New York in 1997, as the state senate prepared to discuss the banning of the activity, the rules, such as they were,

were revealed. There are no rest periods, no gloves, no headgear, no fighter is allowed to gouge eyes, bite or kick in the throat. And that's about it. Anything else goes.

At least seven American states have banned it as barbaric, but it has continued to flourish thanks to TV shows – tournaments are available on Pay-Per-View, and apparently do good business – and spin-offs like videos, internet sites and computer games.

One competitor in the Cobo Hall, Detroit, in 1996 was a former Olympic wrestling gold medallist, Mark Schultz. According to the reports, Schultz won by straddling a Canadian named Gary Goodridge, pinning him down and hitting him repeatedly in the face. Goodridge gave up. Reports suggest as well as from wrestling, competitors come from other martial arts codes, including boxing – but so far I have not heard of any boxers of significance taking part.

I found the official website of the Ultimate Fighting Championship, which claimed to be the 'premier mixed martial arts event in the world'. It talks of its ring as a proving ground. The major news was of a tournament in Lake Charles, Louisiana, in March 2000 in which one Kevin 'The Monster' Randleman was billed to fight Pedro 'The Rock' Rizzo for something called the 'Ultimate Fighting Championship heavyweight title'. The hype was similar to boxing, but there was a cosmetic tone to it. Randleman and Rizzo were described as 'athletes', which somehow switched the attention to their physical fitness and not what they were about to do to each other. The site included 'in-depth profiles' of both fighters and at the time which I visited it, a poll predicting the winner had apparently attracted 3,588 votes.

'Ultimate Fighting' is obviously a young product aimed at a relatively young audience – and in spite of its great public relations efforts via its website, still has a long way to go in the persuading of authorities that it is a viable sport. There were signs that it is in its infancy in terms of organisation. For example, the website also announces boldly: 'John Perretti is the matchmaker for the Ultimate Fighting Championship. If you are interested in fighting, click here.'

In other words, its principle is that anybody can have a go.

Videos of fights are readily available, again most easily through the internet. An example of one in a catalogue claiming to extend to 800 pages was of the 'Ultimate Fighting Championship: Japan'. The synopsis was remarkably different to the pre-fight cosmetic hype and concentrated, not on athleticism or skill, but on the extent of the violence on offer and on the machismo of the competitors. The point of the tournament in Yokohama, Japan, was to discover 'who has what it takes' and it boasted to the prospective buyer: 'Skull-cracking, back-breaking action is guaranteed ...'

One name I did recognise from gloved boxing was Tony Halme, who is apparently featured in 'The Ultimate Fighting Championship XIII: The

Mark 'The Hammer' Coleman: one of a new generation and type of fighting star.

Ultimate Force'. Halme is a Finnish heavyweight boxer of around 21st of very limited ability – a long way short of European title level, for example. This is not to say that he can't handle himself in a free-for-all, but if he qualifies for the selling tag as one of the 'toughest competitors to ever enter the octagon ring', then it doesn't say much for the rest. Looking through the list of videos, there was no doubt that there are plenty of competitors on offer, and that it is organised enough to be taken seriously in the context of where bare-fist fighting has gone since the demise of pugilism. It has some stars – or at least its website would have us believe that to be the case. Steve Jennum appears to be one, along with Randy Couture, a kick-boxing expert named Maurice Smith and one Mark 'The Hammer' Coleman.

There is a comparison in that 'Ultimate Fighting' is struggling to persuade the lawmakers of the United States that it has validity, just as bare-knuckle boxing did in the last century. And if those who saw some of the early rough-and-tumble battles in the USA – for example, the 1816 anything-goes-brawl between Jacob Hyer and Tom Beasley – were able to watch an 'Ultimate Fighting' video, no doubt there would be more than a passing similarity.

Wrestling was once accepted as a part of pugilism. The cross-buttock throw was an art in itself until the sport died out and was overtaken by gloved boxing as we know it. Wrestling evolved separately and produced its own great champions, though in Britain its image eventually suffered terribly when it became a choreographed TV entertainment in the 1960s. A far cry from the purist Olympic wrestling codes like Graeco-Roman, these contests for small money in small halls attracted good crowds and contained plenty of drama. Characters were stereotyped: the bad, the good; the ugly, the handsome; the brutal giant, the skilful 'ordinary' man. And so on. Audiences knew their heroes and villains and people turned out. Middle-aged ladies in coats and hats would occasionally get over-excited, scream and shout and poke at competitors with their umbrellas or try to give them a whack with a trusty handbag. It came into the category of innocent fun, and died out with the era it reflected.

In the last 15 years or so, wrestling has become huge with the arrival of the 'World Wrestling Federation' style of show-business. Its bronzed, sculpted competitors play to massive crowds and draw enormous pay-per-view television audiences. What's more, they can fight. While these shows do nothing for me, they thrill millions. The fights may or may not be choreographed, and certainly the heroes are serious ham-actors who know how and when to fall, who shout and stomp about inside and outside the ring, wear elaborate, gaudy costumes and act out roles with obvious relish. Sport? Of course not. It's high entertainment. But the wrestling ring remains a hazardous place. Wrestlers get hurt, occasionally badly, and the fights, as over-dramatised as they are, take their toll on the bodies of their heroes. One of the great drawcards of recent times is the recently-retired Mankind. His huge-selling autobiography listed his injuries. It seemed that over the years he had broken just about everything there was to break.

Former international class boxer Steve Foster, a popular Commonwealth light-middleweight champion in the 1990s, did a one-off job as a referee on a major wrestling show at the Manchester Evening News Arena. For his £1,000 fee, he was required to flatten the 'bad guys' of the show, two brothers named Harris, who were both about 6ft 7in tall.

Foster said: 'Wrestling's pantomime. I expected the crowd to start saying "He's behind you!" But they had 22,000 people there, whereas I'm happy to pull in 500 for a boxing show. What do you make of that?

'All I can say is that it was hilarious. We rehearsed moves in the dressing room and everyone had a great time. It also proved to my youngest son, Anthony, who is 12, that wrestling's definitely fake. He used to love it, but has switched his attention to boxing.'

Wrestling and boxing occasionally cross over. Muhammad Ali acted out a 15-round bore with a Japanese wrestler, Antonio Inoki, in Tokyo in the 1970s. This was a waste of time. From time to time boxer-wrestler matches happen but make little impact. During his exile from boxing after he bit Evander Holyfield's ears, Mike Tyson was invited to referee a WWF bout. There was also a crazy story concerning 1970s contender Chuck Wepner, the man whose fight with Ali in 1975 is said to have inspired Sylvester Stallone to make 'Rocky'. Wepner was apparently at a wrestling show when he took offence at something, climbed through the ropes and, unscripted, knocked one of the supposed hard men spark out. This tale may, or may not, be apochryphal.

However, that's about as close as it gets. Pugilism is dead – and, in spite of the adaptations it has made in the 130 years since gloved boxing began to replace it, the signs are that we will not see its like again.

BIBLIOGRAPHY

Source books and documents included *Ring Magazine*, *Boxing* and *Boxing News*, as well as a variety of long dead newspapers and journals, principally *The Sporting Magazine*, *Bell's Life In London* and *Famous Fights Past & Present*. Further reading, all of which were used as sources for this book and to which debt is acknowledged, include:

A Treatise Upon The Useful Science of Defence (Godfrey) 1743
Pancratia (Oxberry) 1812
Book of Sports (Egan) 1832
Fights for the Championship & Other Battles (Dowling) 1855
The Champions of the American Prize Ring (Harding) 1893
Fights For The Championship – The Men And Their Times (Henning) 1899
Boxers and their Battles (Thormanby) 1900
The National Sporting Club (Bettinson/Outram) 1901
Pugilistica (Miles) 1906
Sporting Days & Sporting Ways (Nevill) 1910
Famous Fights & Fighters (Platt) 1920
Fisticuffs & Personalities of the Prize Ring (Cleveland) 1924
John L Sullivan (Dibble) 1925
My Sporting Memories (Angle) 1925
The Naked Lady (Falk) 1934
John Gully & His Times (Darwin) 1935
John The Great (Chidsey) 1947
John L Sullivan (Fleischer) 1952
The Frightful Punishment (Brier) 1969
The Victorian Underworld (Chesney) 1970
Bucks and Bruisers (Reid) 1971

Prizefighting (Ford) 1971
The Great Prize Fight (Lloyd) 1977
The Fighting Irish (Myler) 1987
John L Sullivan & His Times (Isenberg) 1988
Bare Knuckles (Brailsford) 1988
The Last Great Prize Fight in England (Insley) 1988
Fifty Years a Fighter (Mace/McInnes) 1989
Manly Art (Gorn) 1989
Jack Scroggins (Hartley) 1989
Australian Boxing (Kieza) 1990
Up To Scratch (Collard) 1992
The Milling Men of the Old Prize Ring (MacDonald)
Tom Sayers (Wright) 1994

PICTURE CREDITS

INDEX